Christopher
ISHERWOOD

a reference guide

ROBERT W. FUNK

George Prior Publishers, London, England

G.K. HALL &CO.

70 LINCOLN STREET, BOSTON, MASS.

Available for sale in the British Commonwealth from
George Prior Publishers, 37-41 Bedford Row, London, W.C.1, England
ISBN (U.K.)   0 86043 260 2

Copyright © 1979 by Robert W. Funk

Library of Congress Cataloging in Publication Data

Funk, Robert W   1937 -
    Christopher Isherwood: a reference guide.

    (Reference publications in literature)
    Bibliography: p.
    Includes index.
    1. Isherwood, Christopher, 1904 - — Bibliography.
I. Series.
Z8441.F85 [PR6017.S5] 016.823'9'12 78-10199
ISBN 0-8161-8072-5

This publication is printed on permanent/durable acid-free paper
MANUFACTURED IN THE UNITED STATES OF AMERICA

Contents

Introduction

Christopher Isherwood has always been a problem for the critics. An obviously talented writer, he has refused to exploit his artistry for either commercial success or literary status. Instead of producing the grand-scale novel which might have brought him the unqualified critical acclaim that has never been accorded his works, Isherwood has quietly insisted upon adhering to the doctrine that "less is more." Since his strongest gifts--ironic wit, penetrating insight into motive, pellucid prose--might have easily dissipated in works of monumental structure, Isherwood scaled his literary efforts to appropriate proportions. Early in his career he discarded plans for an epic treatment of pre-Nazi Berlin (to be entitled <u>The Lost</u>) and offered, rather, a series of incisive character studies and fictionalized journals. These intriguing pieces beguiled reviewers and the general public alike, but their fragmentary character inhibited the critics in their estimation of the author's importance in the world of letters. Isherwood was adjudged a "promising writer"--a designation that he has not been able to outrun even to this day. It is still a cliché of Isherwood criticism to say that he never fulfilled his early promise.

The obstacles to reputation are, for Isherwood, closely allied to the features of his works which make them difficult to interpret and evaluate. These qualities involve both form and content: his technique is deceptive and subtle; his subject matter is unconventional and off center. The casual reader may well fail to grasp the complexity of an Isherwood novel simply because the author does not call attention to his ideas with a dazzling or portentous style. Even the serious critic may be apt to misread or undervalue writing which appears to be so simple and fluent. Of course, there are those who appreciate the understated and who see the problematic characteristics of Isherwood's writings as virtues. But the fundamental division between those who rank Isherwood in the first class of writers and those who dismiss him as second-rate or lower exists, to a great extent, because his ironic, refined presentation eludes many readers and does not satisfy their desire for extensive productions. In any case, five decades of Isherwood criticism present a history of sharply divided opinion.

The major technical stumbling block in Isherwood's work is his highly subtle, almost delicate manipulation of narratorial stance. From the outset, Isherwood's detached narrator/persona has drawn widely divergent reactions--from high praise to nonplussed exasperation. The ambiguity of the narrator's role within Isherwood's fictional schemes is augmented by the seeming identification of author with narrator.

The point of view in the early novels and sketches raised questions about the function of the narrator: does his cool detachment imply a judgment, moral or otherwise, about such obviously flawed individuals as Sally Bowles and Mr. Norris? or does his uninvolved presence suggest a neutral, even amoral acceptance of the weakness and corruption which are depicted in his narratives? The answers to these questions often shaped the critical responses to All the Conspirators, The Memorial, and the Berlin books. Many reviewers who applauded the smooth style and the astute observations qualified their assessments because, in their opinion, the "camera eye" was insufficiently engaged and the moral point of view, therefore, undeveloped and incomplete. Edith Walton (1939.91), for example, felt that Isherwood skimmed "lightly and subtly over the most intangible of surfaces" but that Goodbye to Berlin was "incommensurate in force with the importance of its theme." Similarly, Basil Davenport (1939.31) praised the "uncanny accuracy" and "impartial sensitivity" of Goodbye but complained that Isherwood "merely let impressions come to him" (see also 1939.64). These commentators, apparently, did not respond fully to the judgmental implications of the outside observer's clear and penetrating vision. But Geoffrey Grigson (1939.42) did: he saw that Isherwood "exhibits values without stating them by illustrating their absence." And so did Alfred Kazin (1939.49), who perceived that the author's "intention is always fixed on those little details which summon up the flavor of a way of life."

As Isherwood's career developed, such critical issues intensified. What early critics, such as Cyril Connolly (1938.9), David Garnett (1939.38), and John Lehmann (1939.53), had praised as original, imaginative, and deeply serious, G. H. Bantock (1947.5) dismissed as limited, negligible, and lacking in moral commitment. Richard Mayne (1953.3) concluded that while Isherwood's talents were well suited for comic novels such as The Last of Mr. Norris, he had not yet been able to produce serious fiction; but Jean Weisgerber (1958.6) pointed out that Isherwood always focuses on "des problèmes individuels."

When Prater Violet appeared in 1945, it was almost universally praised for its smooth style and the subtle interplay between the first-person narrator (Christopher) and the vital object of his narration (Friedrich Bergmann). But the book was judged too slight to be a major novel. Orville Prescott (1945.11) summed up this critical reservation when he said that Prater Violet "may be so slight as to be almost trivial, its satirical moral so obliquely conveyed as to be without much force or significance." The views of Joseph Frank

(1946.21) and Isaac Rosenfeld (1946.30) demonstrate how critical reactions divided on the specific issue of the narrator: to Frank the
"I" was isolated and possessed a "lack of center" which prevented the
author from developing his vision and imposing a structure on his observations; to Rosenfeld the "I" of the narrative embodied Isherwood's "master theme" of alienation.

In The World in the Evening, Isherwood abandoned the peripheral
narrator and told the story through the eyes of one of the main characters (Stephen Monk). Reactions once again divided along the matter
of point of view. One side saw the interior persona as a significant
advance over the uninvolved mouthpiece. Thom Gunn (1954.19), for in-
stance, thought that "Isherwood is venturing something far more serious, far more complex, than before"; John Wain (1954.45) said that
for the first time the "I" was a "real, suffering, developing human
being"; and Wayland Young (1954.51) saw the "savagely antiseptic
neutrality" of the Berlin books being replaced by "compassion" and
"immediacy." The other side, however, felt that Isherwood had sacrificed the advantages of an outsider's perspective for the less artistic vision of an insider. Richard Hayes (1954.23) explained the
negative position this way: "In The World in the Evening, 'I' is
active, divided, subject as well as object, and the novel has conse-
quently neither aesthetic nor intellectual coherence." Isaac Rosenfeld (1954.43) saw that Isherwood was trying to go beyond The Berlin
Stories and Prater Violet by "giving full character to his observer
and keeping him in the center of the action," but the results, ac-
cording to Rosenfeld, were not successful: "the novel itself might
as well have been a case history, for all that Isherwood was able to
do with it." Several reviewers echoed these opinions by noting that
the camera eye was involved or turned inward and that the heretofore
sharp, sensitive perspective had become distorted (1954.33) or
blurred (1954.37).

Later Isherwood works did not clarify this problem of narratorial
function for the critics. As the distinction between fiction and
autobiography seemingly diminished, the concerns about tone and authorial stance increased. The narrator of Down There on a Visit
(1962) was once again the fictional Christopher, but this time he
appeared to be more closely identified with the author and more involved with the other characters than previous personae. Alan Wilde
(1971.19) describes the interpretational dilemma that Down There presented to the critics:

> There is the usual danger of confusing Isherwood with
> his narrator. Christopher even in his final phase re-
> mains, in terms of the novel's religious and ethical
> norms, insufficiently responsive to what he recognizes
> to be right. But his understanding of and belief in
> Isherwood's values make him at least a more reliable
> surrogate for his creator than any of his predecessors.

Quite understandably, some reviewers were unable to resist the autobiographical features of this work. Herbert Mitgang (1962.72), for
example, concluded that Isherwood "turned the camera on himself this
time, and the image is frightening." Likewise, William Peden
(1962.77) felt that "the main subject of the book is Isherwood himself, as depicted in retrospect from youth to middle age." While
this emphasis on biography did not necessarily diminish critical appreciation, it sometimes led to confusion--"The author distorts his
writer-narrator...so that one is puzzled to know which is the real
Isherwood," complained Robin Douglas (1962.36)--and to some rather
specialized readings--the Time magazine reviewer (1962.6) felt that
"there is too little fiction for a novel, too little truth for autobiography" and that the book "sometimes seems little else than a
portrait of the artist as an aging adolescent"; whereas the reviewer
for TLS (1962.3) thought that the book could be read as "an apologia
for the whole Herr Issyvoo myth." Nonetheless, other critics were
able to take a less limited view of Isherwood's use of narrator in
Down There: Gerald Sykes (1962.94) thought that "out of his literary
detachment" the author had fashioned "a deeply intelligent and quietly compelling story," and Naomi Bliven (1962.19) saw that the novel
"often harshly judges its narrator" and "has the tone of a penitent,
slightly exhibitionistic confession."

In A Single Man (1964), Isherwood employed a third-person narration. But George, the central character, resembled the author in a
number of ways, a fact that encouraged some reviewers, such as Robert
Ostermann (1964.55), to see the novel as "an emotional and intellectual
portrait of the author, with the dramatic externals secondary to this
self-revelation" (see also, 1964.58, 63). More analytical critics,
however, recognized that there was a crucial distance between author
and main character and that a satirical point of view informed the
intimate revelations and personal insights. David Daiches (1964.22),
for one, saw that while A Single Man was "not the sort of novel that
Christopher Isherwood's earlier works have led us to expect," it
still contained "something of the quietly savage dead-pan observation
that we find in [the] famous Berlin stories." And Carolyn Heilbrun
(1970.12) decided that the point of view was the key to the work's
comic purpose: "We watch George as though we were some mocking god,
tolerant but supercilious."

Opinion divided, too, on the question of how Isherwood's openly
homosexual protagonist affected the worth of A Single Man. Sybille
Bedford (1964.12) put forth the negative case most clearly and directly: "The protagonist's homosexuality is, in my opinion, the
book's main artistic flaw because it impairs what might have been the
august universality of the theme." Phoebe Adams (1964.1) decided
that "George is not a man, in the sense of being a true individual,
at all. In every circumstance, he is first of all a member of a de-
viant minority, and both George and his creator find this a boring
and hampering condition." To Anthony Burgess (1964.15), however,
homosexuality was not one of the book's main issues: "the love for

Christopher
ISHERWOOD
a reference guide

A
Reference
Publication
in
Literature

Ronald Gottesman
Editor

dead Jim is the love for dead anyone; the particular loneliness may
serve as an emblem for the loneliness of all single men." For many
critics, though, the main character's sexual preference was a central
but troublesome consideration, as these discrepant opinions indicate:

> Nowhere does Isherwood countenance homosexuality as the
> more excellent way (Alfred Gross, 1964.37).

> The only false note which intrudes from time to time is
> when [Isherwood's] stream of consciousness elevates homo-
> sexuality to a doctrine (Alan Pryce-Jones, 1964.59).

> The treatment of homosexuality...is honest but mercifully
> not "frank" (John Gross, 1964.38).

> One grows tired of the sentimental assumption that inver-
> sion is an absolute prerequisite for any sense of--and
> share in--the nightmare of mortality (George Greene,
> 1964.36).

> For once we are asked to believe that homosexuals are as
> good as anyone else, not better (Daniel Curley, 1965.13).

> The homosexual as an outcast is the theme of this Isher-
> wood novel with the coyly ambiguous title, and it will
> appeal most to readers who wish to follow the sad, un-
> happy career of a sexual deviate (Ervin Gaines, 1964.32).

A Meeting by the River (1967) did little to close the rift in the
responses to Isherwood's works, although the sides shifted. Critics
who valued the subtleties of the earlier Isherwood were put off by
what they saw as an overly schematic allegory (see 1967.18, 23, 31
and 68). Other commentators, who had perhaps been perplexed by the
ambiguities of previous works, discovered an almost transcendent
clarity in the novel's religious theme (see 1967.40, 44). Many reviewers again pointed out that the novel wasn't long enough to sus-
tain its serious argument (1967.2, 3). As usual, technique provided
a basic dividing line: for some the epistolary method was mechanical
and deadening (1967.26, 60); for others the letters and diaries were
the most appropriate form for a fictionalized account of a spiritual
debate (1967.64, 67).

Isherwood's two principal works of the 1970s have been out-and-
out biographies. This straightforward generic designation, however,
does not mean that the presentation is totally unambiguous. Kathleen
and Frank (1971) employs diary entries which are supplemented by the
remarks of the author as commentator, and, as many critics noted, the
real-life persons in this work are treated a lot like characters in a
novel. In Christopher and His Kind (1976), Isherwood has split himself into a present-day persona (the "I" of the book) and his past-
time object of consideration (once again named Christopher). As one

can see, these techniques do not differ in kind from the detached observers and fictionalized Christophers of previous works. Nonetheless, the critics did feel more confident in approaching these books as non-fiction. Thomas Lask's characterization of <u>Kathleen and Frank</u> as "a memoir that is also an apology" (1972.36) was a typical response, one that Robert Kirsch echoed when he termed the book "part a memoir of [Isherwood's] parents, part an essay in self-analysis" (1972.33). The evaluative effect of such secure views of the work's nature is suggested by Arthur Cooper's remark that "Isherwood's confrontation with the past seems beneficial indeed" (1972.18). As for <u>Christopher and His Kind</u>, Timothy Fox's estimate that the book "is at its best...when it offers us material that is new" (1976.10) is representative of the positive responses which critics had to the work's historical and biographical revelations. The reactions to both books were more uniform in their appreciation of Isherwood's artistry and less disparate about the meaning and purposes of his treatment of materials than responses to previous works had been. <u>Kathleen and Frank</u> enjoyed an especially warm critical reception.

What reviewers did find disturbing about these most recent works was their candor. This objection is not a new one for Isherwood—his subject matter has always been unacceptable to some (<u>vide</u> the reviewer who said that <u>Down There</u> "begins in a compost heap and ends in a dunghill"—1962.32), and his fondness for the outcasts and eccentrics of the world has often earned him adverse criticism (the reviewer from the <u>Wall Street Journal</u> thought that <u>Down There</u> was "peopled with an extraordinarily depressing assortment of deviates, perverts and alcoholics"—1962.83). Even critics who complained about the detachment of the Berlin stories were sometimes objecting to the lack of censure that the tone implied (<u>see</u> 1929.12). Frequently literary commentators are not able to get beyond personal prejudice in forming their judgments. But this tendency is particularly evident in Isherwood criticism because his works so often deal with homosexuality. It is no longer intellectually acceptable to disapprove of homosexuals, however; so recent critics have sometimes resorted to disingenuous analyses in order to avoid a direct expression of bias. (Not a single reviewer of <u>Christopher and His Kind</u>, in the forty-seven reviews that I read, expressed outright distaste for gay people.) Negative feelings are instead directed at another, closely related target. Mary Ellmann, for example, in her review of <u>Christopher</u> (1977.14), affirmed that "No one will ask Isherwood to go back to the closet"; but she then complained that "absolute honesty takes on in him a somewhat disagreeable quality." The critic preferred the "elusive quality which unstatedness" gave to <u>Lions and Shadows</u>. Don't go back in the closet, Mrs. Ellmann said; just try to write more as you did in 1938. The irony of such a position is that the "elusive" style of <u>Lions</u> and other earlier works was often criticized for being too oblique and indirect in its expression of the author's views. In a remarkably similar maneuver Penelope Mesic (1976.23) aimed her objection to <u>Christopher and His Kind</u> at Isherwood's frankness, which she found "almost embarrassingly intimate."

Isherwood has, in fact, written about homosexuals throughout his career, but he often handled them with such indirection and obliquity that many readers were not really aware of what they were reading. As the cultural climate made it possible for Isherwood to be more open and frank, homosexuality has become central to his writing. In Kathleen and Frank he admitted his own sexual preference, and in Christopher and His Kind he gave an extensive account of his homosexual affairs in the 1930s. Unfortunately critical objectivity and acceptance have not kept pace with either Isherwood or the times. It appears that many commentators preferred not to know the truth. Several urbane, educated reviewers, such as C. P. Snow (1977.34), Richard Ellmann (1977.14a), and Auberon Waugh (1977.39), found the revelations that Isherwood made about his sexual behavior and that of his friends to be "unpleasant" or "off-putting" or "unattractive" or "distasteful," even though they admitted that Isherwood wrote about this behavior beautifully. Others applauded the author's candor but expressed relief that he had not made a crusade out of his sexuality (1976.4). Such schizophrenic responses say as much about the critics as they do about the literature under examination. Unpleasant subject matter has never been a detriment to good writing. The fact of the matter is that Isherwood does not regard homosexuals and homosexuality as unpleasant, unattractive, or distasteful. And it is this attitude which distresses those critics who complain about the candor or the "unworthy" subject matter of such masterful creations as Down There on a Visit, A Single Man, and Christopher and His Kind. Isherwood is delivering a message that many people simply do not want to hear—and he is doing so with such intelligence and good humor that it is doubly difficult for a reviewer to object openly.

To be fair, one must admit that many critics, such as Peter Stansky (1976.35) and Gabriele Annan (1977.2), have taken Isherwood's honesty in stride and have found his candor admirable and enriching. Yet the irrationality of homophobia has surely had a significant effect on Isherwood's critical reputation. The common criticism is that his writing is limited in appeal, his novels are not universal. When this judgment is made of such a humane and deeply affecting novel as A Single Man, one can only conclude that homophobia has set in. Some readers do not regard homosexuals as fully and unreservedly human, and until they do, the works of Christopher Isherwood will not be completely accessible to these people.

Christopher Isherwood: A Reference Guide is the most complete bibliography about the author to date, containing 1109 entries for criticism published from 1928 through 1977 (with one citation for 1978). All of these items refer to writings about Isherwood, not to works by him. I have not included editions or translations of the author's work, since such materials properly belong in a primary bibliography.

This secondary bibliography contains almost every item of criticism listed in previous bibliographies about Isherwood, his literary associates, and the movements in literary history of which he was a part. I have tried to include all autobiographical material from Isherwood's friends and associates. All traceable references to the collaborative works of Auden and Isherwood have been included, even though many of them treat Auden as the principal or exclusive author. Mardi Valgemae (1968.15) and Edward Mendelson (1976.22) have established that the collaboration on the plays was much closer and more balanced than previously assumed, and the criticism of these efforts must now be re-evaluated, especially in respect to what might be revealed about Isherwood's abilities and interests. I have also made available the reviews from American newspapers that are in my collection of clippings about Isherwood from the 1930s through the 1960s. These references to Christopher Isherwood and his works in the popular press are highly significant for assessing the course of the author's critical reception, especially at the precise times when his books were published. These materials have more than doubled the previously known writings about Isherwood.

I cannot, of course, take sole credit for all of the material enumerated and annotated in this reference guide. All previous Isherwood scholars, and many Auden scholars as well, have provided leads to the many discussions of Isherwood that appear in general works and works about other authors. Unpublished dissertations and theses (included herein) have also provided new sources of Isherwood material. I owe particular thanks to Brian Finney, Roger Austen, Kay Parkhurst Easson, and W. I. Scobie for help in obtaining data on items that were not readily available to me.

Christopher Isherwood: A Reference Guide is arranged chronologically; within each year entries are arranged alphabetically by author's name. Items for anonymous or unidentifiable authorship are grouped under the heading "Anon." and occur wherever "Anon." comes alphabetically in each annual list. All items have been examined, except those preceded by an asterisk. In the annotations I have attempted, as much as possible, to excerpt the author's own words instead of offering my summary of the material.

All entries are identified by year of publication and the number which corresponds to the item's alphabetical position within the year. Cross-references guide the reader to reprintings. The entry numbers are used instead of page numbers in the index, which contains references to authors, periodicals, individuals, Isherwood's publications, and works of a creative nature. There are three other headings in the index: Bibliography, Biography, and Interviews. Finally, the many references to newspaper material about Christopher Isherwood (presented with page numbers where available) requires that papers published in towns and cities of obscure or ambiguous location be identified by the two-letter abbreviations for states used by the United States Postal Service.

Introduction

I would like to acknowledge my indebtedness to the University of Illinois Library (Urbana-Champaign campus) and the Newberry Library of Chicago, and to David Doman and the staff of Milner Library of Illinois State University. I also wish to thank Ray Lewis White for help with publications in German and Walter Gallas for aid with materials in Spanish. I must assume personal responsibility for materials in French and Danish. And for his continuing advice, encouragement, and inspiration throughout this project, I thank my friend and colleague, Professor Ray Lewis White of Illinois State University.

Primary Works of Christopher Isherwood

Detailed descriptions of the various editions are in Selmer Westby and Clayton Brown, Christopher Isherwood: A Bibliography 1923–1967 (1968) and Paul Piazza, Christopher Isherwood: Myth and Anti-Myth (1978). See also Stathis Orphanos' checklist in Twentieth Century Literature, 22 (October 1976), 354–358, for recent information about reprints and reissues. Dates given below are for the first publication only.

Novels
> All the Conspirators (1928).
> The Memorial: Portrait of a Family (1932).
> Mr. Norris Changes Trains (1935). In Berlin Stories.
>> American title: The Last of Mr. Norris (1935).
> Sally Bowles (1937). In Berlin Stories.
> Goodbye to Berlin (1939). In Berlin Stories.
> Prater Violet (1945).
> The Berlin Stories (1945). Includes Mr. Norris Changes Trains,
>> Sally Bowles, and Goodbye to Berlin.
> The World in the Evening (1954).
> Down There on a Visit (1962).
> A Single Man (1964).
> A Meeting by the River (1967).
> The Berlin of Sally Bowles (1975). Same as Berlin Stories.

Autobiography
> Lions and Shadows: An Education in the Twenties (1938).
> Kathleen and Frank (1971).
> Christopher and His Kind 1929–1939 (1976).

Plays
> The Dog Beneath the Skin (1935). With W. H. Auden.
> The Ascent of F6 (1936). With W. H. Auden.
> On the Frontier (1938). With W. H. Auden.

The Adventures of the Black Girl in Her Search for God (produced,
    1969). Adaptation of the novel by G. B. Shaw.
A Meeting by the River (produced, 1972). With Don Bachardy.
Frankenstein: The True Story (1973). Screenplay; with Don
    Bachardy.

Travel
Journey to a War (1939). With W. H. Auden.
The Condor and the Cows; A South American Travel Diary (1949).

Other
An Approach to Vedanta (1963).
Ramakrishna and His Disciples (1965).
Exhumations: Stories, Articles, Verse (1966).
Essentials of Vedanta (1969).

Editings
Vedanta for the Western World (1945).
Vedanta for Modern Man (1951).

Translations
Baudelaire, Charles. Intimate Journals (1930).
Brecht, Bertolt. A Penny for the Poor (1937). Translated only
    the verses; text translated by Desmond Vesey.
Bhagavad-Gita: The Song of God (1944). With Swami Prabhavananda.

Writings about Christopher Isherwood, 1928-1977

1928

1   ANON. "Books." <u>The Sphere</u> (21 July), p. 138.
<u>All the Conspirators</u> is marked by "modern cleverness" and is the work of a young but talented writer.

2   ANON. Review of <u>All the Conspirators</u>. <u>Times Literary Supplement</u> (14 June), p. 452.
<u>All the Conspirators</u> "reads like an exercise in novel writing, a first sketch of a novel, rather than a complete and rounded novel itself."

1932

1   ANON. Review of <u>The Memorial</u>. <u>Times Literary Supplement</u> (14 April), p. 272.
In <u>The Memorial</u> "there is very little 'plot' or story, but the book grips the reader from the sheer interest of the characters themselves; Mr. Isherwood deals in shades and shadows, in the half and quarter tones of human relationships, but each facet of a personality he shows is in itself a vivid portrait."

2   JONES, E. B. C. Review of <u>The Memorial</u>. <u>The Adelphi</u>, NS 4 (May), 565-566.
"<u>The Memorial</u> has one great virtue rare in psychological novels, that of being immensely readable.... Mr. Isherwood is a serious writer, but...has a sense of humour and is far from ingenuous."

3   R., G. Review of <u>The Memorial</u>. <u>Oxford Outlook</u>, 12 (May), 139-142.
"<u>The Memorial</u> is to be read with pleasure and admiration, it is, I think, one of the few novels worth reading which has been published lately."

1933

1   WALPOLE, HORACE. "Books I Have Liked Best Since the War--A
    Symposium." Sunday Times (12 November), p. iii.
        All the Conspirators is one of the eight or nine "un-
    justly neglected books of the twenties."

1935

1   ANON. "A Dramatic Experiment." Times Literary Supplement
    (11 July), p. 444.
        The Dog Beneath the Skin contains "richness of language,
    a teeming range of subject-matter and types (if no charac-
    ters), and eminent diversion...."

2   ANON. "A Rare Character." New York Times Book Review
    (12 May), p. 7.
        The Last of Mr. Norris "offers interesting sidelights on
    certain aspects of the feverish Berlin of 1931-33. It tem-
    pers the picture of an unappetizing scoundrel with nervous
    humor and innocent merriment."

3   ANON. Review of The Dog Beneath the Skin. Hartford Courant
    (8 December).
        The Dog Beneath the Skin "is wild and whirling satire,
    irresistibly entertaining and stimulating to read....
    Mr. Auden and Mr. Isherwood had a grand time writing this
    uproarious, audacious and savage satire; the intelligent
    reader will have a grand time reading it."

4   ANON. Review of The Dog Beneath the Skin. Listener, 13
    (19 June), 1067.
        The Dog Beneath the Skin "is a morality play in inten-
    tion, and reminiscent of the old morality plays in its
    verse structure. It has the vivid, irrational consistency
    of a dream sequence: but the achieving of this consistency
    leads to an occasional damping-down of the dramatic cri-
    ses."

5   ANON. Review of The Dog Beneath the Skin. Philadelphia In-
    quirer, (7 December).
        "Auden and Isherwood, using everything they have in the
    way of learning and barbaric wit, have constructed an ab-
    surd piece of drama, part musical comedy, part Greek trag-
    edy, part farce, part solemn pageant, which allows them in
    a series of fantastic and biting scenes to say just what
    they think about the world today."

*6   ANON. Review of <u>The Last of Mr. Norris</u>. <u>Boston Evening
       Transcript</u> (12 June), p. 3.
            Cited: <u>Book Review Digest 1935</u>, p. 510.

7   ANON. Review of <u>The Last of Mr. Norris</u>. <u>Nation</u>, 141 (24
       July), 112.
            "The account of Mr. Norris and his haunts and habits in
       fatigued London and decadent Berlin is as accurate as farce
       should be.... Unfortunately...the work lacks that which is
       essential to any fictional venture into international es-
       pionage--a good, involute intrigue plot."

8   ANON. Review of <u>Mr. Norris Changes Trains</u>. <u>Times Literary
       Supplement</u> (14 March), p. 161.
            "In 'Mr. Norris Changes Trains' [Isherwood] has made his
       plans and built his scaffolding much more carefully [than
       he did in <u>The Memorial</u>], while the same descriptive powers
       and psychological insight distinguish his book.... But it
       is chiefly as a picture of Berlin just before the Nazi
       regime that the book is valuable."

9   BARNES, T. R. "Poets and the Drama." <u>Scrutiny</u>, 4 (September),
       192-195.
            In <u>The Dog Beneath the Skin</u>, "Messrs. Auden and Isher-
       wood are neither cold nor academic; on the other hand, they
       are...more up-to-date than genuinely new.... On the stage,
       parts of it might come off, but very little of the play
       stands up to cold solitary perusal." The play is not suc-
       cessful on the level of political satire.

10   BENÉT, WILLIAM ROSE. "Contemporary Poetry." <u>Saturday Review
       of Literature</u>, 13 (30 November), 16.
            "...I cannot say that I think 'The Dog Beneath the Skin'
       is wholly successful, even in its satire. There are dull
       passages. There are some very British moments. The struc-
       ture groans and creaks. But in spite of this the poem-play
       has one very considerable virtue to me--it is interesting
       to read."

11   BOGAN, LOUISE. "Action and Charity." <u>New Republic</u>, 85
       (27 November), 79.
            In <u>The Dog Beneath the Skin</u>, Auden has written, "with
       the competent aid of Christopher Isherwood, a long, highly
       amusing revue, whose satire is so deft that it may stand,
       without cutting a sorry figure, beside the early Gilbert."

*12 BRIDSON, D. G. Review of <u>The Dog Beneath the Skin</u>. <u>Time and
       Tide</u>, 16 (17 August), 1204.
            Cited: Bloomfield and Mendelson, 1972.11, p. 16.

3

1935

13 CONNOLLY, CYRIL. Review of <u>Mr. Norris Changes Trains</u>. <u>New Statesman and Nation</u>, 9 (2 March), 284.
   The story of Mr. Norris is not the most important element of the novel: "while the stream of the book flows along round the mystery of Mr. Norris, the strong undertow carries the reader towards the problems of his young friend, whom we see first as a rather over-weening undergraduate, with a bias toward tolerance and elasticity, and then, through his relations with Norris, we are made to realise after all how intolerant and inelastic he is."

14 GARRETT, JOHN. Review of <u>The Dog Beneath the Skin</u>. <u>Criterion</u>, 14 (July), 687-690.
   "Anyone who saw the film 'Little Friend,' for the dialogue of which Mr. Christopher Isherwood was responsible, will recognize in the prose scenes of [<u>The Dog Beneath the Skin</u>], the same unerring instinct for exactly the right word, idiom, and cadence of phrase."

15 GILMORE, WILLIAM S. "A Burlesque from Britain." <u>Brooklyn Daily Eagle</u> (3 November).
   <u>The Dog Beneath the Skin</u> "is a very amusing play in spite of the nature of what is being satirized. No extravagant claims can be made for it, nor can it be truthfully said that it 'will make people think,' since all people who do think think every day on the problems of which Auden and Isherwood treat, and certainly these young men present no novel viewpoint."

16 HEMRICK, HAROLD. "Rolling Stones Flock." <u>Atlanta Constitution</u> (11 August).
   "There must be some moral to this delightful story [<u>The Last of Mr. Norris</u>], but it is none of the conventional ones. In fact, the failure of the author to become serious and attempt to make a moral lesson is one of the most attractive features of the book."

17 HOLLIDAY, TERENCE. "A Late Victorian in Berlin." <u>New York Herald Tribune Books</u> (19 May), p. 2.
   In <u>The Last of Mr. Norris</u>, the picture of the title character "is also the portrait of a period wholly alien to him. We may relish him or not, but we cannot ignore, nor deny the validity, for him, of the queer, twisted appetites and satisfactions that he wrings from his hostile environment."

18 HOLMES, JOHN. Review of <u>The Dog Beneath the Skin</u>. <u>Boston Evening Transcript</u> (9 November), p. 5.
   "With chorus describing each setting in ominous tones, and strong contemptuous satire in every exaggerated symbolic episode, any Savoyard alive or dead would shiver in his shoes at a performance of this grim and noisy farce...."

4

19 JACK, P[ETER] M[ONRO]. "An Extravaganza." <u>New York Sun</u>
     (12 October).
          <u>The Dog Beneath the Skin</u> "is a merry and sad play of
     poetry and burlesque, with overtones of the sheerest ab-
     surdity and undertones of disaster."

20 JONES, E. B. C. Review of <u>Mr. Norris Changes Trains</u>. <u>The</u>
     <u>Adelphi</u>, NS 10 (June), 186.
          "When I saw and heard the praise lavished on <u>Mr. Norris</u>
     <u>Changes Trains</u> by the critics of the B.B.C. and lowbrow
     Press, I began, with inverted snobbery, to wonder whether
     my first enthusiastic view of it were mistaken; but the
     book remains, on second reading, quite outstandingly good,
     with an almost flawless consistency in accomplishing what
     it sets out to do; and it is astonishingly inoffensive
     considering that its subject is one which many people would
     consider repulsive."

21 L., F. K. Review of <u>The Dog Beneath the Skin</u>. <u>Birmingham</u>
     <u>News</u> [AL] (29 December).
          "Sheer poetry it is not, nor was meant to be; but cer-
     tainly as a travesty on every known failing, ancient or
     modern, 'The Dog Beneath the Skin' wears a bigger and more
     madly cut fool's cap than does any recent work of its
     kind."

22 LECHLITNER, RUTH. "For the Under Dog." <u>New York Herald Trib-</u>
     <u>une Books</u> (1 December), p. 38.
          Review of <u>The Dog Beneath the Skin</u>: "It is true that
     certain radical playwrights would profit by a little more
     of the wit characteristic of the Auden-Isherwood combine.
     Since this, however, is a play best adapted to an audience
     of intellectual Leftists, the latter may object to its lack
     of sustained poetic quality--that impassioned lyricism, for
     instance, of Stephen Spender's 'Vienna.'"

23 M., A. L. "Shocked Satirists." <u>Daily Worker</u> (3 July), p. 4.
          <u>The Dog Beneath the Skin</u> offers "criticism, often
     pointed and effective, of a Europe distracted by Fascism
     and crisis."

24 M., J. Review of <u>The Dog Beneath the Skin</u>. <u>High Point Enter-</u>
     <u>prise</u> [NC] (3 November).
          <u>The Dog Beneath the Skin</u> "is an ironic diatribe against
     hypocrisy and vulgarity and meanness, against narrowness
     and pretense." The form of the play may not meet with
     popular success, but it could prove to be a "fresh and
     stimulating" approach to theatre.

1935

25 MATTHEWS, T. S. "Publishers' Properties." New Republic, 83
    (22 May), 54.
        The Last of Mr. Norris is a "pot-boiler," and "it reads
    like a sturdy attempt to make a publisher's purse out of a
    left-wing ear.... It is like a dirty story that is more
    embarrassing than funny."

26 MUIR, EDWIN. "New Novels." Listener, 13 (13 March), 468.
        "Mr. Norris Changes Trains is an extraordinarily amusing
    book, and without ever drawing on the conventional sources
    of comedy.... The book is too slight to judge Mr. Isher-
    wood's powers.... But there can be no doubt of the origi-
    nality of his vein of humour or of the genuineness of his
    talent."

27 PARSONS, I. M. "Poetry, Drama and Satire." Spectator, 154
    (28 June), 1112, 1114.
        "The Dog Beneath the Skin is a shoddy affair, a half-
    baked little satire which gets nowhere." The play "is set
    out with a great deal of extravagant pretension"; the sat-
    ire is "so crude that it completely misses fire"; and the
    objects of the satire "have been objects of ridicule for
    the last ten years or more."

28 PLOMER, WILLIAM. "Fiction." Spectator, 154 (1 March), 346.
        Mr. Norris Changes Trains is recommended for the high
    quality of sustained irony. "The book, which is continu-
    ously amusing and intelligent from the first page to the
    last, may be described as a full-length portrait with
    numerous implications--social, political, and psychologi-
    cal."

29 REDMAN, BEN RAY. "Problem for the Book Reviewer." Saturday
    Review of Literature, 12 (11 May), 18-19.
        In The Last of Mr. Norris, Isherwood writes "of vice and
    viciousness with candor and a lightly pervasive irony....
    [H]e [has] so dealt with them that they excite laughter and
    a kind of compassionate sympathy, rather than repulsion."

30 REES, RICHARD. Review of The Dog Beneath the Skin. The Adel-
    phi, NS 10 (July), 246-248.
        "Once I started to read [The Dog Beneath the Skin] I did
    not stop until I reached the last page. It is interest-
    ing.... Messrs. Auden and Isherwood have certainly carried
    the movement, or whatever it is they adorn, a stage further
    by writing this play."

31 RICE, PHILIP BLAIR. "Toward a Poetic Drama." Nation, 141
    (27 November), 626.
        The structure of The Dog Beneath the Skin "resembles a
    club sandwich," but it is not because of the collaboration

so much as the difficulty in cajoling a modern audience
"into swallowing poetry at all." The solution is "to pre-
scribe it in small but frequently repeated doses."

*32 SLATER, MONTAGUE. "The Turning Point." Left Review, 2
     (October), 20-22.
         Review of The Dog Beneath the Skin. Cited in Hynes,
     1977.20, p. 184.

33 STONE, GEOFFREY. Review of The Dog Beneath the Skin. Ameri-
    can Review, 6 (November), 126-128.
        "What strikes one most about The Dog Beneath the Skin is
    its shallowness. All, it says, is not for the best in our
    world, and we may agree; but the diagnosis comes from no
    clear perception of the malady--it is based on an odd learn-
    ing compounded of Laurentianism, Marxism, and sophisticated
    wit."

1936

1 A[LLOTT], K[ENNETH]. "Not So Hot." New Verse, no. 19 (February/
   March), p. 15.
       The Dog Beneath the Skin is a "pot-pourri" and "diffuse"
   in form, but its verse contains some "incidental beauties."

2 ANON. "The Ascent of F6." Group Theatre Paper, no. 6 (December), p. 5.
       "In Ramson, the leader of the expedition to F6, we have
   a complex study of the hero of action, a figure which has
   so often attracted the attention of the English theatre.
   But it is the hero of action in contemporary terms; who
   reminds us not of Tamburlaine or Agamemnon or Antony, but
   of T. E. Lawrence, or the dictators of the continent."

3 ANON. "Group Dog." Left Review, 2 (March), 273.
       Review of the Group Theatre production of The Dog Be-
   neath the Skin: "The writing and production of the first
   act are excellent, and the former could well be taken as a
   guide for those writers who are still interested in the
   possibilities of the modern stage. The latter part of the
   play becomes somewhat too episodic and disjointed...; the
   result seems more like a newsreel than a play."

4 ANON. "Parnassus or F6?" Times Literary Supplement (7 November), p. 902.
       "Mr. Auden and Mr. Isherwood continue their brave attempt
   to revive the poetic play.... [In The Ascent of F6] for
   the first time characters are essayed.... The chief person
   is Michael Ransom...; but though he has been removed from

1936

the cartoon level it must not be assumed that he has become
a character who absorbs us or is memorable. Nor is he
universal."

5   ANON. Review of The Dog Beneath the Skin. Christian Science
     Monitor (11 March), "Weekly Magazine Section," p. 11.
          "'Dog Beneath the Skin' is both a satire on contemporary
     life and a pointer to salvation.... That this particular
     shot does not come off is due largely to the fact that the
     marksmen have not stood far enough back."

6   ANON. "Westminster Theatre: 'The Dog Beneath the Skin.'"
     London Times (31 January), p. 12.
          "One is made aware by the moral earnestness of the two
     commentators or 'witnesses' that Mr. Auden and Mr. Isher-
     wood have propaganda up their sleeve, but let it be said
     that this has not prevented them from writing an entertain-
     ing revue.... [W]hen they speak their mind and, in the
     comments of the Witnesses, point the moral of their satire,
     they do so in passages which...are often genuinely eloquent
     and seldom wilfully freakish."

7   ARMITAGE, GILBERT. Review of The Ascent of F6. English Re-
     view, 63 (November), 526-527.
          The most significant feature of The Ascent of F6 is the
     character of Ransom. He is "a convincingly heroic hero."

8   BEEVERS, JOHN. "Topical Morality." New Statesman and Nation,
     12 (10 October), 531.
          In The Ascent of F6, "Auden and Isherwood have pumped
     life into a dead literary form.... [T]hey are the only men
     writing topical moralities--plays which present and comment
     on urgent problems affecting society and the individual and
     use allegory and symbolism to hammer home their point."

*9   BELFRAGE, C. "Dog's Eye View of Modern Life." London Daily
     Express (3 January).
          Review of The Dog Beneath the Skin. Cited: Jurak,
     1968.9, p. 69n.

10   BONNEROT, LOUIS. Review of The Dog Beneath the Skin. Revue
     Anglo-Américaine, [13] (April), 16.
          This "revue," written with gusto, has just been produced
     by Rupert Doone and the Group Theatre at the Westminster
     theatre with vivid success. The Dog Beneath the Skin pro-
     ceeds from the same vein as The Dance of Death, but the
     satiric intentions, while more vigorous, are here less ef-
     fectively realized by the "fabulation." [In French]

11   C[ONNOLLY], C[YRIL]. "The Muse's Off Day." New Statesman and
     Nation, 11 (8 February), 188.
          Review of the Rupert Doone production of The Dog Beneath
     the Skin: "If a play has got to be written in doggerel
     which often breaks into song, the only thing to do is to
     treat it as comic opera.... Handed over to Messrs. Cole
     Porter, Cecil Beaton, and Oliver Messel with a cast of
     singers and a lavish production something might be made of
     it...."

12   COOKMAN, A. V. "The Theatre." The London Mercury, 33 (March),
     529.
          "All who wish to see poetry find its way back to the
     Theatre may be recommended to see The Dog Beneath the Skin.
     If they go in an austere spirit of inquiry it is possible
     that they may stay to be entertained. This satiric revue...
     makes its point through an interesting and largely success-
     ful juxtaposition of burlesque action on the stage and
     serious poetic commentary."

13   DAVIDSON, DONALD. "Six Poets: A Study in Magnitudes."
     Southern Review, 1 (Spring), 884-886.
          Reviewed with five other poetic works, The Dog Beneath
     the Skin is examined mainly for its poetic choruses: "I
     know of nothing in modern literature that surpasses [the
     play's middle] scenes in relentlessness of satire, in sheer
     disillusionment and horror.... Although...'good theatre,'
     I doubt whether it is a good play." Yet "the poems borrow
     strength from the play, and the play from the poems."

14   DAY-LEWIS, C. "Autumn Verse." Life and Letters, 15 (Winter),
     37-38.
          "Technically, "The Ascent of F6' is a great advance on
     'The Dog Beneath the Skin.' The construction is firmer,
     the satire as vigorous but less crude, while the morality
     is rendered more explicit without loss of balance or incon-
     sistency of texture."

15   DUKES, ASHLEY. "The English Scene: A Word about the Left."
     Theatre Arts Monthly, 20 (April), 269.
          The Dog Beneath the Skin "is far from being a good play,
     judged by any conceivable standard.... The Left sentiment
     that permeates it is shy-making.... But the whole is vigor-
     ously directed by Rupert Doone...; and it never ceases to
     be vital and challenging."

16   DYMENT, CLIFFORD. "Auden, Isherwood, and Day Lewis." Time
     and Tide, 17 (17 October), 1452.
          "The Ascent of F.6 has drama, but it is a drama of ideas,
     and ideas in themselves are not satisfyingly visual. But

1936

the play is a notable piece of work: it is skilfully constructed, it holds the attention, and it is very relevant
to our day and our problems."

17 ELLIS-FERMOR, UNA. "Dramatic Notices." English, 1, no. 2,
155-156.
    When read, The Dog Beneath the Skin "leaves a deep, in-
tentionally conflicting series of impressions," but "the
fact remains that something was destroyed by the theatre;
some of the delicate half-tones and connectives that give
in the reading an impression of urgency and significance
were lost in the bolder selective emphases of the theatre...."

18 "ERIC." "At the Play." Punch, 190 (12 February), 189.
    "As a theatrical experiment [The Dog Beneath the Skin]
is full of interest, but viewed as an entertainment, an
edifier or a work of art...it must be set down as uneven....
Parts of the commentary show great poetic feeling and a
joint ability to attack with felicity of phrase and considerable wit...; but what is noticeably lacking is the
humour which makes prolonged satire palatable."

*19 EWART, G. Review of The Ascent of F6. University Forward, 3
(November), 16.
    Cited: Bloomfield and Mendelson, 1972.11, p. 22.

20 FORSTER, E. M. "Chormopuloda." Listener, 16 (14 October),
"Autumn Book Supplement," vii.
    "'The Ascent of F.6' is a tragedy in a modern mode, full
of funniness and wisecracks. It is not an entertainment for
all its lightheartedness, because its details fit in to its
general plan. It is a tragedy." [Slightly abridged version of this essay appears in 1951.2.]

21 GREGORY, HORACE. "Poets in the Theatre." Poetry, 48 (July),
226.
    "The pace of [The Dog Beneath the Skin] is sometimes too
rapid, and if read as a continuous performance it is obviously uneven. If there is a slight falling off on one
page, the next page is likely to reveal an excellent chorus
or song...."

22 H., D. "Drama." Colosseum, 3 (March), 81-82.
    "The dramatic precedents...of The Dog Beneath the Skin
[are] chiefly Morality and Folk-play.... Messrs. Auden and
Isherwood have successfully experimented in musical comedy
pastiche. I hope it will be followed up with a firmer
grasp and that the music, instead of imitating popular lyr-
ic, will be a significant creation as in Facade."

23   LEAVIS, F. R. "Mr. Auden's Talent." Scrutiny, 5 (December),
     323-327.
         "For corroboration of the surmise that the habits of
     the group-world are intimately associated with the failure
     of Mr. Auden's talent to mature we have the new play [The
     Ascent of F6] that he has written with Christopher Isher-
     wood." The play is pretentious and the verse is bad.
     These faults indicate "a complete absence of exposure to
     criticisms" and "a confident awareness of an encouraging
     audience."

24   M., J. Review of The Dog Beneath the Skin. Janus, 1 (May),
     30.
         "The general trend of [The Dog Beneath the Skin] is
     revolutionary, but apart from one easily adapted scene the
     fascist helmet fits almost as well as the communist cap."

25   POWELL, CHARLES. Review of The Ascent of F6. Manchester
     Guardian (6 November), p. 6.
         "The tragedy of the subtitle is a tragedy so diluted
     with satire, modern realistic incongruities, and music-hall
     jingles that, so far from putting our emotions through or-
     deal by the fire that refines and exalts them as the true
     tragedy can, it hardly touches them."

26   P[OWELL], D[ILYS]. "Heroic Tragedy." The London Mercury, 34
     (October), 561.
         The Ascent of F6, "though it has the satirical inter-
     ludes and the indirect comments from stage-box which are
     still apt to flummox the general public, is in essentials
     a direct heroic play. It is the tragedy of a man sacri-
     ficed for the people (the hanged god again?): a man, how-
     ever, at fault in allowing himself to be sacrificed."

27   RANDALL, E. D. "Speaking Personally." Action, no. 1 (21 Feb-
     ruary), p. 10.
         The Dog Beneath the Skin "is brilliant, and contains
     some magnificent verse. As a jocular superficial satire of
     the society of our day the whole production is clever and
     very funny."

28   RODMAN, SELDEN. Review of The Dog Beneath the Skin. Common
     Sense, 5 (February), 29.
         The Dog Beneath the Skin "is a fanciful play in three
     acts, outwardly in the humorous Gilbert and Sullivan man-
     ner, but profoundly a bitter satire on our times with a
     symbolical answer.... Its choruses...rise to great heights;
     its thrusts at sham and barbarism are rapier-like; its
     humor, except where exasperatingly English, is superb."

1936

29　SAYERS, MICHAEL. "Drama: The Dog Beneath the Skin." New
English Weekly, 8 (13 February), 354-355.
"It is worth reflecting on the fact that in order to
make The Dog Beneath the Skin fit for staging...Mr. Doone
has had to omit nearly everything that made it peculiarly
good to read.... One must conclude that Auden-Isherwood
just haven't taken the trouble to study their medium."

30　SAYERS, MICHAEL. "A Year in the Theatre." The Criterion, 15
(July), 655-657.
In production The Dog Beneath the Skin proved to be a
disappointment: "One felt that Mr. Auden had a lot of
poetry to get off his chest, and that Mr. Isherwood liked it
and wanted Mr. Auden to have a platform from which to de-
liver it, and so they constructed a play as an excuse for
a public recitation. The recitation was very pleasant and
the play was very silly."

31　SPENDER, STEPHEN. "Fable and Reportage." Left Review, 2
(November), 779-782.
"The weakness of [The Ascent of F6] is that the drama
does not realise and externalise in action the most important implications of Ransom's character.... One is left
feeling that instead of the truth about Ransom having been
realised, it has only been explained: the tragedy culmi-
nates in an acute piece of analysis." [An abridged version
of this article appears in 1937.37.]

32　T., G. M. "Poetry and Revolution." Colosseum, 3 (December),
312-314.
The Ascent of F6 "provides a welcome opportunity for a
fresh onslaught, in the best pro-Marxist manner, on poli-
ticians, bankers and the Press lords. The idea of using
the method of the morality play to criticize modern civilization is a brilliant one; but the morality play was the
product of a primitive civilization and needs to be carefully adapted to contemporary needs."

33　VERSCHOYLE, DEREK. "The Theatre." Spectator, 156 (7 February), 211.
The Dog Beneath the Skin "is a satirical study of a society which has surrendered to unreason and attempts to
conceal from itself the symptoms of its own decadence."
The satire is precise and pointed but the play's "grave
fault" is that it offers no "constructive substitute" except "a vague and doctrinaire outline of a priggish and
watery Utopia."

1937

1   ALLOTT, KENNETH. "Auden in the Theatre." New Verse, nos. 26-
    27 (November), pp. 17-21.
        "I do not believe that the dramatic pieces of Auden, or
    of Auden and Isherwood, are good plays: but The Dog Be-
    neath the Skin and The Ascent of F6 are exciting and in-
    teresting (if mainly for irrelevant reasons).... I want
    to show that the plays would be better if Auden and Isher-
    wood were free of certain pre-conceptions."

2   ANON. "New Play." New York Times (9 March), p. 21.
        Collaboration with Isherwood on The Ascent of F6 may
    have helped clear up some of Auden's difficult poetic
    symbolisms, "but it does not help a great deal; secret
    Audenisms still abound." The play combines "sonorous and
    Shakespeare-like blank verse, very effective, with a curi-
    ously banal sort of doggerel and plain, unadorned prose.
    There are passages both sardonic and acidly humorous, and
    long stretches of what probably is philosophy."

3   ANON. "Other Books: Selected List, Fiction." The London
    Mercury and Bookman, 37 (November), 94.
        "In this long short story [Sally Bowles], written with a
    classic simplicity, Mr. Isherwood has done for a completely
    amoral woman what he did in Mr. Norris Changes Trains for
    a completely amoral man.... [Sally] is no good to anyone,
    yet Mr. Isherwood, with his instinct for humanity as a
    good-in-itself, has made her touching, likeable, a creature
    to haunt the mind."

4   ANON. "A Play in Verse." London Times (20 March), p. 12.
        News item: "The Ascent of F6...has been so well at-
    tended since it was first performed at the Mercury Theatre
    a few weeks ago that Mr. Ashley Dukes has decided to trans-
    fer it to Central London as soon as he can find a suitable
    theatre."

5   ANON. "Plays and Pictures: 'The Ascent of F6,' Mercury Thea-
    tre." New Statesman and Nation, 13 (6 March), 368.
        "This time Auden and Isherwood have brought it off. The
    Ascent of F6 is a poetical drama containing some brilliant
    comedy, deep psychology, and a central theme--the exploita-
    tion by imperialists of all that is best in the youth of
    the Empire...."

6   ANON. Review of The Ascent of F6. London Times (27 February),
    p. 10.
        "Embedded in its doctrine [The Ascent of F6] contains a
    fable that is in itself interesting and coherent. The

1937

dramatists need not blush to find themselves story-tellers, however doctrinaire their chief purpose may be.... The whole play seems to be written less with a desire to wound and contemn than to understand."

7   ANON. Review of <u>Sally Bowles</u>. <u>Times Literary Supplement</u> (23 October), p. 781.
     "[I]t would be harsh to accuse [Isherwood] of having written this story just for the sake of bringing in a few of Sally's pert and shocking remarks; but it is difficult to find much other excuse for it."

*8   ANON. "Something to Bite on." <u>London Daily Sketch</u> (3 May). Review of <u>The Ascent of F6</u>.
     Cited: Jurak, 1969.12, p. 17n.

9   BELITT, BEN. "Rugby and the Tragic Muse." <u>Nation</u>, 144 (17 April), 439-440.
     <u>The Ascent of F6</u> offers "polite 'revolutionary' farce for the salon rather than the open market, conceived on the principle of the rugby match, wherein a symbol serves the function of a football, in a contest of endurance between the actors, the authors, and a handful of selected visitors including Shakespeare, Noel Coward, W. S. Gilbert, and T. S. Eliot."

10   BENÉT, WILLIAM ROSE. "Contemporary Poetry." <u>Saturday Review of Literature</u>, 16 (8 May), 20.
     "It has, I think, been pointed out that the trouble with Auden and Isherwood as satiric dramatists is that they don't know how to write for the stage.... 'The Ascent of F6' is to me merely a curiosity of literature."

11   BOGAN, LOUISE. Review of <u>The Ascent of F6</u>. <u>New Yorker</u>, 12 (13 February), 64-65.
     "'The Ascent of F6' is not...the achievement it might well have been.... [I]t falls, in scheme and tone, between satire and tragedy. Its theme...is a theme for satire. But the authors have sheered off from satire and presented, from time to time, short glimpses into everyone's subconscious."

12   COLUM, MARY M. "The Propaganda Plays." <u>Forum and Century</u>, 97 (June), 355.
     <u>The Ascent of F6</u> is the kind of "social criticism" play which "attacks subtly the whole spiritual structure of modern life and whose authors have no panacea to offer." Its theme is "that life is not worth while."

13   COOKMAN, A. V. "The Theatre." The London Mercury and Book-
      man, 35 (April), 619.
          "In The Ascent of F6 the Mercury Theatre has discovered
      another poetic play of quality. The authors...have a doc-
      trine to inculcate, but like all wise preachers in the
      theatre, they do not fail to tell an interesting story.
      It is a story of a leader of men who despises the motives
      that cause others to accept his leadership and praise his
      achievements."

14   DAY-LEWIS, C. "Paging Mankind." Poetry, 49 (January), 225-
      227.
          "The Ascent of F6 shows a marked forward development
      from...The Dog Beneath the Skin.... The authors' preoccu-
      pation with motives is consistent; but when the interpre-
      tation of motives is elevated into a morality, that morality
      is apt to be negative, defeatist, and dangerous."

15   DREW, ELIZABETH. Discovering Drama. New York: W. W. Norton
      & Co., pp. 199-200, 209-211.
          "...Auden and Isherwood in The Ascent of F6 have created
      a powerful tragedy from the ironic clash between the public
      view of a romantic and courageous hero, and the real mind
      of the man--moved by complex and conflicting motives and
      emotions of which he himself is only half aware."

16   DUKES, ASHLEY. "The English Scene: Tragedy Returns." Theatre
      Arts Monthly, 21 (May), 353, 355-356.
          The mountain in The Ascent of F6 "typifies the struggle
      with existence, the Hamlet-struggle with a world of meaning-
      less action, as opposed to the struggle for existence which
      [Ransom's] just mind perceives in all the starkness of its
      cruelty. The authors are themselves concerned with both
      struggles, which means that they are both philosophers and
      interpreters of history in terms of materialism good enough
      for any Marxist."

17   GREGORY, HORACE. "The Liberal Critics and W. H. Auden." New
      Masses, 23 (20 April), 25-27.
          "The Ascent of F6 shows us again how profoundly the
      young poet accepted the teachings of the Lawrentian aes-
      thetic. The very theme of Sons and Lovers is reënacted on
      the stage; and at the end of the play, as in the novel,
      there is the same 'drift toward death' that Lawrence knew
      so well...."

*18   H., E. B. Review of The Ascent of F6. Cambridge Review, 58
      (30 April), 365.
          Cited: Bloomfield and Mendelson, 1972.11, p. 22.

1937

19 H., H. Review of The Ascent of F6. London Observer (28 Feb-
p. 17.
"It would be easier to praise this play extravagantly
than to do it justice.... [T]he ascent of F.6...becomes an
adventure of the soul on which Hamlet might have made per-
tinent observations, and which Lear might have endorsed."

*20 HOLMES, JOHN. Review of The Ascent of F6. Boston Evening
Transcript (10 July), p. 3.
Cited: Book Review Digest 1937, p. 41.

21 HUMPHREYS, A. R. "The Ascent of F6." Cambridge Review, 58
(30 April), 353-355.
The confusions of The Ascent of F6 are caused by the
mixture of psychological analysis with glib satire, by the
complicated borrowings from Eliot, by the shifting symbol-
isms, superimposed on a physical adventure, and by the
surrealistic representation of hysteria.

22 JACK, PETER MONRO. "A Disturbing Drama by W. H. Auden." New
York Times Book Review (30 May), p. 3.
The "quixotic adventure" depicted in The Ascent of F6
"has its inexorable economic and political causes and effects, none of which Auden and Isherwood spare us. Briefly, it is the tragedy of the individual in a capitalistic
and imperialistic world."

23 JOAD, C. E. M. "Notes along the Way." Time and Tide, 18
(8 May), 603-604.
In The Ascent of F6, "Auden and Isherwood have succeeded
in restoring something of the sense of strangeness to life.
There are dignity in the play and nobility; there is also
a profound wisdom; but above all, there is a sense of the
wonder and significance of being alive."

24 LECHLITNER, RUTH. "Satire and Symbolism in Modern Verse."
New York Herald Tribune Books (8 August), p. 2.
The Ascent of F6 "is not distinguished by its poetic
form; nor do Auden and Isherwood...intend it to be. What
these young men are anxious to put across, even at the ex-
pense of form, are ideas of social import. And much of
what they have to say should interest all people who think
seriously about contemporary problems."

25 M., J. Review of The Ascent of F6. High Point Enterprise
[NC] (4 July).
The Ascent of F6 "is quite likely to discourage the
timid reader before he is well started. It is, as a matter
of fact, highly doubtful, that this play would ever prove a
'success' on the legitimate stage: the average audience
would stare in amazement, leave in bored disgust."

26   MORGAN, CHARLES. "London's Two New Plays." New York Times
        (28 March), section 11, p. 2.
            The satire in Auden/Isherwood's The Ascent of F6 is
        often "no better and no worse than the ordinary undergradu-
        ate charade, but their main argument is lucid, their main
        action is straightforward, their poetic language at its
        best has pressure and rhythm."

27   MUIR, EDWIN. "New Short Stories." Listener, 18 (10 Novem-
        ber), 1039.
            Sally Bowles "has such a rightness that one despairs of
        finding any other quality in it. The writing is sufficient
        and nothing more. The selection of incidents seems obvi-
        ous, the way in which they are set down, natural. It is a
        perfect little work."

28   NATHAN, GEORGE JEAN. "Theater." Scribner's Magazine, 102
        (September), 66, 68.
            The Ascent of F6 "is insistently, exaggeratedly, and
        monotonously pessimistic and defeatist in the treatment of
        its theme.... That there are isolated moments when the
        inner power of the play's theme triumphs over the treatment
        is not to be gainsaid. But I fear that, as a whole, [it]
        makes dramatically a molehill out of a mountain." [Re-
        printed in 1938.16]

29   NIXON, BARBARA. "Theatre." Left Review, 3 (May), 254.
            "Auden and Isherwood have yet to write a play which will
        sustain the level of the first act until the end. As in
        The Dog Beneath the Skin, in the first act of F6 the satire
        is witty and to the point, the dialogue concise, and the
        whole entertaining. But where, in the second half, the
        construction needs to get firmer, where the plot needs to
        gather speed and compactness, it does the reverse and be-
        comes more diffuse."

30   PORTEUS, HUGH GORDON. "Auden Now." Twentieth Century Verse,
        no. 1 (January), [pp. 12-16].
            "What precise contribution Mr. Isherwood's talent has
        lent to The Ascent of F.6 is not apparent. That, I hope,
        is a compliment, of a kind one would pay to the good produc-
        er or performer who does not interpose his personality in
        the play. It is very much an Auden play: a parable about
        power."

31   PORTEUS, HUGH GORDON. "F.6." New English Weekly, 10 (11
        March), 432-433.
            "'The Ascent of F.6,' as performed at the Mercury...is
        both better and worse than the book promised." Auden and
        Isherwood have succeeded "in combining and contrasting

contemporary stage realism with traditional poetic drama.
Probably nobody to-day writes better contemporary dialogue
than Mr. Isherwood."

32   QUINN, KERKER.   "Poets into Playwrights."   Virginia Quarterly
     Review, 13 (Autumn), 618-619.
          "'The Ascent of F6' is inferior to [The Fall of the
     City] in power and poetic beauty. But it succeeds quite as
     admirably in objectifying the action so that on the sur-
     face at least it seems to develop naturally, spontaneously,
     rather than through the poet's complex perception of the
     action...."

33   RODMAN, SELDEN.   Review of The Ascent of F6.   Common Sense, 6
     (June), 27-28.
          The Ascent of F6 is ambitious but not potentially popu-
     lar because of "its sophisticated imagery and needless
     psychopathological symbolism." The verse "occasionally
     rises to great heights, the idea is arresting, but the con-
     clusion is too absurd to make it either good drama or good
     propaganda."

34   S., J.   "New Novels."   London Times (22 October), p. 10.
          Sally Bowles is an "unimportant but revealing portrait....
     Sally is not a character large enough for a full novel, and
     Mr. Isherwood teaches other writers a lesson in restricting
     his book to the size of the subject."

35   SHAWE-TAYLOR, DESMOND.   "New Novels."   New Statesman and Na-
     tion, 14 (23 October), 646, 648.
          "Sally Bowles does not go so deep as The Novaks, and
     naturally has not time to develop the larger lunacy of
     Mr. Norris Changes Trains. But as a specimen of the easy-
     going, good-natured conte it is irresistible, and its read-
     ability is fabulous...."

36   SMITH, JANET ADAM.   Review of The Ascent of F6.   Criterion,
     16 (January), 329-333.
          "The question implicit in F6...is one which Mr. Auden
     has asked explicitly elsewhere: what shall the self-
     conscious man do to be saved? There is no hint that Ran-
     som's friends were wrong in climbing the mountain, that it
     offered them any temptation; it is Ransom, who comes to
     know himself and his motives, who is judged and condemned."

37   SPENDER, STEPHEN.   "The Poetic Drama."   Living Age, 351
     (January), 450-452.
          An abridged version of 1936.31.

38 SYMONS, JULIAN. Review of The Ascent of F6. Twentieth Century Verse, no. 3 (April/May), pp. 59-60.
   As a book The Ascent of F6 seemed dull "with a few good
passages, cluttered up with a pretentious symbolism and
full of the half-deliberate but still regrettable clumsi-
ness and jingo Communism...." But on stage "all, or almost
all, is successful, all is justified."

39 VERSCHOYLE, DEREK. "The Theatre." Spectator, 158 (5 March),
403.
   Review of Rupert Doone's production of The Ascent of F6:
"The first act, which ends with Ransom's decision to lead
the expedition, is remarkably good; but from that point
the play decreases in coherence and force until it dies in
the muddle of the final scene."

40 W., D. "At the Play." Punch, 192 (10 March), 272.
   "The Ascent of F.6...has a very ambitious theme and
flings a wide net. It is concerned with exceptional
achievement under modern conditions, and it seeks to find
the human causes which make individuals want to achieve
these great feats...."

41 WHISTLER, LAURENCE. "A Note on the New Auden." Poetry Review, 28:7-13.
   In The Dog Beneath the Skin, "the fine verse of the Chorus is offset by the amazing crudity of the satire in the
action.... Nor does there seem to be much improvement in
The Ascent of F6.... It is no good making melodrama-
villains out of the characters you hate. Their villainy in
actual life is a very much more subtle affair than Messrs.
Auden and Isherwood give them credit for."

42 WHITE, E. W. Review of A Penny for the Poor. Life and Letters, 16 (Summer), 161-162.
   Isherwood's translations of the verses and mottoes that
decorate the chapter heads of Brecht's A Penny for the Poor
are "sympathetically" done, but the translator forgot or
ignored that they were meant to be sung.

43 WILSON, EDMUND. "The Oxford Boys Becalmed." New Republic, 90
(24 February), 77-78.
   "The Ascent of F-6 suffers even more [than The Dog Beneath the Skin] from the flimsiness of amateur theatricals;
and here Marxism has been forgotten for a relapse into
Freudianism. The theme is a sort of psychoanalytic version
of a career like that of Colonel Lawrence." [Reprinted in
Shores of Light, 1952.12]

44   WYATT, EUPHEMIA VAN RENSSELAER. "Post War Poets and the
      Theater." Catholic World, 145 (August), 602-604.
          "Since Auden has begun to collaborate with Christopher
      Isherwood, his plays have gained in coherence." The Ascent
      of F6 "is far ahead of any of Auden's other dramatic excur-
      sions. The story is good straight theater but for the
      reader its philosophical conclusions are distinctly taxing
      to follow."

                              1938

1   ANON. "Cambridge Arts Theatre: 'On the Frontier.'" London
      Times (16 November), p. 12.
          "The early stages of [On the Frontier] deal with the
      situation in a light vein, but inevitably the antagonism
      between the adjoining States...becomes dominant.... Com-
      edy turns to tragedy and the lighter vein of the opening
      reverts to grim revolutionary scenes."

2   ANON. "Music by Wireless." London Times (12 December),
      p. 25.
          "The Ascent of F6...was heard in a broadcast version
      last week, produced by Miss Barbara Burnham. Much of it
      came through very well, but it is a little complicated for
      the microphone.... The weakness of the play has always
      been the ending, and Messrs. Auden and Isherwood seem to
      have written a new ending for this performance, which dif-
      fered from both the theatre version and the published text,
      and was not really satisfactory."

3   ANON. "A Poetic Drama of To-day: Parody of Public Life."
      Times Literary Supplement (29 October), p. 689.
          On the Frontier is "a drama so much absorbed with char-
      acteristic world events that the play hardly stays in the
      theatre at all. Its whole reference is outside. We, the
      audience, are present at a running commentary...."

*4   ANON. Review of On the Frontier. Cambridge Review, 60
      (25 November), 134.
          Cited: Bloomfield and Mendelson, 1972.11, p. 35.

5   BARNES, T. R. "Auden and Isherwood." Scrutiny, 7 (December),
      361-363.
          "Messrs. Auden and Isherwood continue to follow their
      principle of putting Marxist pap into bourgeois bottles.
      They call this repast a melodrama in three acts, but un-
      fortunately it doesn't deserve that title. On the Frontier
      is a tract, similar in formula to their other productions,
      but duller."

6 BROWN, IVOR. Review of On the Frontier. Manchester Guardian
   (2 December), p. 7.
      On the Frontier "shows no advance on their past experi-
   ments and its 'Left-wingishness' seems to offer no ideas
   which are not familiar to a schoolboy Socialist. But is
   done with the customary drive and mastery of an effective
   phrase."

7 CALDER-MARSHALL, ARTHUR. Review of Lions and Shadows. Life
   and Letters, 18 (Summer), 184-185.
      In Lions and Shadows, Isherwood succeeds in describing
   "a typical literary education of the twenties"; the book
   has a witty, impersonal style and avoids sentimentality
   without becoming superficial.

8 CAMERON, MAY. "England's White-Haired Literary Boys...Talk of
   China and Themselves." New York Post (9 July).
      Auden and Isherwood discuss their collaboration on what
   they call "simply a war travel book": "Obviously we
   couldn't say anything authoritative about China, who's
   going to win and all that. We were just two strangers and
   we hope to present our impressions."

9 CONNOLLY, CYRIL. Enemies of Promise and Other Essays. New
   York: Macmillan, pp. 89-91, 94-96, 105, 107, 134, 176.
      "In England the ablest exponents of the colloquial style
   among the younger writers are Christopher Isherwood and
   George Orwell, both left-wing and both, at the present
   level of current English, superlatively readable." Isherwood's readability may prove "fatal," but he also possesses
   "the mastery of form, the imaginative content of a true
   novelist...." [The revised edition of the book, 1948.8,
   does not alter the comments on Isherwood.]

10 [DAY-LEWIS, C.] Review of On the Frontier. Listener, 20
   (24 November), 1145.
      On the Frontier seems "the least successful of the Auden-
   Isherwood plays" because it lacks both "the vitality and
   invention" of The Dog Beneath the Skin and "the deeply
   realised moral conflict" of The Ascent of F6.

11 DUKES, ASHLEY. "The Ascent of F6 in Norwich." Theatre Arts
   Monthly, 22 (April), 258.
      "The poetic drama by W. H. Auden and Christopher Isher-
   wood was included by Nugent Monck among the recent productions at Maddermarket Theatre. This piercing and somewhat
   disillusioning examination of man's most vaunted qualities
   has been hailed by the critics as the authors' finest work
   and a milestone toward the drama of the future."

1938

12 EMERSON, DOROTHY. "Poetry Corner." <u>Scholastic</u>, 31 (15 January), 23E.
     Brief comments on verse-plays of the twentieth century and excerpts from <u>The Ascent of F6</u>.

13 GOLDIE, GRACE WYNDHAM. "Broadcast Drama: Half Way up." <u>Listener</u>, 20 (15 December), 1326.
     Review of the B.B.C. broadcast of <u>The Ascent of F6</u> (4 December 1938): "The quality of mind behind [the play] is unmistakable. The authors are using the theatre to state the problem of contemporary youth, that swing away from detachment and towards action which is combined with a distrust both of the motives of action and of the forms that it takes."

14 GRIGSON, GEOFFREY. "Education in the Twenties." <u>New Verse</u>, no. 29 (March), pp. 18-19.
     <u>Lions and Shadows</u> is "very simple, very human, and very interesting" and will be a key reference book on the "Auden Age" and the so-called Auden circle.

15 MacNEICE, LOUIS. "The Theatre." <u>Spectator</u>, 161 (18 November), 858.
     Review of the Group Theatre production of <u>On the Frontier</u>: The theme is similar to that of <u>The Ascent of F6</u>, "but the treatment is rather facile and seems to fall between two stools as if the authors could not decide whether they were writing a straight play or a crooked one. Compared with <u>The Ascent of F6</u>, there is less sparkle, less poetry, less thought and even more embarrassment."

16 NATHAN, GEORGE JEAN. <u>The Morning after the First Night</u>. New York: Alfred A. Knopf, pp. 168-171.
     Reprint of review of <u>The Ascent of F6</u>, 1937.28.

17 PAINE, TOM. "On the Frontier." <u>New Statesman and Nation</u>, 16 (19 November), 826-827.
     "The first night of <u>On the Frontier</u> was a great success at the Cambridge Arts Theatre. The play is precisely topical.... The verse is admirable and the music effective.... [I]t is dramatically much more mature than <u>The Ascent of F.6</u>."

18 SMITH, NAOMI ROYDE. "Mr. W. H. Auden and Others." <u>Time and Tide</u>, 19 (19 November), 1619-1620.
     In <u>On the Frontier</u>, Auden and Isherwood "use and revivify the conventions and experiments of the stage." They give their theme "the drive of news-value" and heighten it "with the poignancy of an immediate danger." The "direct and realistic satire" alternates with more symbolic scenes, and the "two contrasted methods of writing for the stage" are linked with music and drama.

19 SOUTHWORTH, JAMES G. "Wystan Hugh Auden." <u>Sewanee Review</u>,
    46 (April-June), 189-205.
    "A reading of Mr. Isherwood's <u>Mr. Norris Changes Trains</u>
    throws some light on the possible characteristics of his
    contributions to the plays. If Mr. Auden has written the
    poetry, it is Mr. Isherwood who has furnished many of the
    ideas of surprising pungency."

20 SPENDER, STEPHEN. "The Poetic Dramas of W. H. Auden and
    Christopher Isherwood," in <u>New Writing</u>, NS 1 (Autumn).
    Edited by John Lehmann. London: Hogarth Press, pp. 102-
    108.
    "An encouraging start has been made by Auden and Isher-
    wood to solve the problems of creating a contemporary po-
    etic drama. The most important of these problems--that of
    finding an audience--they have solved better than anyone
    for a generation. They have concentrated--quite justifi-
    ably--on providing entertainment; but since they are also
    creating a form and presenting a view of the world, one
    has to realize how many of the problems of presentation
    they have evaded."

21 VERSCHOYLE, DEREK. "Mr. Isherwood's Growing Pains." <u>The Lon-
    don Mercury and Bookman</u>, 37 (April), 660.
    "<u>Lions and Shadows</u> in no way succeeds in what is de-
    clared to be its purpose [to present "the education of a
    novelist"]. Nor does it satisfy overmuch in pursuing its
    secondary aim [presenting Isherwood's early life]. Neither
    Mr. Isherwood's childhood nor his adolescence differed as
    much as he appears to suppose from the childhood and ado-
    lescence of the average person."

22 WRIGHT, RALPH. "'Heroes' Who Were Afraid." <u>Daily Worker</u>
    (30 March), p. 7.
    Both <u>Lions and Shadows</u> and Edward Upward's <u>Journey to
    the Border</u> "are remarkable for their descriptions of an
    adolescent mind, dominated by fear, and out of touch with
    its environment."

                            1939

1   ADLER, HENRY. "A Political Charade." <u>The London Mercury</u>, 39
    (January), 368.
    <u>On the Frontier</u> "should be effective when staged because
    it does compress topical and essential issues into a neat,
    if narrow, dramatic form, even if it cramps them. It is a
    skilfully composed political charade, enacted by trim, flat
    puppets who moralize pithily if not profoundly."

1939

2   A[LLOTT], K[ENNETH]. "A Tract." New Verse, NS 1 (January),
    24-25.
        On the Frontier is an ineffective play: it presents "a
    false front of simplification."

3   ANON. "Ace Collaborators." San Francisco Argonaut (18 Au-
    gust).
        Review of Journey to a War: "The observations are re-
    corded in lively style. Lacking is the credulous onlookers'
    stamp. These gentlemen might hail from Missouri. They
    know their legs were pulled, but aren't sure just when."

4   ANON. "Auden and Isherwood in China: Diary and Poetic Com-
    mentary." Times Literary Supplement (18 March), p. 158.
        Journey to a War "is a nourishing and sharply flavoured
    sandwich of a book. It contains a rich, thick slab of
    travel diary transcribed by Mr. Isherwood.... [H]is simple
    and telling precision exactly fits a narrative which, to be
    true, must be disconnected."

5   ANON. "The Bad Earth." Time, 34 (7 August), 59.
        Review of Journey to a War: "In high holiday humor,
    this bright, fast, pert reporting rollicks along almost as
    if there were no war in China.... More startling than any-
    thing they report about the East is what they report, often
    unconsciously, about themselves."

6   ANON. "Briefly Noted: Fiction." New Yorker, 15 (18 March),
    69-70.
        Goodbye to Berlin is a "series of sketches which thor-
    oughly illuminate the background of Hitler's success.... A
    pitying and understanding book."

7   ANON. "Briefly Noted: Verse." New Yorker, 15 (18 March), 72.
        On the Frontier is "a decided letdown from these col-
    laborators' first dramatic effort.... It conforms exactly
    to a by now well-worn dilute-Leftist stereotype, and its
    purpose, which seems to be pure indoctrination, flattens
    the characters into puppets and the writing into medioc-
    rity."

8   ANON. "China at War: Travel Diary and Commentary." London
    Times (17 March), p. 10.
        In Journey to a War, "the merit of Mr. Isherwood's rec-
    ord is its sharp and unprejudiced objectivity. In these
    pages a strange country and a strange people are seen for
    the first time by four uncommonly open eyes."

9   ANON. "Group Theatre: 'On the Frontier.'" London Times
     (13 February), p. 10.
        "Though, in its bitter end, [On the Frontier] does not
     go beyond an advocacy of hatred and of heroic death on the
     barricades, and is, therefore, slashed across by the famil-
     iar confusion of those who will not or cannot distinguish
     between a political dislike of war and a spiritual percep-
     tion of the futility of all violence, it is conspicuously
     more mature and, in the highest sense, more charitable than
     the dramatists' other work."

10   ANON. "A Present Day Parallel." Chicago Tribune (8 April),
     p. 12.
        "If Hitler had never lived, [On the Frontier] would be
     merely a Graustarkian melodrama with some unpleasant social
     implications and some amusing satires on government and the
     ways of international finance and politics. But because
     one of the characters, The Leader, is almost a caricature
     of Hitler, it is tempting to identify his nation...and its
     rival...and their war with some current events and forces
     in Europe."

11   ANON. Review of Goodbye to Berlin. Boston Evening Transcript
     (22 April), p. 2.
        "The structure is loose; the writing direct if immature.
     Isherwood intended these sketches as little more than a
     notebook for an ambitious novel he had conceived. Realiza-
     tion of the project would require months of reworking, syn-
     thesis and emotional vitalization."

12   ANON. Review of Goodbye to Berlin. Times Literary Supplement
     (4 March), p. 133.
        In Goodbye to Berlin the "air of inflexible integrity is
     not unattractive. At the same time, however, it has the
     notable drawback that Mr. Isherwood is continually drawing
     the reader's attention to Mr. Isherwood.... [H]aving taken
     his stand in the witness-box, his imagination tends to stop
     short at the contemplation of himself."

13   ANON. Review of Journey to a War. Booklist, 36 (1 September),
     4.
        "Admitting no special knowledge of the country, [Auden
     and Isherwood] recorded both the commonplace and the un-
     usual with honesty, mild humor, and some bitterness...."

14   ANON. Review of Journey to a War. North American Review, 248
     (Autumn), 203.
        Journey to a War "avoids omniscience and brilliantly re-
     cords first impressions"; it is "a book of sublimated re-
     portage which one reads greedily."

1939

15   ANON. Review of Journey to a War. Springfield News [MA]
      (1 November).
          "It is inevitable that such a journey would produce [a]
      depressive effect, yet, although there is horror and trag-
      edy in abundance, [Journey to a War] is often relieved by a
      semiobjective humor and contrasting events."

16   ANON. Review of On the Frontier. Birmingham News [AL]
      (16 April).
          By most standards On the Frontier is the best of the
      three Auden/Isherwood plays: "The prose scenes are com-
      pactly pointed and yet conversational in their satire, and
      several of the verse choruses, such as the opening chant...
      are full of the spontaneous pithiness of the people."

17   ANON. Review of On the Frontier. Booklist, 35 (1 May), 287.
          "An ironic play, in prose and verse, about life in a
      totalitarian state, and in its neighboring country."

*18   ANON. Review of On the Frontier. Cleveland Open Shelf (June),
      p. 11.
          Cited: Book Review Digest 1939, p. 39.

19   ANON. "Seeing War in China." Pasadena Star News (19 August).
          Journey to a War is a factual account, yet "the authors
      plainly show that their sympathies are not with the Japan-
      ese."

20   ANON. "Striking." San Francisco Argonaut (7 July).
          "These two young poet-playwrights are doing more and
      more to bring themselves into international notice. This
      three-act melodrama [On the Frontier] is a stirring piece.
      Satire, tragedy and idealism meet in the plot of intrigue."

21   ATKINSON, BROOKS. "Insurgent Penmen." New York Times
      (9 April), section 10, p. 1.
          "[O]ne comes up from a reading of 'On the Frontier' with
      a sense of dissatisfaction. The play never goes doggedly
      to grips with either the theatre or its theme. After a
      single-minded approach to the subject-matter it scatters
      fire in double talk and caterwauling, asking the audience
      and the actors to perform impossible tasks; and it con-
      cludes with a supernatural orgy of verse."

22   BERTRAM, JAMES. "'Patrons Pour la Chine.'" Listener, 21
      (16 March), "Spring Book Supplement," vii.
          "Journey to a War is a book that no one will want to
      miss, and it would be merely pedantic for anyone with a
      rather longer experience of China than the authors to point
      out its inaccuracies of detail, futile to wish that they
      had seen more than they did see."

23   BISSON, T. A. "Two Poets in China." Saturday Review of Lit-
        erature, 20 (5 August), 6.
            In Journey to a War, Auden and Isherwood have written
        "a brilliant commentary on the Sino-Japanese War. Isher-
        wood's narrative of their travels...sparkles with a gaiety
        seemingly unforced, yet playing continually against a som-
        ber undertone."

24   BOIE, MILDRED. Review of Journey to a War. Atlantic, 164
        (November), in unpaged preliminary section.
            Journey to a War is "readable and in spots exceedingly
        interesting.... The accounts of the people...are sharp
        and precocious"; and the analyses of China's problems "are
        unpretentious and neat but not original or profound sum-
        maries of what they were told and observed in so short a
        visit...."

25   BROWN, IVOR. Review of On the Frontier. London Observer
        (19 February), p. 13.
            The best thing in On the Frontier is "the realistic
        psychological study of Westland's dictator, a weak man
        ridden by his own fantasies of greatness.... [It is] sad
        that the whole theatrical effect should have to be sub-
        jected to and spoiled by the anti-realistic elements."

26   CAMERON, MAY. "A Joint Diary of Road to War." New York Post
        (1 August).
            Journey to a War "struck me as being astonishingly triv-
        ial in many of its pages.... [A]ny one who wishes any very
        solid and meaty information about war-time China had better
        search elsewhere."

27   COLLIS, MAURICE. "Abandoned by His General and His Lice."
        Time and Tide, 20 (22 April), 510.
            Journey to a War is filled with illuminating touches and
        curious but delicious anecdotes. The pungent effects of the
        writing "are produced by the quantity of unusual detail,
        a smiling subtlety, perfect good humour and a power of
        catching the peculiar Chinese approach to actuality."

28   CONNOLLY, CYRIL. "Introduction" to All the Conspirators.
        London: Jonathan Cape, pp. 7-10.
            All the Conspirators "is a key to Isherwood and the
        Twenties. It is as mature, as readable, as concentrated,
        as perceptive as anything he has written since, and intro-
        duces a dominant theme of his work, the Evil Mother, fierce,
        obstinate, tearful, and conventional, who destroys her son
        in All the Conspirators as ingeniously as in The Memorial
        or The Ascent of F.6."

1939

29   CONROY, JACK. "Anti-Fascist Melodrama." <u>San Francisco Peo-</u>
      <u>ple's World</u> (25 March).
           "<u>On the Frontier</u>, with its Freudian nuances and other
      intellectual influences, is yet melodrama of a sort, though
      not of the ten-twenty-and-thirty variety. It reads flu-
      ently, and it should act that way, too."

*30   DARLINGTON, W. A. "War Play by Two Poets." <u>London Daily</u>
      <u>Telegraph</u> (13 February).
           Review of <u>On the Frontier</u>. Cited: Jurak, 1969.12, p. 41n.

31   DAVENPORT, BASIL. "Atmosphere of Decay." <u>Saturday Review of</u>
      <u>Literature</u>, 19 (15 April), 14.
           In <u>Goodbye to Berlin</u>, "Isherwood combines an uncanny
      accuracy of observation and ability to convey his impres-
      sions with a universal sympathy almost unknown in English
      literature.... One feels that this impartial sensitivity
      has in it a certain defect of its own; the book leaves one
      with the feeling that Mr. Isherwood merely let impressions
      come to him; one cannot help wishing that he had looked
      for more shades of opinion and character...."

32   DEUTSCH, BABETTE. "Melodrama of Fascism." <u>New York Herald</u>
      <u>Tribune Books</u> (26 March), p. 19.
           "Reading [<u>On the Frontier</u>] is one of the most exciting
      experiences that Left-Wing English writers have provided.
      There is a promise that it will be staged in New York later
      this season. But as a matter of fact, it is being staged
      in the offices and sitting rooms, the prisons and dance
      halls of Europe at this moment."

33   DEXTER, CHARLES E. "Auden-Isherwood Journey to China." <u>San</u>
      <u>Francisco People's World</u> (26 August).
           The tone of <u>Journey to a War</u> is "polite." Isherwood is
      a "master of banter" and his descriptions "glow with real-
      ism and humor. It is not until he reaches Shanghai that
      they glow with indignation."

34   DUFFUS, R. L. "An Illuminating Journey to the War in China."
      <u>New York Times Book Review</u> (6 August), pp. 1, 15.
           <u>Journey to a War</u> "is not a whole and cannot be reviewed
      as a whole. If the prose is taken first, we find a travel
      diary which is annoying (to an American, at least) in some
      respects, and highly entertaining in other respects."

35   DUKES, ASHLEY. "In Paris and London." <u>Theatre Arts Monthly,</u>
      23 (January), 20-24.
           A performance of <u>On the Frontier</u> is reviewed as part of
      a survey of current European theatre: "The play should be
      freed of its accretion of artistic character, mostly bogus.

And if the dramatists hope to interpret the rhythms of the modern world significantly, they must think more deeply and individually."

36   DUPEE, F. W.   "Two Refined Oxonians Tour the Chinese War Scene...."   New York Sun (2 August).
Review of Journey to a War: "Discriminating about the Chinese as individuals, Isherwood is likewise quietly intelligent about the war as a whole. He is an artist, not a mouthpiece for any cause; he tells you only what he sees himself."

37   GANNETT, LEWIS.   "Books and Things."   New York Herald Tribune (1 August), p. 13.
Journey to a War "is Britishly intelligent and Britishly bright and, sometimes, Britishly debonair. Mr. Auden contributes some poems in a disillusioned late Aldous Huxley vein, Mr. Isherwood a straightforward prose diary à la Peter Fleming."

38   GARNETT, DAVID.   "Books in General."   New Statesman and Nation, 17 (11 March), 362.
Isherwood has the power "to impose a personal vision of the world on the reader." But in Goodbye to Berlin, he "no longer achieves his effects by plunging the reader into the unpleasant, but by leading him gently by the hand."

39   GREEN-ARMYTAGE, A. H. N.   "A Valuable Failure."   Colosseum, 5 (January), 66-68.
On the Frontier "is less successful than The Dog Beneath the Skin, but for an honorable reason. It is less of a caricature.... Mr. Auden and his collaborator are perhaps the ablest writers of the post-war generation, and it is therefore most heartening to find them preaching...that we are all members one of another, and therefore jointly responsible for our own disasters...."

40   GREENBERT, CLEMENT.   "The Beggar's Opera—After Marx."   Partisan Review, 6 (Winter), 120-122.
"Isherwood's versions of Brecht's own poems which are set at the chapter heads [of A Penny for the Poor] are brave efforts, but inadequate since they coarsen Brecht's colloquialisms to the point of banality, something which is entirely absent from the German."

41   GREENSPAN, JEANNETTE.   "Trail of Terror in China."   Brooklyn Citizen (22 September).
Review of Journey to a War: "In place of the analytical objectivity which characterizes the usual run of war correspondence, it seems that Auden and Isherwood have deliberately colored their report with their sympathy for the

Chinese cause, their idealogical [sic] interest in the
Eighth and New Fourth Armies, and their furious indignation
at the policy and war methods of the Japanese."

42 GRIGSON, GEOFFREY E. Review of Goodbye to Berlin. New Verse,
      NS 1 (May), 54.
        In Goodbye to Berlin, Isherwood "exhibits values without
      stating them by illustrating their absence. This book is a
      brilliant lesson in how to be serious by means of charm...."

43 G[RIGSON], G[EOFFREY] E. "Twenty-Seven Sonnets." New Verse,
      NS 1 (May) 47-49.
        Review of Journey to a War: "Good as Isherwood's prose
      travel-diary is, as a description of the bigness of China
      and the War, not jazzed up into the dramatic, know-all,
      pseudo-significant pattern of the journalist, it is really
      rather small beside the moral and imaginative weight and
      tenderness of Auden's poems...."

44 HAWKINS, DESMOND. Review of On the Frontier. Purpose, 11
      (January March), 55-57.
        "Mr. Isherwood has had his uses as a dilution and a
      lubricant: his experience as a scenarist has been of con-
      siderable value in matching the substance to the medium.
      But what is now important to the bystander is whether the
      authors will continue to hash up increasingly facile ver-
      sions of their political burlesque...or whether Auden will
      find the stamina to measure himself against the tragic-
      heroic theme which appears to haunt him."

45 JACK, PETER MONRO. "Auden & Isherwood." New York Times Book
      Review (16 April), p. 16.
        "The brilliant collaboration of Auden and Isherwood,
      whose plays are still unaccountably absent from Broadway,
      has turned from poetry to straight political melodrama....
      The hilarious fantasy and the tragic symbolism of the ear-
      lier plays are dropped in favor of simple exposition. It
      may be likely that 'On the Frontier' is their best stage
      play at the moment, with its violent dramatic situations,
      strong characterization, and shrewd theatre."

46 JACKSON, JOSEPH HENRY. "China in Wartime Informatively De-
      picted by Two Englishmen." San Francisco Chronicle
      (11 August).
        Journey to a War "is a great deal more than just a
      travel book, chiefly because China is at war. Admitting
      that they knew nothing about the Far East...these two young
      men have tried to record for the benefit of the reader who
      has never been to China some impressions of what he would
      be likely to see and of what kind of stories he might be
      likely to hear."

47   JONES, HOWARD MUMFORD. "Eminently Readable." Boston Evening
      Transcript (5 August), p. 1.
          Journey to a War "has an odd effect of good humor and
      gayety. It is the product of hopefulness, despite the sur-
      face cynicism of its authors, for they see in the struggle
      part of the eternal march of mankind towards 'human jus-
      tice, the contribution of our star.' They have written an
      eminently readable book."

48   K., E. C. "Young Englishmen Write Feelingly of the War in
      China." Milwaukee Journal (20 August).
          In Journey to a War, Auden and Isherwood were sympa-
      thetic to the Chinese cause, but "they were not greatly
      impressed by Chinese morale or Chinese customs.... [T]he
      China they saw is a land of confusion and disorder."

49   KAZIN, ALFRED. "Leaves from Under the Lindens." New York
      Herald Tribune Books (12 March), p. 10.
          "One does not find in [Goodbye to Berlin] anything like
      a major study; the scale is restricted to the lives of a
      few Berliners.... But [Isherwood's] touch is so sure that
      something of the central quality of Berlin life is gath-
      ered. They gain by pungency what they lack in scope...."

50   KIRSTEIN, LINCOLN. "Poets under Fire." Nation, 149 (5 Au-
      gust), 151-152.
          Journey to a War "is ostensibly a record of a trip
      through wartorn China by two of the most talented young
      English writers of our day. But primarily it is a book
      about the conscience of a Western ruling class faced with
      the agony of an Oriental people to whom they feel respon-
      sibility. It is funny, brilliant, fierce, tragic, and
      technically superb."

51   KRONENBERGER, LOUIS. "Two Travellers and Thirty-eight Philo-
      sophers." New Yorker, 15 (12 August), 53.
          "'Journey to a War' is, in a sense, trivial.... But, as
      a whole, it is by no means unobservant or even unreflective.
      The point is, here is war as experienced by civilians, and
      China observed by tourists; under such circumstances, war
      is bound to seem a little too decorous and China a little
      too picturesque."

52   LECHLITNER, RUTH. "Two English Poets See the War in China."
      New York Herald Tribune Books (6 August), p. 3.
          Journey to a War "is the work of mature, very much in
      earnest writers. But it is the amateur status of the trip
      and the telling--never glorified, always casual, real, in-
      timate--that gives 'Journey to a War' its charm, its thor-
      ough aliveness." [This review also appeared in the Wash-
      ington Post (6 August), p. 10.]

1939

53   LEHMANN, JOHN. "Christopher Isherwood and Berlin," in his
      New Writing in England. New York: Critics Group Press,
      pp. 24-31.
          "The implication of Christopher Isherwood's work is en-
      tirely revolutionary, humanist in the most active sense of
      the word, though he is never explicitly propagandist.
      Isherwood is one of the first prose artists of his genera-
      tion to receive the full impact of fascist-menaced Europe,
      and the first perhaps who neither turned away from this
      sight to write of other subjects nor was deflected by it
      into more obviously propagandist and political activities."
      [Revised and expanded in 1940.6.]

54   LEHMANN, JOHN. "Experiment in Drama," in his New Writing in
      England. New York: Critics Group Press, pp. 32-36.
          The Dog Beneath the Skin and The Ascent of F6 both suf-
      fer from private allusions and jokes, although the latter
      is more dramatic in structure and clearer in theme. On the
      Frontier is an indication "that these highly gifted col-
      laborators may one day soon write a play that is as rich as
      their earlier work but far wider in its appeal and clearer
      in its thought...." [Revised and expanded in 1940.5.]

55   LELAND, MARION. "Speaking of Books." Greenwich Press [CT]
      (12 October).
          Review of Journey to a War: "Sensitive and alertly in-
      telligent, the observations and adventures of Poet Auden
      and Author Isherwood are entertaining as well as revealing
      commentaries."

56   LINKE, LILO. Review of Goodbye to Berlin. Life and Letters,
      21 (April), 118-119.
          Isherwood shows a complete understanding of Berlin and
      its people; he "can write in the most admirable way, always
      the right words, and never a word too many."

57   McEACHERAN, F. "Topical Drama." The Adelphi, NS 15 (Janu-
      ary), 201-203.
          "On the Frontier will come as a disappointment to many
      people.... [T]here is little poetry, very ordinary psychol-
      ogy (though quite good), satire hardly equal to that in the
      Dog, little vitality and not even that sense of 'getting
      somewhere' which often retrieves a drama." Furthermore,
      the political message is not clear.

58   MacF., R. P. "Two Brilliant Young Writers Record Their Travels
      in China's War Zone." Chicago Tribune (26 August), p. 15.
          "With the traditional British phlegm, these two brilliant
      young writers took their camp beds through China's war zone,
      having tea with their air raids, dashing off sonnets between

visits to the front lines, and then writing about their experiences in a book which lets considerable light in on the
true situation in that unhappy land."

59   MacLEOD, JOSEPH GORDON. "Notes on the Frontier." Townsman, 2
     (January), 22-24.
          Auden and Isherwood "may feel with the workers, but [On
     the Frontier] rings false. Perhaps from lack of technique,
     perhaps from a failure of creative power. Not good realis-
     tic stuff, not good abstracted stuff. A manipulation of
     images to rouse sentiment fashionable among the not-too-
     active left wing of the middle-class."

60   MANN, KALUS. "Berlin, Pre-Swastika." Nation, 148 (22 April),
     473-474.
          In Goodbye to Berlin, "Isherwood is neither a reporter
     nor a preacher of morals...."; yet he "aspires to portray
     the decay and rapid transformation of the German capital,
     in epic form. He tries to make clear how it happened. In
     many passages he most impressively succeeds."

61   MERLIN, MILTON. "Agony of China Described by Poet and Novel-
     ist." Los Angeles Times (1 September).
          In Journey to a War, Auden and Isherwood "disregard
     journalistic tradition of reporting flat facts and present
     instead a lively personal account of experiences and inter-
     views, sights and events."

62   MOULT, THOMAS. Review of Goodbye to Berlin. Manchester
     Guardian (24 March), p. 7.
          "Judged solely as art, the six pieces, including frag-
     ments of a diary, are vague and uneven, and as personal
     impressions they are overegoistic and too lacking in the
     saving grace of humour...."

63   MUIR, EDWIN. The Present Age from 1914. Introductions to
     English Literature, V. 5, edited by Bonamy Dobrée. London:
     Cresset Press, pp. 120, 122, 145, 178-179, 216, 265.
          "The Ascent of F6 is a clever construction which keeps
     the reader guessing, and therefore occupied, from scene to
     scene.... [But Ransom's] fine sentiments, his disinter-
     ested service of his country, were mere disguises of a
     mother-fixation, it seems...."

64   O'BRIEN, KATE. "Fiction." Spectator, 162 (3 March), 364.
          "For the manner of Goodbye to Berlin...there can be
     nothing but praise, but whether the content is consistently
     worth the beautiful work expended is a question....
     [W]hile reading the book one was wearied sometimes by sus-
     tained closeups of small neuroses."

1939

65   P., J. M. D. Review of <u>Journey to a War</u>. <u>Manchester Guardian</u>
      (19 May), p. 7.
          In <u>Journey to a War</u>, "the prose account is light, amus-
      ing, flippant, and almost, one may say, under-graduate....
      Mr. Isherwood cannot write badly. His light and simple
      style and observant imagination make him...the ideal lit-
      erary reporter."

66   PEFFER, NATHANIEL. "War on the Yellow River." <u>New Republic</u>,
      100 (27 September), 221-222.
          <u>Journey to a War</u> provides "[g]ood observation, good
      documentary material, good war reporting and good fun to
      read. Only the snobbish will find it trivial."

67   PLOMER, WILLIAM. "Journey to a War." <u>The London Mercury</u>, 39
      (April), 642-644.
          <u>Journey to a War</u> is "a various and lively commentary; no
      bouquet of recollections in tranquillity...; but a collec-
      tion of snapshots by two extremely animated minds, and like
      any collection of snapshots uneven and miscellaneous."

68   PRITCHETT, V. S. "Auden and Isherwood in China--A London Let-
      ter." <u>Christian Science Monitor</u> (29 April), "Weekly Maga-
      zine Section," p. 10.
          In <u>Journey to a War</u>, "Mr. Isherwood does the prose. He
      has the detached, bird-like eye, a way of writing which
      suggests that he heard and saw everything and was so unob-
      trusive that nobody knew he was there."

69   PRITCHETT, V. S. "Post-War Germany." <u>Christian Science Moni-
      tor</u> (8 April), "Weekly Magazine Section," p. 11.
          Isherwood's stories in <u>Goodbye to Berlin</u> "are studies of
      groups. The Landauers are rich Jews, the Nowaks are a
      working-class family. Yet, though he is, as a foreigner,
      outside them..., he manages to get an extraordinary illu-
      sion of wholeness in his portraits."

70   RAHV, PHILIP. "A Variety of Fiction." <u>Partisan Review</u>, 6
      (Spring), 107-108.
          <u>Goodbye to Berlin</u>, "though it communicates the strain of
      the period through casually presented details of melancholy
      and derangement, has an undertone of humor which in a way
      measures its degree of detachment.... [Isherwood's] prose
      manners are those of an impressionist."

71   REINER, MAX. "Queer People." <u>Canadian Forum</u>, 19 (April), 29.
          In <u>Goodbye to Berlin</u>, "Mr. Isherwood has a very deft pen
      and an observant eye. If he tells us little about Berlin,
      he makes us live and feel very fully with a curious assort-
      ment of human beings...."

72   RHODES, ARTHUR. "Two Englishmen View Hell in China." Brook-
        lyn Daily Eagle (8 August).
           In Journey to a War, Auden and Isherwood "plucked infor-
        mation there and everywhere--at least wherever they thought
        they could cull the reliable.... And they report their
        wanderings with candor and often with wit and sparkle."

73   RODMAN, SELDEN. Review of On the Frontier. Common Sense, 8
        (May), 25-26.
           On the Frontier is "less tricky and far more playable"
        than the previous Auden-Isherwood plays, but "in avoiding
        the sur-realist situations and fine writing that may have
        weakened the earlier plays," the authors "have achieved
        mere clever caricature."

74   ROVERE, RICHARD H. "Far Eastern Diary." New Masses, 32
        (15 August), 25-26.
           Journey to a War is "an exasperating book." The writing
        is beautiful and the authors are quite sensitive, but they
        "went through China like a pair of frivolous Boy Scouts--
        or better, perhaps, like the 'silly ass' Englishmen of
        Wodehouse...."

75   S., J. "New Novels." London Times (3 March), p. 21.
           "Isherwood has never seemed to claim more than unworld-
        liness for his Berlin figures, some of whom are reassembled
        here in Goodbye to Berlin.... [E]ven when...they should be
        more than mildly shocking, they are so spontaneous and un-
        critical of themselves that it is impossible to be dis-
        pleased."

76   SCHILLER, SISTER MARY B., O.S.F. "Trends in Modern Poetic
        Drama in English, 1900-1938." Ph.D. dissertation, Univer-
        sity of Illinois, pp. 230-242.
           "There is more constraint and form to The Ascent of
        F6.... The rollicking humor and the savage satire of The
        Dog Beneath the Skin give way to an unhealthy pessimism and
        a milder scorn for the aristocratic class." On the Fron-
        tier is "a propaganda play cast in a melodrama pattern.
        Its emphasis is on situation not on character."

77   SELBY, JOHN. "'Journey to a War' Told in Bold Type." Memphis
        Commercial Appeal (20 August).
           In Journey to a War "it is apparent that although Messrs.
        Auden and Isherwood found little the newspapers have not
        said long ago, they write their findings very well indeed."
        The travel diary "is an amusing, quickly stepping chunk of
        prose...." [This review also appeared, anonymously, in
        the Utica Press [NY] (1 August), the Charlotte News [NC]
        (13 August), and the Charlotte Observer [NC] (20 August).]

1939

78   SMITH, JANET ADAM. Review of On the Frontier. Criterion, 18
      (January), 322-323.
          "On the Frontier is far more of a charade than a play.
      Each scene lights up a different aspect of the general sit-
      uation, but the scenes are not organically connected...."

79   SNYDER, LOUIS L. "Behind the Swastika." Living Age, 356
      (July), 498-499.
          "One who lived in Berlin during the period described by
      Mr. Isherwood will recognize in [Goodbye to Berlin] an ad-
      mirable account of the spirit and temper of the German
      people during an era of emotional transition."

80   S[OUTHWORTH], J. G. Review of On the Frontier. Saturday Re-
      view of Literature, 19 (18 March), 20, 22.
          "'On the Frontier' fulfills more definitely and more ef-
      fectively what was only tentative in the earlier plays of
      Auden and Isherwood. They have discarded theatricality...."
      They have also "heightened the dramatic suspense" and
      "given greater depth to their treatment of the subject."

81   STONIER, G. W. "The Ascent of F.6." New Statesman and Nation,
      18 (1 July), 13.
          "The Ascent of F.6, whatever misgivings one may have had
      about its appeal with a large audience, succeeds brilliant-
      ly. There was a full house, and I was astonished to notice
      how quickly jokes were taken up by the gallery...."

82   STONIER, G. W. "Auden and Isherwood." New Statesman and Na-
      tion, 17 (18 March), 428, 430.
          "[W]hat makes [Journey to a War] so different from a
      hundred others of the moment is that it avoids omniscience
      and brilliantly records first impressions.... Isherwood's
      diary...is extraordinarily vivid."

83   SWINGLER, RANDALL. "Two Intellectuals in China." Daily
      Worker (29 March), p. 7.
          "Many people will, I think, be annoyed by [Journey to a
      War].... [O]n the whole the authors are too preoccupied
      with their own psychological plight to be anything but
      helplessly lost in the struggle of modern China."

84   SYMONS, JULIAN. "About Frontiers." Twentieth Century Verse,
      nos. 15-16 (February), p. 164.
          "There is not much to say about the verse in On the
      Frontier: it is made to fit a play, and its virtue depends
      on its effectiveness. I think the verse will be exceed-
      ingly effective, and dramatic, on a stage...."

85   SYMONS, JULIAN. "Auden and Poetic Drama 1938." Life and Let-
         ters, 20 (February), 70-79.
             Isherwood's contributions to the plays written in col-
         laboration with Auden can be seen in "the increased techni-
         cal skill, the increased suavity of the jokes, the attempt
         at some sort of plot."

86   SYMONS, JULIAN. Review of Journey to a War. Life and Let-
         ters, 21 (May), 158-162.
             The travel diary of Isherwood is "amusing, superficial,
         subjective." Auden's verse is the outstanding feature of
         Journey to a War.

87   THOMPSON, RALPH. "Books of the Times." New York Times
         (1 August), p. 15.
             Journey to a War, "for all the gravity of its subject
         and scene, is no less fresh and high spirited." Isher-
         wood's prose "can rarely have shown more facility and wit."

88   TODD, RUTHVEN. "Two Wars and Mr. Campbell." Twentieth Cen-
         tury Verse, no. 17 (April-May), pp. 20-21.
             "Journey to a War is much more than an ordinary travel
         book--a bit of Peter Fleming negligence or Evelyn Waugh
         blaseness; it deals with men and not with imaginary maps
         in the brains of the travellers. Isherwood's Travel-Diary
         is a first-class piece of journalism (using the word as a
         compliment and not in its snobbish sense)...."

89   T[RAVERS], P. "Drama: On the Frontier." New English Weekly,
         14 (23 February), 302-303.
             In On the Frontier, Auden and Isherwood "have made a new
         communication. New, that is, in the sense that it is new
         to them. Unfortunately, for all our stay-at-homeness, it
         is no news to us. The particular piece of country they
         seek to reveal is already depressingly familiar."

*90   T[RAVERS], P. Review of The Ascent of F6. New English Weekly,
         15 (20 July), 223-224.
             Cited: Bloomfield and Mendelson, 1972.11, p. 22.

91   WALTON, EDITH. "Berlin on the Brink." New York Times Book
         Review (19 March), pp. 23-24.
             "When it comes to the actual merits of 'Goodbye to Ber-
         lin,' they seem...to be definitely minor. Mr. Isherwood
         skims lightly and subtly over the most intangible of sur-
         faces. Though he does, it is true, convey something of
         the hysteria, the tension, the breakdown of morale which
         preceded Hitler's rise to power...."

1939

92 WAUGH, EVELYN. "Mr. Isherwood and Friend." <u>Spectator</u>, 162
    (24 March), 496, 498.
        "Mr. Isherwood writes a smooth and accurate kind of de-
    motic language which is adequate for his needs; he never
    goes butterfly-hunting for a fine phrase. It is no fault
    of his technique that <u>Journey to a War</u> is rather flat; he
    is relating a flat experience, for he is far too individual
    an artist to be a satisfactory reporter."

91 WILSON, EDMUND. "Isherwood's Lucid Eye." <u>New Republic</u>, 99
    (17 May), 51.
        In <u>Goodbye to Berlin</u>, Isherwood's observation is "accu-
    rate, lucid and cool; and it is a faculty which brings its
    own antidote to the hopelessness and horror he describes."
    His prose is "a perfect medium for his purpose"--it allows
    the reader "to look right through Isherwood and to see what
    he sees."

                            1940

*1 ANON. Review of <u>Journey to a War</u>. <u>Pratt Institute Quarterly</u>
    (Winter), p. 20.
        Cited: <u>Book Review Digest</u> 1939, p. 39.

2   BONNEROT, LOUIS C. Review of <u>Journey to a War</u>. <u>Etudes</u>
    <u>Anglaises</u>, 4 (January-March), 75-77.
        Isherwood's diary portion of <u>Journey to a War</u> makes
    very endearing reading. The authors' purpose is not to
    make history, not even to present commentary, much less
    propaganda, but modestly to relate the impressions of their
    trip. [In French].

3   BONNEROT, LOUIS C. Review of <u>On the Frontier</u>. <u>Etudes Ang-</u>
    <u>laises</u>, 4 (January-March), 77-78.
        <u>On the Frontier</u> is a melodrama which intends to leave us
    with the impression that the modern world is one of confu-
    sion and disorder, that no idea, not even that of the fron-
    tier, has lasting value. [In French].

4   CONNOLLY, CYRIL. "Comment." <u>Horizon: A Review of Literature</u>
    <u>and Art</u>, 1 (February), 68-71.
        "[T]he departure of Auden and Isherwood to America a
    year ago is the most important literary event since the
    outbreak of the Spanish War.... They are far-sighted and
    ambitious young men..., who have abandoned what they con-
    sider to be the sinking ship of European democracy, and by
    implication the aesthetic doctrine of social realism that
    has been prevailing there."

5   LEHMANN, JOHN. "Adventures in Drama," in his <u>New Writing in
     Europe</u>. Harmondsworth: Penguin Books, pp. 65-72.
     Revised and expanded version of 1939.54.

6   LEHMANN, JOHN. "Refitting the Novel," in his <u>New Writing in
     Europe</u>. Harmondsworth: Penguin Books, pp. 46-56.
     Revised and expanded version of 1939.53.

7   MacNEICE, LOUIS. "The Poet in England Today." <u>New Republic</u>,
     102 (25 March), 412.
          "...certain sophisticated poets carefully dragooned
     themselves into the narrow (but easy) paths of slogan-
     poetry--'up the barricades!' Auden and Isherwood wrote a
     bad play, 'On the Frontier,' in the belief that writing
     down in literature is the best way up in life."

8   ROSTEN, NORMAN. "The Theatre." <u>One Act Play Magazine</u>, 3
     (January) 85-87.
          "[I]n <u>On the Frontier</u> we do not have a logical growing
     organism but rather a loose set of character and action
     mutations, often rhetorical, usually naive. We are con-
     fronted with a treatment dangerously poised between an in-
     tellectual stance and a serious attack."

9   ZABEL, MORTON D. "Two Years of Poetry: 1937-1939." <u>Southern
     Review</u>, 5 (Winter), 590-591.
          "<u>On the Frontier</u> is a political cartoon of the flattest
     type. Its characters are cardboard, its settings have the
     blankness that became a bore in German films ten years ago,
     its conflicts slump into the tritest effects of left-wing
     oratory, and its writing...acts as a final dissipation of
     dramatic force and emphasis."

                              <u>1942</u>

1   KUNITZ, STANLEY J. and HOWARD HAYCRAFT, eds. <u>Twentieth Century
     Authors: A Biographical Dictionary of Modern Literature</u>.
     New York: H. W. Wilson, pp. 707-708.
     Brief biographical sketch. Supplemented in 1955.4.

2   SHORT, ERNEST. <u>Theatrical Cavalcade</u>. London: Eyre & Spottis-
     woode, pp. 133-134.
          Auden and Isherwood employ the methods of Expressionism
     in order to convey the scope of the conflict in <u>On the
     Frontier</u> and to fill in the picture of two national states
     on the verge of war. [Comment is repeated in 1951.8.]

1944

1 SAVAGE, DEREK S. "The Strange Case of W. H. Auden," in his
The Personal Principle: Studies in Modern Poetry. London:
Routledge, pp. 155-182.
The Dog Beneath the Skin "is a series of episodes rather
than a drama, each caricaturing some hypothetical aspect of
a decadent bourgeois society. The play itself may be inter-
preted as a middle-class allegory." [Reprinted: 1969.19.]

1945

1 ANON. "Fable of Beasts & Men." Time, 46 (5 November), 102-
106.
"Prater Violet, like all good books, adds up to a lot
more than the sum of its parts.... In Friedrich Bergmann,
Author Isherwood sees a giant of a passing generation--a
mature, tough, revolutionary artist in whom the will to
live and feel is practically indestructible."

2 ANON. Review of Prater Violet. Virginia Kirkus' Bookshop
Service, 13 (1 September), 375-376.
"[A]n item for collector of moderns, but not a book for
a wide public.... Here--in satire, parable, are the forces
at work in the early '30's, the foreshadowing of the ter-
rors to come, as in minuscule the pattern of European conflict is reflected in a moving picture studio...."

3 ANON. Review of Vedanta for the Western World. Virginia
Kirkus' Bookshop Service, 13 (15 November), 500.
In the introduction, Isherwood, through dialogue technique, "convinces himself (and presumably the reader) of
the value in personal in-knowing, of the mystical experience, of the use of yoga...."

4 ANON. "Universal Cult." Time, 45 (12 February), 94-100.
Bhagavad-Gita, The Song of God "is a distinguished literary work.... [T]he translators have presented a version
of the great dialogue that does some violence to the original flavor of the poem, but makes it easily understand-
able to the common reader."

5 ANON. "The Year's Books." Time, 46 (17 December), 101.
"...probably the year's best novel was Britisher Christopher Isherwood's Prater Violet, a crisp close-up of life
in a British movie studio. This book sold out its first
edition within ten days of publication."

6   BERNSTEIN, WALTER. "A Novelist's Search for Truth in the Mal-
    aise of the Thirties." New York Times Book Review (28 Oc-
    tober), p. 3.
        "The simplicity of the plot [of Prater Violet] is decep-
    tive. This is a complex work, operating on more than one
    level. It is not merely a fable of the artist in relation
    to a commercialized mass medium. It deals with the rela-
    tion of man to other men and the world around him."

7   DEUTSCH, BABETTE. "The Unrealities of Movie Life." New York
    Herald Tribune Weekly Book Review, 22 (11 November), 3.
        Prater Violet "is worth attention not merely because it
    is a witty and painful exposition of contemporary and an-
    cient evils, but because Isherwood steps out of his role of
    'ventriloquist's dummy' to speak intimately of fundamental
    things...."

8   ISHERWOOD, CHRISTOPHER. Letter to the editor. Time, 46
    (17 December), 4.
        Disclaims being "the original, or part-original" of
    Larry in Somerset Maugham's The Razor's Edge.

9   LECHLITNER, RUTH. "The Odyssey of Auden." Poetry Magazine,
    66 (July), 209-210.
        The Ascent of F6 illustrates another point in Auden's
    search for faith; the play's mother-symbol extends the
    Freudian concept into a universal symbol for evil, in which
    power becomes the "mother of humanity."

10 LEWIS, ELAINE L. Review of Prater Violet. Library Journal,
    70 (15 October), 979.
        "Super writing...[Isherwood] has the sensitivity of a
    poet and the courage of a decent human being."

11 PRESCOTT, ORVILLE. "Books of the Times." New York Times
    (31 October), p. 21.
        Prater Violet "may be so slight as to be almost trivial,
    its satirical moral so obliquely conveyed as to be without
    much force or significance, but nevertheless it is most
    artfully done."

12 PURDY, THEODORE M. "Isherwood Again." Saturday Review of
    Literature, 28 (17 November), 34.
        "What distinguishes 'Prater Violet' from a hundred other
    cinema satires is the author's ability to see the studios
    and their denizens as significant and alarming symptoms of
    the world's present malaise."

1945

13 TRILLING, DIANA. "Fiction in Review." Nation, 161 (17 November), 530-532.
    Prater Violet is a "charming novel" which "reverberates with the widest and deepest meanings": it is "a novel of narrative and social observation," "a study in sensitivities," "a study in dedication," "a study in the relation of the individual to society," and "a novel about man's relationship to himself."

14 WILSON, EDMUND. Review of Prater Violet. New Yorker, 21 (10 November), 93.
    "'Prater Violet'...is one of [Isherwood's] longish short stories, which resembles the episodes in 'Goodbye to Berlin' and keeps up the same high level of excellence. It is perhaps a little more dramatic and more of a deliberate historical parable than the earlier stories were."

15 YOUNG, MARGUERITE. "Parable Told in a World of Illusions." Chicago Sun Book Week, 4 (25 November), 5.
    "Isherwood's 'Prater Violet' is an unambitious novel but curiously, within its restricted framework, a tragicomedy filled with symbolic meanings which may escape our last analysis. It is a series of beautiful propositions which cannot be reduced to true or false but which move forever in a realm of meaningful ambiguity."

1946

1 ANON. "Behind the Film." Times Literary Supplement (1 June), p. 257.
    "The quality of craftsmanship and nice divination of human feeling...draw out [Prater Violet] from the undistinguished amble of day-to-day fiction: it is only in a wider aspect that it disappoints."

2 ANON. "Briefly Noted: Fiction." New Yorker, 22 (30 November), 134.
    The Memorial is "about an ineffectual English county family and some of their friends during the unsettled years after the first war."

3 ANON. "Germany before Hitler." Book-of-the-Month Club News (April), p. 24.
    The first half of The Berlin Stories "consists of a tale of adventure and mystery, though without exciting incident"; the second half "is a sort of combination of stories and sketches. Both books...vividly depict the decadence of German society."

4 ANON. "Meaning of Vedanta." Nashville Banner (8 May).
   "The appeal of [Vedanta for the Western World] will vary
   with the tastes and interests of the reader. Carefully and
   excellently edited and very readable, it should find a wide
   field of followers."

5 ANON. "Obsessed with Evil." Hartford Courant [CT] (7 April).
   "'The Berlin Stories,' case histories of will-less,
   decadent Europeans who just let themselves succumb to the
   prevailing between-wars miasma, can safely be shelved among
   the literary charivaria and trivia."

6 ANON. Review of The Berlin Stories. Commonweal, 43 (15 February), 461.
   "These stories are even more effective now than when
   they first were written, for, from the deeps we have
   plumbed since 1932, we can better appreciate the deeps in
   Mr. Isherwood's characters, and perhaps, from them, learn
   something of the cavities in our own."

7 ANON. Review of The Memorial. Miami Herald (1 December).
   "Isherwood tells about the Vernon family and the feudal
   aristocracy of England in a short, graphically told novel
   that is as vivid as a series of camera flashes."

8 ANON. Review of Prater Violet. Booklist, 42 (15 January),
   165.
   Prater Violet "is well written; in spite of brevity it
   is a telling satire on the whole film industry and a study
   of the frustration of an artist in the modern world."

9 ANON. Review of Vedanta for the Western World. Booklist, 42
   (15 March), 220.
   "The dominating note is a challenge to materialism and
   an emphasis on the need for a spiritual experiment."

10 ANON. Review of Vedanta for the Western World. New Yorker,
   21 (9 February), 91.
   "The book is another proof of the curious fact that, as
   the British hold on world power relaxes, more and more
   English intellectuals are retiring into exotic mysticisms."

11 ANON. "Violet Vitriol." Hobbs News [NM] (8 March).
   Review of Prater Violet: "Master of satire and brilliant denunciation, Mr. Isherwood has this time used the
   tycoons of the moving picture studio to lambast, at the
   same time writing...a picture of a Europe bound by tradition and racked by confusion, tottering before the onrush
   of Fascism."

1946

12   BOLAND, CHARLES. "Isherwood's Vernons." <u>Philadelphia Record</u>,
      (1 December).
          <u>The Memorial</u> is "well-told in spots" but tends to ram-
      ble, and some of the characters "seem to wander around
      waiting for entrance cues. Once on stage, they don't do
      much of anything."

13   BRANCH, E. DOUGLAS. "A Minor Isherwood That Has Its Appeal."
      <u>Chicago Sun Book Week</u> (8 December), p. 12.
          "[T]his story of the entanglements of a family with the
      unsynchronized strands of time has a quiet validity of its
      own. Minor Isherwood though 'The Memorial' is..., nothing
      by and very little about Isherwood can be uninteresting."

14   CAHOON, HERBERT. "Christopher Isherwood." <u>Briarcliff Quar-
      terly</u>, 3 (April), 83-84.
          "The common criticism that the writing of Isherwood is
      indistinguishable in style from that of several of his con-
      temporaries, such as Hemingway, Steinbeck, and Orwell, is
      less valid in considering <u>Prater Violet</u>.... Isherwood no
      longer stands completely on the sidelines as a colorless
      narrator; he takes a positive role...."

15   COURNOS, JOHN. "Christopher Isherwood's Story of Disintegra-
      tion." <u>New York Sun</u> (15 November).
          <u>The Memorial</u> "is not a great novel nor even wholly sat-
      isfactory as a story. But the man can write and this novel
      as writing is simply superb."

16   CULLEN, MARY MISSETT. "Disintegration of a Family." <u>Phila-
      delphia Inquirer</u> (17 November).
          "In 'The Memorial' Christopher Isherwood has written
      poignantly of the disintegration and decadence to be found
      in one English family and its group of friends after the
      First World War. It is not a pleasant subject, though the
      author handles most of it with skill." [This review also
      appeared in the <u>Cleveland News</u> (23 November).]

17   DUFFY, CHARLES. Review of <u>The Memorial</u>. <u>Commonweal</u>, 45
      (27 December), 284.
          "The fragmentary episodes, half-depicted characters, un-
      resolved situations all aim to evoke a memory of the be-
      wildering chaos of the twenties. In this sense [<u>The Memo-
      rial</u>] is an appropriate memorial to that brecciated era."

18   DWIGHT, OGDEN G. "Writes with Confusion." <u>Des Moines Regis-
      ter</u> (22 December).
          <u>The Memorial</u> "seems to have an expert obliqueness,
      though lacking the satire of 'Prater Violet' and the impact
      of the 'Berlin Stories.'" Isherwood "writes very subtly
      and skillfully in shadows and overtones...."

19 EDWARDS, NORMAN. "Monument in Words to a Passing Britain and
Its Moral Order." Milwaukee Journal (29 December).
The Memorial "is cold and hard in style, like the stone
of the war monument which is being dedicated. Little
poetic glow envelops the scenes and the sense of things
past."

20 FARRELL, JAMES T. "The Movies and Monopoly Capitalism." The
Call, 13 (25 February), 4-5.
"To me, the central theme of [Prater Violet] is the position of the artist and the status and role of art in the
period of monopoly capitalism. The author develops this
theme by the clever use of a contrapuntal structure by
which he shows how shabby motion-picture art presents coun-
terfeit images of life at the same time that the real world
of history is one of terrible drama." [Reprinted, somewhat
revised, 1947.11.]

21 FRANK, JOSEPH. "Fiction Chronicle." Sewanee Review, 54
(July-September), 538-539.
Review of Berlin Stories and Prater Violet: "What the
'I' feels is isolation.... This lack of any center in
himself makes it simple for the 'I' to appreciate eccentric
types without discomfort; he feels close to them because
they, too, are declassed and isolated; but, for lack of a
center, it has never been possible for him to develop his
snapshots into a larger montage...."

22 FREMANTLE, ANNE. "Explaining Vedanta." New York Herald Tribune Book Review (12 May), p. 16.
Vedanta for the Western World is "an admirable primer
for all who know that Yoga is something other than the
light-hearted practice of a few...exercises, yet who did
not know with which of the many books about it they should
begin."

23 G., J. B. Review of The Memorial. Hartford Times [CT]
(16 November).
"For all its taste and deftness, 'The Memorial' is over-
the-shoulder writing. Here again a fine contemporary style
has been sacrificed on an altar where already more defini-
tive social exposés have been offered."

24 KAZIN, ALFRED. "Christopher Isherwood, Novelist." New York
Times Book Review (17 February), pp. 1, 33.
Review of Berlin Stories: Isherwood is not a political
writer, but a novelist; he doesn't tell his readers anything but rather makes them see. "And what is visible in
his work above all else is the creative power of his fra-
ternity, his free and inquisitive admission of himself into
the total German--and European--picture."

1946

25   LEWIS, CARL. "Isherwood Writes of His Homeland in New Novel."
     Indianapolis Star (17 November).
          The Memorial "is quite different from [Isherwood's] pre-
     vious [novels], which might gain for the author a new group
     of admirers. Yet, in a sense, it is strangely familiar....
     It is not as satisfying as 'The Berlin Stories'..., yet it
     has real merit...."

26   LINDLEY, DENVER. "Vedanta: Its Meaning and Its Solace." New
     York Times Book Review (14 April), pp. 5, 38.
          "For the Western reader interested in the universal as-
     pects of Indian thought, from its highest to its simplest
     expression, [Vedanta for the Western World] is a lively and
     well-balanced introduction."

27   LOWREY, JACOB H. "'Prater Violet' Rated One of Neatest Writ-
     ing Jobs." Columbia State [SC] (13 January).
          "Although there is neither mysticism nor monasticism in
     'Prater Violet' there is some sort of magic afoot in its
     pages. It is, I think, the author's ability to conjure up
     scenes and personalities with marked economy of words...."

28   MIRRIELEES, EDITH R. "A Bewildering English Family." New
     York Times Book Review (24 November), p. 7.
          "What occupies the author [in The Memorial] is neither
     the following of a course of action nor the making of his
     different characters individually memorable. His concern
     is with a mood, a collective state of mind, one which is
     perhaps more accurately named a state of nerves...."

29   R., M. C. "In Memory of World War I in England." Washington
     Evening Star (17 November).
          The Memorial "is rather much the usual thing about the
     types of that well-advertised period [the twenties]....
     Nothing much happens in any direction. The futility is not
     confirmed but neither is the hope. Even so, it is a read-
     able book."

30   ROSENFELD, ISAAC. "Isherwood's Master Theme." Kenyon Review,
     8 (Summer), 488-492.
          Review of Berlin Stories and Prater Violet: "What...
     distinguishes Isherwood's writing from journalism...is the
     all-important minor role the narrator plays in his fiction.
     ... There is a silence about the 'I,' a weight almost of
     non-entity.... The 'I' thus becomes symbol in addition to
     narrator: he is the alienated man, in whom alienation is
     embodied as the master theme." [Reprinted in 1962.85.]

31   S., L. J. "Oriental Religious Philosophy Presented for West-
      ern Readers." San Diego Union (17 March).
           Vedanta for the Western World "is a good book for anyone
      to read, regardless of race, creed or color.... There is
      considerable repetition..., but this serves the more strong-
      ly to emphasize the thorny path which must be traveled by
      those who seek a better life than this material one...."

32   SMITH, HARRISON. "Disintegrating World." Saturday Review of
      Literature, 29 (9 March), 11-12.
           "Not all of 'The Berlin Stories' is concerned with Mr.
      Isherwood's investigation of weird and suffering human be-
      ings. He remains perfectly conscious of what is going on
      around him in the 1930's in Berlin, though he never seems
      aware that a new world war is in the making."

33   S[QUIRES], R[ADCLIFFE]. Review of Prater Violet. Chicago
      Review, 1 (Winter), 39.
           Isherwood's technique is "a paradigm of modulation and
      good taste." The "subduance" of "the old Isherwood ghosts
      which arise from the spiritual failure of homosexuality and
      the collapse of dual standards and confused morals...marks
      an important progression for Mr. Isherwood."

34   STEVENSON, ELIZABETH. "Pre-Supposing Other Religions." At-
      lanta Journal (14 April).
           "The special emphasis of the Western, non-Indian writers
      in [Vedanta for the Western World] has been to establish
      points of contact between this Indian philosophy and Chris-
      tian mysticism and to transplant the idea into the familiar
      thought environment of the average American or English
      reader. With the exception of Isherwood, these English and
      American writers seem to be dwelling in a mental void."

35   STRACHEY, JULIA. "Selected Notices: New Novels." Horizon:
      A Review of Literature and Art, 14 (July), 63-64.
           "The main point of [Prater Violet] is the portrait of
      Bergmann.... And an excellent portrait it is.... Alto-
      gether a most elegant piece of journalism this. We don't
      get the mark of the artist--significant architecture. But
      we do get a most stylish little prefabricated house...."

36   SUPPLE, J. O. Review of Vedanta for the Western World. Chi-
      cago Sun Book Week (24 February), p. 14.
           "Regardless of what a reader may think of Oriental mysti-
      cism 'Vedanta for the Western World' deserves considerable
      respect and careful reading."

37   TRILLING, DIANA. "Fiction in Review." Nation, 163 (14 Decem-
      ber), 702.
           Merely notes publication of the New Directions edition
      of The Memorial.

1946

38 VIERTEL, BERTHOLD. "Christopher Isherwood and Dr. Friedrich
    Bergmann." Theatre Arts, 30 (May), 295-298.
        "Prater Violet turned out to be, in spite of its satiri-
    cal vein, one of the most sincere literary attempts to take
    picture work seriously.... I am the last one to judge
    Bergmann. I can neither assert nor deny an identity which
    some of my friends find flattering, others rather deplor-
    able."

39 WEBSTER, HARVEY CURTIS. "2 Isherwood Novels on Prewar Berlin."
    Louisville Courier-Journal (31 March).
        "It is good to have these sensitive and intelligent nov-
    els [Berlin Stories]...in print in America at this time.
    They are not as closely knit or as effective as Mr. Isher-
    wood's recent success, 'Prater Violet,' but they are unu-
    sually good and illuminating reading for a generation that
    tends to think rather fast and loosely about the German
    problem...."

40 WEEKS, EDWARD. "Hollywood in England." Atlantic, 177 (Janu-
    ary), 151, 153.
        In Prater Violet, "Mr. Isherwood's virtuosity disguises
    the fact that his narrative is pretty thin.... The por-
    trait of Bergmann is one to remember, and the warning im-
    plicit in this smoothly written but not very substantial
    book is how oblivious we all were to the real meaning of
    the rape of Vienna."

41 WOODBURN, JOHN. "Artlessness Perfected and Tangled." Satur-
    day Review of Literature, 29 (14 December), 15-16.
        The Memorial "is intended as an ironic and pitiful memo-
    rial to Isherwood's selected group of survivors, who have
    survived the war only physically, and who are its traumatic
    and untended casualties."

                              1947

1   ANON. "Briefly Noted: Fiction." New Yorker, 23 (29 Novem-
    ber), 140.
        Lions and Shadows "is a very pretty piece of satirical,
    gently self-mocking writing."

2   ANON. "Cultivated Hysteria." Time, 50 (3 November), 106, 108.
        "Christopher Isherwood calls Baudelaire's Intimate Jour-
    nals 'a warning and an inspiration to us all' and pays them
    the tribute of an excellent translation."

3   ANON. Review of Lions and Shadows. Booklist, 44 (15 December),
    150.
        Lions and Shadows "gives a fascinating picture of the Eng-
    lish male literati who grew up in London during the 20's...."

4   ANON. Review of <u>Lions and Shadows</u>. <u>Virginia Kirkus' Book-</u>
     <u>shop Service</u>, 15 (15 November), 645.
         "Chatty, pleasant and at times the English equivalent to
     zany, Isherwood follows his typical English education....
     Appeal largely to 'snob audience'--as with previous books."

5   BANTOCK, G. H. "The Novels of Christopher Isherwood," in
     <u>Focus, V.4: The Novelist as Thinker</u>. Edited by B. Rajan.
     London: D. Dobson, pp. 46-57.
         Since he left Cambridge without taking a degree, Isher-
     wood has become a drifter, a time-waster, a morally uncom-
     mitted man. Therefore, Isherwood's novels are rootless
     and have no moral commitment behind them.

6   CALLAHAN, JOSEPH. Review of <u>The Memorial</u>. <u>The World in Books:</u>
     <u>A Magazine of Life and Letters</u>, 2 (January), 4.
         "Although the quick, sharp style is on a level with his
     other work, <u>The Memorial</u> is not by a long shot Isherwood's
     best. It is great reading, however, for those who still
     like to ponder the wonderfully sad state of things in Eng-
     land during the twenties."

7   CAPETANAKIS, DEMETRIOS. "Notes on Some Contemporary Writers,"
     in his <u>The Shores of Darkness</u>. London: J. Lehmann,
     pp. 135-146.
         Isherwood, "the most talented, perhaps, of all the young
     prose writers of the 'thirties," seems to have recently
     taken to mysticism, in an attempt "to get rid of intellect"
     and "sink into the depths of night." But this is "a much
     too easy and much too doubtful way to truth." [Reprinted
     in 1949.5; 1969.5.]

8   CARVER, CATHERINE. "Still Life." <u>Partisan Review</u>, 14 (Jan-
     uary/February), 95-96.
         "...<u>The Memorial</u> fails to commemorate. For while it is
     nervously moving about, objectifying in its motion the psy-
     chic predicament of its characters, it is at the same time
     slighting them of full reality in their situation by its
     impatient, fragmentary treatment of them."

9   DEMPSEY, DAVID. "Connolly, Orwell, and Others: An English
     Miscellany." <u>Antioch Review</u>, 7 (March), 142-150.
         Primarily a review of Cyril Connolly's <u>The Condemned</u>
     <u>Playground</u>, this essay discusses the writers of the thir-
     ties, including comments on three Isherwood novels: <u>Prater</u>
     <u>Violet</u>, <u>The Memorial</u>, and <u>The Berlin Stories</u>. Most of
     Isherwood's characters are damned; but because the author
     does not moralize about them, "his lost people have out-
     lived their moral betters through fifteen years of revolu-
     tion and war and remain, even after their defeat, our own
     spiritual contemporaries."

1947

10   E., N.   "Isherwood Describes Growth as a Writer."   <u>Milwaukee</u>
     <u>Journal</u> (28 December).
          In <u>Lions and Shadows</u>, "Isherwood's forte is honest por-
     traiture in which the people seem very much like actual
     people, but with an almost imperceptible edge of carica-
     ture."

11   FARRELL, JAMES T.   "When Graustark Is in Celluloid," in his
     <u>Literature and Morality</u>.   New York: Vanguard Press,
     pp. 125-132.
          Reprint, somewhat revised, of 1946.20.

12   FREEDLEY, GEORGE.   "England and Ireland," in <u>A History of Mod-</u>
     <u>ern Drama</u>.   Edited by Barrett H. Clark and George Freedley.
     New York: D. Appleton-Century, pp. 215-216.
          In <u>The Dog Beneath the Skin</u>, satire "combines with gen-
     uine poetry of the disillusioned Eliot school to make a
     drama of real importance."   <u>The Ascent of F6</u> is "a bril-
     liant and cruel indictment of imperialism and opportunism,"
     and <u>On the Frontier</u> "is a warning against the futility of
     war when no high principles are involved."

*13 HINKEL, CECIL E.   "A Production Study and Text of the Auden
     and Isherwood <u>The Ascent of F6</u> as Presented at Catholic
     University."   M.F.A. thesis, Catholic University.
          Cited in Bloomfield and Mendelson, 1972.11, p. 360.

14   HOLLIDAY, TERENCE.   "The Last of Mr. Isherwood."   <u>New Repub-</u>
     <u>lic</u>, 117 (22 December), 29.
          In <u>Lions and Shadows</u>, Isherwood "has welded refractory
     characters and improbable events into a smooth and credible
     tale, cast in a pleasing form and endued with the animating
     power of a vigorous and original imagination."

15   JAMES, EDITH.   Review of <u>The Memorial</u>.   <u>San Francisco Chronicle</u>
     (26 January).
          In <u>The Memorial</u>, Isherwood writes "bitterly and wist-
     fully" of a tradition-bound English family which is "be-
     wildered by the upsetting of old feudal balances."

16   L, G. K.   "English Life, Types."   <u>New Orleans Times-Picayune</u>
     (5 January), section 2, p. 9.
          "Mr. Isherwood has a genius for suggesting individual
     character, for establishing mood--and he has a happy facil-
     ity with the English language.   Readers who value these
     gifts will enjoy [<u>The Memorial</u>]."

17   LEWARS, KENNETH.   "The Quest in Auden's Poems and Plays."
     Master's thesis, Columbia University, pp. 57-102.
          The second period of Auden's poetic development includes
     his dramatic collaboration with Isherwood.   In this period

the questing hero becomes involved with the guilt of his society and discovers that his own deeds only serve to fulfill the guilty purposes of society.

18 McLAUGHLIN, RICHARD. "Isherwood's Arrival and Departure." Saturday Review of Literature, 30 (27 December), 14-15.
    Lions and Shadows "is the enchanting story of how a young man made himself into an important writer of his age." Isherwood is the "legitimate chronicler of the mental growing pains" of "the Auden generation."

19 MORRIS, LLOYD. "Englishmen in a Dissolving World." New York Herald Tribune Weekly Book Review (5 January), p. 6.
    The characters in The Memorial "are a group of well born, well bred English people...who are confronted by the disintegration of their world. The story relates what, in this circumstance, they make of their lives."

20 NICOLL, ALLARDYCE. British Drama: An Historical Survey from the Beginnings to the Present Time. 4th edition, revised. London: George G. Harrap, p. 482.
    The value of the Auden/Isherwood plays is not doubted, "yet the strange paradox is to be noted that the more these two authors have tried to incorporate the colloquial in their work the less popular has their dramatic work become." [Revised in 5th edition, 1963.2.]

21 OLSON, LAURENCE. "What War Did to a Family." Chicago Tribune Magazine of Books (12 January), p. 4.
    "What marks [The Memorial] as different from others using similar material is its lack of satire, its tender treatment of the elder generation..., and its clear cut limits. A group of real people are firmly drawn; issues that matter to us are presented, without our being told how they must be taken."

22 PHELAN, KAPPO. "On-Stage." Commonweal, 46 (29 August), 475-476.
    The Dog Beneath the Skin, "a kind of Brechtian mix-drix-- was written in 1935 at a time when, I think it is fair to say, the authors were still securely locked in their rosy (parlor pink?) schoolboyhood.... Nevertheless, the piece seemed to me surely reversibly, if not conclusively moral."

23 PLANT, RICHARD. "Mr. Isherwood Candidly Looks Back." New York Times Book Review (14 December), p. 3.
    "In 'Lions and Shadows' it's impossible to determine where truth ends and fiction begins--impossible and unnecessary because the very ambiguity makes the charm of the book."

1947

24   PRIOR, MOODY E. The Language of Tragedy. New York: Columbia
      University Press, pp. 367-372.
          "The Dog Beneath the Skin is probably the most thorough-
      going attempt to adapt popular stage and motion-picture
      genres to the ends of the serious poet...." The variations
      between verse and prose in The Ascent of F6 and On the
      Frontier add poignancy to the plays and augment their thea-
      trical symbolism.

25   PRITCHETT, V. S. "Men of the World," in The Penguin New Writ-
      ing, No. 30. Edited by John Lehmann. Harmondsworth: Pen-
      guin Books, pp. 135-141.
          Three living English novelists deal with "the man of the
      world"--Maugham, Aldous Huxley, and Isherwood. "In Prater
      Violet, an amusing book which moves one in the end, Isher-
      wood drops the man of the world, and one stands in the mod-
      ern world of film slosh and toughness."

26   R., W. G. "Story about English Changes." Columbus Dispatch
      [OH] (2 February).
          "The lesson of [The Memorial] is all the more ominous
      from the fact that there has been still another war since
      the one the disastrous effects of which Isherwood describes
      sensitively."

27   TINDALL, WILLIAM YORK. Forces in Modern British Literature,
      1885-1946. New York: A. A. Knopf, pp. 53, 57, 61, 62, 89,
      211-212, 328-329, 345, 357. [Reprinted: 1956.4.]
          "Christopher Isherwood's excellent novels of pre-Nazi
      Berlin..., less narratives than character studies, deal in
      the prose of Hemingway with people whose sexual aberrations
      complicate their social complexity." Also discusses the
      Auden/Isherwood plays.

28   TURNER, W. J. "Christopher Isherwood," in Living Writers.
      Edited by Gilbert Phelps. London: Sylan Press, pp. 48-57
          "Isherwood may not be a great writer...but at least he
      is a real writer and not a pretentious bore." He is "far
      more human" than Aldous Huxley and "the best comic writer--
      apart from Evelyn Waugh--living today."

29   VANDORE, EDRIE. "Unique Literary Era Recalled by Isherwood."
      Hartford Times [CT] (27 December).
          Lions and Shadows "should be a valuable addition to
      those interested in modern literature. It is more than an
      autobiography; it is a record of an era unique for breadth
      of freedom in literary thought."

30   WILSON, EDMUND. Review of <u>The Intimate Journals of Baudelaire</u>.
      <u>New Yorker</u>, 23 (1 November), 93, 94, 96.
          "[W]hen Eliot and Auden and Isherwood invoke the example
      of Baudelaire, they are appealing to a passion for litera-
      ture which has managed to burn pure and intense through
      suffering and degradation." [Reprinted: 1950.4.]

31   YEISER, FREDERICK. "English Novelist Publishes Autobiography
      When at the Ripe Old Age of Thirty-five." <u>Cincinnati En-</u>
      <u>quirer</u> (27 December).
          "Though [<u>Lions and Shadows</u>] is by no means everyone's
      cup of tea, it does give one an idea--and in most diverting
      fashion--how one of the best of the younger British writers
      got that way."

32   YOUNG, MURRAY. "The Fiction of Youth." <u>Brooklyn Daily Eagle</u>
      (28 December).
          "As a document of the England of the twenties [<u>Lions and</u>
      <u>Shadows</u>] has a certain value; disillusioned, rather sad,
      acutely aware of not belonging, Mr. Isherwood gives a
      fairly accurate picture of what life was like for members
      of his class and his generation in the difficult years be-
      tween the two wars."

                              <u>1948</u>

1   ANON. "Briton Wins Praise for Fine Prose." <u>Miami Herald</u>
      (18 January).
          <u>Lions and Shadows</u> "adds to [Isherwood's] stature as an
      English writer and, we hope, as a maturing novelist."

2   ANON. "Cambridge Charmer." <u>San Francisco Argonaut</u> (26 March).
          The compelling feature of <u>Lions and Shadows</u> is its
      charm: "It is a delightful feast for the literary con-
      noisseur."

3   ANON. "Introduction to Isherwood." <u>Nashville Tennessean</u>
      (4 April).
          <u>Lions and Shadows</u> requires "some detective elan to
      fitting one's own facts to the fiction here," but the book
      offers "a foreshadowing of some of the best Isherwood work
      in novel form."

4   ANON. "Isherwood Remembers Undergraduate Days." <u>Denver Post</u>
      (4 January).
          Reviews of <u>Lions and Shadows</u>: "The struggle of an artist
      toward self expression always has meaning and importance.
      And whatever material Isherwood may choose to draw from, he
      can be depended upon to compel interest by the exceptionally
      adroit and stimulating prose with which it is clothed."

                              53

1948

5   BALAKIAN, ANNA. "Precursor." <u>Poetry</u>, 72 (July), 228-231.
      "Isherwood's translation of the posthumous prose frag-
    ments of Charles Baudelaire appears as a welcome reprint
    and should prove fascinating reading to the French poet's
    ever increasing number of American enthusiasts."

6   BUCKMAN, GERTRUDE. "Some Lions, Some Shadows." <u>Partisan Re-
    view</u>, 15 (April), 504-505.
      In <u>Lions and Shadows</u>, "Isherwood regards his youth with
    indulgent irony; if the indulgence wins out rather too
    often, as, for instance, in his account of the imaginative,
    gothic-tempered, myth-and-language-making games which he
    played during his Cambridge days, he makes up for these
    lapses with much that is purely delightful."

7   C., S. "Isherwood Recalls Younger Days." <u>Pasadena Star News</u>
    (22 February).
      In <u>Lions and Shadows</u>, "Isherwood's quiet laughter is
    directed at himself, but, occasionally, beneath the banter,
    there can be seen the eager, sometimes fearful, heart of a
    young man struggling to find his place in life."

8   CONNOLLY, CYRIL. <u>Enemies of Promise and Other Essays</u>. Re-
    vised edition. New York: Macmillan, pp. 70-71, 74-75, 79,
    81, 101, 133.
      Revision of 1938.9; comments on Isherwood are unchanged.

9   FOULKE, ADRIENNE. Review of <u>Lions and Shadows</u>. <u>Commonweal</u>,
    47 (9 January), 331.
      "'Lions and Shadows' has occasional lively and ironic
    insights but it offers less enlightenment as a study of
    Isherwood as a writer than does the obvious device of read-
    ing his novels and stories...."

10 GREENBERG, SAMUEL. "Auden: Poet of Anxiety." <u>Masses and
    Mainstream</u>, 1 (June), 38-50.
      The four works of the Auden/Isherwood collaboration il-
    lustrate the authors' disenchantment with aristocratic
    values and document a struggle between Marxist ideology
    and the authors' emotional attachments with the aristocracy.

11 HUGHES, ELINOR. "Isherwood Novel off Beaten Track." <u>Boston
    Traveler</u> (11 February).
      "Some of [<u>Lions and Shadows</u>] will irritate you, but much
    of it will amuse you, and if you are familiar enough with
    the London book world to penetrate the aliases of Mr. Ish-
    erwood's friends, you will enjoy it even more."

12   MacRAE, DONALD G. Review of <u>Bhagavad-Gita: The Song of God</u>.
      <u>Life and Letters</u>, 59 (December), 234-235.
          Both the translation and the content are disappointing;
      the English prose is "stilted" and its verse is "Wardour
      Street oriental."

13   MORRIS, LLOYD. "The Education of a Novelist." <u>New York Her</u>-
      <u>ald Tribune Weekly Book Review</u> (4 January), p. 4.
          "As social satire, certain portions of 'Lions and Shad-
      ows' are quite as effective as the early novels of Aldous
      Huxley and Evelyn Waugh.... In few books are you likely
      to find the grub-like stage of a developing literary talent
      reported with greater candor or more pitiless self-
      criticism."

14   PUTZEL, MAX. "Adolescence Described in Slick Prose." <u>St</u>.
      <u>Louis Post-Dispatch</u> (8 February), p. 4B.
          "[W]hat comes out in [the] slick and expert prose [of
      <u>Lions and Shadows</u>] is unlikely to hold the attention of
      readers less determined and bound to read it than Mr. Ish-
      erwood himself...."

15   STEWART, DOUGLAS. "The Rhinoceros's Mother," in his <u>The Flesh</u>
      <u>and the Spirit</u>. Sydney: Angus and Robertson, pp. 60-62.
          An imaginary dialogue between two characters, Mr. Shean
      and Mr. Gallagher; the latter has just seen a production of
      <u>The Ascent of F6</u>. The point of their discussion--that the
      "mother-complex" has been "fantastically over-emphasized in
      contemporary literature"--is summed up in Gallagher's
      claim that he does not have a mother, since the play taught
      him "that men climb mountains because they have a mother-
      complex...."

16   WOOLF, VIRGINIA. "The Leaning Tower," in her <u>The Moment and</u>
      <u>Other Essays</u>. New York: Harcourt Brace, pp. 128-154.
          Study of the Auden group--writers who began to write in
      1925 and came to an end as a group in 1939. [Reprinted:
      1967.70.]

<u>1949</u>

1   ANON. "Mr. Isherwood Changes Trains." <u>Times Literary Supple</u>-
      <u>ment</u> (11 November), p. 727.
          "A book so consistently entertaining as <u>The Condor and</u>
      <u>the Cows</u> should not, perhaps, be used as the text for a
      sermon on Mr. Isherwood's capacities as a novelist.... The
      machinery functions beautifully...; but the level upon
      which these activities are coordinated is the level of film-
      script and magazine."

1949

2   ANON. Review of <u>The Condor and the Cows</u>. <u>Booklist</u>, 46
        (15 November), 95.
             "Candid impressions of six months of travel in the
        northern and western countries and a brief excursion into
        Argentina make entertaining general reading or supplemen-
        tary reference for tourists."

3   ANON. Review of <u>The Condor and the Cows</u>. <u>Virginia Kirkus'</u>
        <u>Bookshop Service</u>, 17 (15 July), 387.
             "The impressions of South America...are at once sharply
        witty, sometimes wicked and at all times fresh-eyed....
        An inquiring mind, a spontaneous interest make this travel-
        ogue stimulating reading...."

4   BOROME, JOSEPH. Review of <u>The Condor and the Cows</u>. <u>Library</u>
        <u>Journal</u>, 74 (1 September), 1196.
             In <u>The Condor and the Cows</u>, Isherwood's "portraits are
        not as sharply etched as his descriptions, but some of them
        will surprise readers, particularly his questioning sketch
        of Haya de la Torre, and his admirable defense of Mme.
        Peron's past."

5   CAPETANAKIS, DEMETRIOS. "Notes on Some Contemporary Writers,"
        in his <u>The Shores of Darkness</u>. New York: Devin-Adair,
        pp. 135-146.
             Reprint of 1947.7; reprinted again 1969.5.

6   FLEMING, PETER. "Mild Earthquakes." <u>Spectator</u>, 183 (9 Decem-
        ber), 828.
             "[T]here are throughout [<u>The Condor and the Cows</u>]
        flashes of brilliant perception and interpretation; and the
        descriptions of people are often (though of places less
        often) extraordinarily good. But something is missing,
        something inhibits the level flow of the narrative...."

7   GOODMAN, ANNE L. "South of the Border." <u>New Republic</u>, 121
        (7 November), 19-20.
             <u>The Condor and the Cows</u> "has fallen directly into the
        pitfall that awaits all travel books unless they possess
        a strong personality of their own or highly specialized
        knowledge of their subject: it gives too much information
        for the reader only casually interested in South America
        and not enough for anyone really concerned...."

8   HERRING, HUBERT. "Mr. Isherwood Takes a Trip South." <u>New</u>
        <u>York Herald Tribune Book Review</u> (4 December), p. 7.
             In <u>The Condor and the Cows</u>, Isherwood does not pretend
        to knowledge of the people or the language, but he "jogs
        down the Andes from the Caribbean to the pampas, seeing,
        hearing, smelling much that any properly equipped associate
        professor would never have thought about."

*9   JACKSON, J[OSEPH] H[ENRY]. Review of The Condor and the Cows.
     San Francisco Chronicle (30 September), p. 22.
       Cited: Book Review Digest 1949, p. 455.

10   KALEM, THEODORE. "South American Safari." Christian Science
     Monitor (20 October), p. 15
       In The Condor and the Cows, Isherwood "is a near-ideal
     tourist who writes with the casual perfection of an angel
     on furlough.... [H]e has the novelists's knack for pro-
     jecting himself into a given set of circumstances without
     sacrificing the detachment of an uninvolved observer."

11   M., P. J. Review of The Condor and the Cows. Manchester
     Guardian (6 December), p. 4.
       The Condor and the Cows "is always readable and occa-
     sionally penetrating.... One would be glad if [Isherwood]
     could some day return to, say, Peru or Ecuador, give him-
     self time to acclimatise, and let his gift of luminous
     sympathy play over this queer juxtaposition of cultures."

12   POORE, CHARLES. "Books of the Times." New York Times (1 Octo-
     ber), p. 11.
       "If you have not been to South America, [The Condor and
     the Cows] will give you a fine vicarious voyage. If you
     have been traveling there, you will want to compare experi-
     ences."

13   PRITCHETT, V. S. "Books in General." New Statesman and Na-
     tion, 38 (19 November), 585.
       "The changing pulse, the quick eye that refuses no sight
     are the making of The Condor and the Cows.... Mr. Isher-
     wood has conveyed the crowded effervescence of being
     there...."

14   PUTNAM, SAMUEL. "Isherwood's South American Diary." New York
     Times Book Review (2 October), p. 41.
       The title of The Condor and the Cows--"with its touch of
     playfulness and underlying seriousness"--"is accurately in-
     dicative of the character of the book.... [I]t is South
     America viewed through a temperament, by a novelist who is
     well up among the best that we have."

15   REYNOLDS, ERNEST R. Modern English Drama: A Survey of the
     Theatre from 1900. London: George C. Harrap, pp. 100-101.
       Auden and Isherwood have "interpreted contemporary life
     in verse." The subject matter of the verse in On the Fron-
     tier is "strictly realistic," while The Ascent of F.6 is "a
     blend of the real and the symbolic."

1949

16 SCARFE, FRANCIS. W. H. Auden. Contemporary British Poets
    Series. Monaco: Lyrebird Press, pp. 22-25.
    Discusses the three plays of the Auden-Isherwood col-
    laboration, primarily from the point of view of the devel-
    opment of Auden's poetic themes. On the Frontier is judged
    the most successful because "the theme is still vital" and
    "Auden and Isherwood had at last achieved a truly dramatic
    unity."

17 SUTTON, HORACE. "Travelers' Tales." Saturday Review of Lit-
    erature, 32 (31 December), 37.
    The Condor and the Cows "is all personalized adventure
    and observation.... The book's rich description should
    give more insight to the countries [Isherwood] covers than
    all the annotated guidebooks."

18 WHITE, ERIC WALTER. Benjamin Britten: A Sketch of His Life.
    London: Boosey & Hawkes, pp. 8-12.
    Brief comments on Britten's incidental music for the
    Auden-Isherwood plays. [Revised edition: 1970.19.]

19 ZABEL, MORTON DAUWEN. "The Uttermost Shore." Nation, 169
    (29 October), 423-424.
    In The Condor and the Cows "the baffling problems of
    races and religions, illiteracy and education, politics and
    cultures, agriculture and foreign exploitation are recog-
    nized, sometimes with brilliant concision and accurate
    suggestion, but they are mostly left at the level of enigma
    and paradox."

1950

1 CHEW, CATHERINE. "No One Now Alive Will Know the Outcome."
   Little Rock Gazette (26 February).
   "One has only to compare this delightful book [The Condor and the Cows] with other travel books covering the same
   territory to realize how excellent and unusual it is--the
   travel diary of a man who is perceptive, witty and educated,
   a writer worth knowing."

2 JENKINS, HAROLD D. "Isherwood Visits South America." Dallas
   Times-Herald (12 February).
   The Condor and the Cows "may not cause a literary flurry,
   but it won't tarnish the glories of Christopher Isherwood.
   It is, in fact, a delightful book--full of beguiling charm
   and information."

3   WILSON, EDMUND. "Christopher Isherwood in South America."
    New Yorker, 25 (14 January), 83.
        The Condor and the Cows "is a kind of travel book that
    flourished brilliantly in the last century but that...has
    become a relative rarity: the personal account of wander-
    ings in unfamiliar countries that sticks close to the in-
    cidents of travel yet aims to convey some accurate ideas
    about the people and localities visited."

4   WILSON, EDMUND. "The Sanctity of Baudelaire," in his Classics
    and Commercials: Literary Chronicle of the Forties. New
    York: Farrar, Straus and Co., pp. 419-422.
        Reprint, somewhat revised, of 1947.30.

                              1951

1   BREIT, HARRY. "Talk with Mr. Isherwood." New York Times Book
    Review (16 December), p. 18.
        Interview: Isherwood discusses the Van Druten play (I
    Am a Camera) based on Sally Bowles; his collaborations with
    Auden; and his work in progress. [Reprinted: 1956.1.]

2   FORSTER, E. M. "The Ascent of F6," in his Two Cheers for Demo-
    cracy. London: Edward Arnold, pp. 271-273; New York:
    Harcourt, Brace, & World, pp. 263-265.
        Reprint, except for the last few sentences, of 1936.20.

3   FORSTER, E. M. "English Prose between 1918 and 1939," in his
    Two Cheers for Democracy. London: Edward Arnold, pp. 280-
    291; New York: Harcourt, Brace, & World, pp. 272-284.
        "Isherwood--who is extremely intelligent--always writes
    as if the reader were equally intelligent. He is an ex-
    ample of democratic good manners. He trusts his public."
    [Reprint of the W. P. Ker Lecture delivered in 1944 at the
    University of Glasgow.]

4   GRIFFIN, HOWARD. "A Dialogue with W. H. Auden." Hudson Re-
    view, 3 (Winter), 575-591.
        Auden comments on the relation of T. E. Lawrence to the
    protagonist of The Ascent of F6.

5   HOGGART, RICHARD. "The Plays, with Christopher Isherwood,"
    in his Auden, an Introductory Essay. London: Chatto and
    Windus, pp. 71-86.
        "The plays offer only a limited satisfaction, because
    even the tenets of 'epic theatre' do not allow Auden the
    kind of scope his mind requires. But in the 'thirties they
    were exciting to see; they were often amusing, and were at
    least attempting something, even though much of their en-
    ergy was only superficially dazzling."

1951

6   ISAACS, JACOB. <u>An Assessment of Twentieth Century Literature</u>.
    London: Secker and Warburg, pp. 141-142, 144-145, 173-174.
        "Perhaps the chief talent of those years [1929-1938], a
    talent which seems, so far as the novel is concerned, to
    have burnt itself out, is Mr. Christopher Isherwood....
    [N]o German writer then or since has captured so accurately
    the atmosphere [of Berlin] of the time." The Auden/Isher-
    wood plays are also discussed.

*7 OZU, JIRO. "Auden to Isherwood [Auden and Isherwood]."
    <u>Engeki Koza</u>, v. 3: <u>Engeki no skimpu</u>. Edited by Kumo no
    Kai. Tokyo: Kawade Shobo, chapter 27.
        Cited in Bloomfield and Mendelson, 1972.11, p. 355.

8   SHORT, ERNEST. <u>Sixty Years of Theatre</u>. London: Eyre &
    Spottiswoode, pp. 355-356.
        Repeats comments from 1942.2.

9   SPEARS, MONROE K. "The Dominant Symbols of Auden's Poetry."
    <u>Sewanee Review</u>, 59 (Summer), 392-425.
        Auden's most famous version of the theme of the narcis-
    sistic nature of sexual love is found in the dummy-
    undressing scene in <u>The Dog Beneath the Skin</u>.

10 SPENDER, STEPHEN. <u>World within World</u>. New York: Harcourt,
    Brace, pp. 47, 91-94, 109-117, 118, 120, 151, 158-159, 226,
    269, 273, 287.
        "Perhaps my greatest debt to Christopher is the confi-
    dence he gave me in my work. He was more than a young
    rebel passing through a phase of revolt against parents,
    conventional morality and orthodox religion. He also rec-
    ognized that nearly everyone wanted something out of life
    which he or she had been taught to conceal. He was on the
    side of the forces which make a work of art, even more than
    he was interested in art itself, and on the side of the
    struggle towards self-realization more than he was interest-
    ed in the happy ending or the success story."

11 WILLIAMSON, AUDREY. <u>Theatre of Two Decades</u>. New York: Mac-
    Millan, pp. 130-134, 136, 144.
        The plays of Auden and Isherwood "never achieved com-
    plete artistic homogeneity." They did, however, have "ele-
    ments of genuine character, an occasional feeling for dra-
    matic shape, a biting, satiric wit, and a sense of the
    world's fear and despair that had, at moments, the ring of
    poetic revelation."

<u>1952</u>

1 ANON. "The Huge Northern Circuit." <u>Times Literary Supplement</u>
   (23 May), p. 344.
      General review of Isherwood's writing up to the publica-
   tion of the opening chapter of <u>The World in the Evening</u> in
   <u>New World Writing</u>: "At first glance...Isherwood would appear to be the type-figure of his generation.... On closer
   examination, however, he proves to be completely outside
   the movement, much less a leading representative...."

2 BAIN, KENNETH BRUCE FINDLATER. <u>The Unholy Trade</u>. London:
   Victor Gollanz, pp. 146-150; <u>151, 153</u>.
      The Auden-Isherwood plays "are interesting today largely
   as topical caricatures of the English intellectual climate
   between the wars, and as landmarks in the development of
   two outstanding writers. But neither Auden nor Isherwood,
   singly or in combination, were [sic] good dramatists, and
   there was no future in their playmaking."

3 HAWES, HENRY. "Christopher Isherwood's Snapshots." <u>Saturday
   Review</u>, 35 (12 April), 38-40.
      Isherwood discusses the play <u>I Am a Camera</u>, its develop-
   ment and the changes that were made from his original stories. He also talks about his recent trip to Berlin, his
   interest in Vedanta, and his work on <u>The World in the Even-
   ing</u>.

4 M., D. "Forecasts and Side Glances." <u>Theatre Arts</u>, 36
   (March), 12-13.
      Reports that the original "Sally Bowles" was instru-
   mental in securing Isherwood's first job as a film writer.

5 MITCHELL, DONALD and HANS KELLER, eds. <u>Benjamin Britten: A
   Commentary on His Works from a Group of Specialists</u>. London: Rockliff Publishing, pp. 12, 289, 298, 299, 311.
      Various comments on Britten's incidental music to the
   plays of Auden and Isherwood. [Reprinted: 1972.42.]

6 MOORE, GEOFFREY. "Three Who Did Not Make a Revolution: A
   Critical Study." <u>American Mercury</u>, 74 (April), 107-114.
      "To look back on the career of Auden-Spender-Isherwood
   since their star first burst upon us is to review the public record of a generation's education."

*7 NAKAGIRI, MASAO. "W. H. Auden, C. Isherwood, <u>Inu ni natta
   otoko</u>: shigekiron no ichibu [<u>The Dog Beneath the Skin</u>:
   On a Poetic Drama]." <u>Shigaku</u>, 7 (April), 60-74.
      Cited: Bloomfield and Mendelson, 1972.11, p. 356.

1952

8 NAKAGIRI, MASAO. "W. H. Auden, C. Isherwood saku <u>Kokkyo nite</u>
   [<u>On the Frontier</u>]." <u>Shigaku</u>, 7 (June), 58-65 and (July),
   54-62.
       Cited: Bloomfield and Mendelson, 1972.11, p. 357.

9 PRITCHETT, V. S. "Books in General." <u>New Statesman and Na-</u>
   <u>tion</u>, 44 (23 August), 213-224.
       Review of reissues of <u>Goodbye to Berlin</u>, <u>Mr. Norris</u>
   <u>Changes Trains</u>, and <u>The Memorial</u>: "Isherwood's sketches
   and novels, if we except <u>The Memorial</u>, seem to be hanging
   in an alarming void. They are suspended there from the
   pathos of Isherwood's personal loneliness.... [B]ut if we
   turn back from [the] German writing to the earlier novel
   <u>The Memorial</u> we see how more soundly based, from a novelists's point of view, it really is."

*10 TAKAGI, NARAHIDE. "<u>On the Frontier</u> no seijiteki fushi: W. H.
   Auden to Christopher Isherwood no gassaku shigeki ni tsuite
   [Political Satire of <u>On the Frontier</u>]." <u>Eigo kenkyu</u>, 4
   (May), 20-23.
       Cited: Bloomfield and Mendelson, 1972.11, p. 357.

11 WILLIAMS, RAYMOND. "Some Verse Dramatists," in his <u>Drama from</u>
   <u>Ibsen to Eliot</u>. London: Chatto & Windus, pp. 247-256.
       "Of all dramatic work that has received serious critical
   attention in this century, the three plays written in collaboration by W. H. Auden and Christopher Isherwood...are
   the most obviously related to a particular, unmistakable
   period: the middle nineteen-thirties in England. This
   fact has limited their more recent appreciation, but the
   plays have a more than temporary importance, and need examination as examples of a lively and influential form of
   verse drama." [Revised: 1968.17.]

12 WILSON, EDMUND. "The Oxford Boys Becalmed," in his <u>The Shores</u>
   <u>of Light</u>. New York: Farrar, Straus and Young, pp. 669-
   673.
       Reprint of 1937.43

<u>1953</u>

1 FRASER, GEORGE S. <u>The Modern Writer and His World</u>. London:
   Derek Verschoyle, pp. 26, 48, 103-105, 112, 113, 152, 162,
   180, 232, 234, 336.
       Isherwood's style "looks easy and simple, it is exactly
   like somebody talking to us, and Isherwood never seems to
   be taking any special pains with his writing, but at the
   same time there is no waste.... This complete lack of
   wastage gives Isherwood's books...a density which they do
   not at first appear to have...." [Revised: 1964.30.]

*2   HOBBS, JOE K. "The Coterie Playwright Then and Now: A Study
      of John Lyly and W. H. Auden." Master's thesis, Columbia
      University.
         Cited: Bloomfield and Mendelson, 1972.11, p. 360.

3   MAYNE, RICHARD. "The Novel and Mr. Norris." <u>Cambridge Jour-
      nal</u>, 6 (June), 561-570.
         The flippant pose that masks the serious side of <u>Mr.
      Norris Changes Trains</u> is the basic dualism in Isherwood's
      work. The writer "seems perpetually torn between his sense
      of the ridiculous and his rather naive solemnity, and has
      often employed a similar disguise."

4   WOOLF, VIRGINIA. <u>A Writer's Diary</u>. Edited by Leonard Woolf.
      London: Hogarth Press, pp. 306-307.
         From the entry for Tuesday, 1 November 1938: "Isher-
      wood and I met on the doorstep. He is a slip of a wild
      boy: with quicksilver eyes: nipped: jockeylike."

<u>1954</u>

1   AMIS, KINGSLEY. "Book Notes." <u>Twentieth Century</u>, 156 (July),
      87-89.
         "When one asks finally what <u>The World in the Evening</u> is
      about, what its centre is, one is hard put to it to answer.
      It is all ingeniously stage-managed and dovetailed, but
      there seems no good reason for any particular feature of
      the book being as it is and not otherwise...."

*2   AMY, EDITH. "British Poetry of Social Protest." Ph.D. dis-
      sertation, University of Pennsylvania.
         Includes comments on the Auden/Isherwood plays.
         Cited: <u>Dissertation Abstracts</u>, 14 (1954), 2061.

3   ANON. "Camera or Conscience?" <u>London Times</u> (19 June), p. 8.
         In <u>The World in the Evening</u>, Isherwood "tries to under-
      stand the fatal magic of these wasted years [between the
      wars], but not, as in the Berlin stories, by penetrating
      deep into his characters and seeing the life around them
      through their eyes, but by setting the period against the
      awesome background of God and eternity, and noting, one by
      one, its numerous shortcomings."

4   ANON. "Record of Experience." <u>Times Literary Supplement</u>
      (18 June), p. 389.
         The <u>World in the Evening</u> "is more a record of experience
      than an individual character-study. At moments Mr. Isher-
      wood writes with surprising sentimentality and at others he
      is unnecessarily and embarrassingly frank, but at all times

he is impressive as a writer who with complete sincerity and to the best of his ability puts his considerable talent to the service of his experience."

5   ANON. Review of The World in the Evening. Booklist, 50 (15 July), 451.
The World in the Evening is an "intricate novel which tells how Stephen Monk, a wealthy Anglo-American expatriate, finally broke out of the chrysalis of his prolonged adolescence to become, at the age of thirty-six, a full-fledged adult...."

6   ANON. Review of The World in the Evening. San Diego Union (27 June).
The World in the Evening "is vivid in drawing the characters of Jane, Stephen, and Elizabeth and the abnormal but plausible life they shared."

7   ANON. Review of The World in the Evening. Vallejo Times-Herald [CA] (26 October).
"This is the story of a turning-point in a man's life; one of those mysterious occasions on which his subconscious will dramatically intervene, warning him to stop, take a look at himself, and see what his actions have made of him."

8   ANON. Review of The World in the Evening. Virginia Kirkus' Bookshop Service, 22 (1 April), 247.
"The festering, first person reconnaissance of Stephen Monk...is an honest examination of emotional transgression...a reassessment of experience--of the truth which hurts but also heals--and it is for the most part intense and immediate."

9   ANON. Review of The World in the Evening. Wilmington News [DE] (19 July).
"Isherwood...can tell a story exceptionally well and if you like stories of philanderings among the idle rich both here and abroad you will certainly enjoy [The World in the Evening]."

10   ANON. "Saxophone Age Orphan." Time, 63 (7 June), 118, 120.
The World in the Evening is "a second-rate novel that sounds no more than an echo to the stories Isherwood told better in Goodbye to Berlin and Prater Violet.... Author Isherwood's prose still has the crisp grace of a good tennis match. He is an exterior decorator of chic and competence...."

11 BARENSFELD, THOMAS. "Hero Dissects Self in New Isherwood Novel." Cleveland Plain Dealer (27 June).
    The World in the Evening "has a vitality and sustained
dramatic unity not heretofore achieved by [Isherwood].
Above all it manages to incorporate for the first time certain of his religious ideas...in an unobtrusive and yet
forceful manner. It is, I think, Isherwood's best novel."

12 BARRON, LOUIS. Review of The World in the Evening. Library
Journal, 79 (1 June), 1051-1052.
    The protagonist of The World in the Evening "is essen-
tially a sensitive bore whose experiences the reader fol-
lows only because of the felicity of Isherwood's writing."

13 BROOKE, JOCELYN. Aldous Huxley. Writers and Their Work,
No. 55. London: Longmans, Green, p. 24.
    The unusual chronology of Eyeless in Gaza "probably
owes something to Christopher Isherwood's The Memorial...."

14 EDWARDS, PAT. "'The World in the Evening' Makes Entertaining
Reading." Fort Worth Star (1 August).
    "As a psychological study, [The World in the Evening]
misses the mark somewhat; as entertaining reading, it's
good stuff."

15 ENGLE, PAUL. "Probing a Self Indulgent Man." Chicago Tribune
Magazine of Books (4 July), p. 4.
    "In his earlier books, Christopher Isherwood revealed an
exact sense of place...and an imaginative sense of people.
In [The World in the Evening] he reveals the same strong
awareness of the flavor of the times in which his characters
live, but his particular concern is with Stephen, his
friends, and his wives."

16 FINNEY, J. L. B. "Many Faults in Latest Isherwood." Boston
Daily Globe (25 July).
    Review of The World in the Evening: "Mr. Isherwood is a
skillful writer, and there are certain scenes that remain
persistently in the mind of the reader. It is well worth
reading the whole book to experience these high moments."

17 GILL, BRENDAN. Review of The World in the Evening. New
Yorker, 30 (10 July), 72.
    The World in the Evening is a "disappointing novel":
"we put down the book with a sense that whatever decision
[Stephen] comes to about his future will be all right with
us, just so we don't have to listen to him going on and on
and on about it."

1954

18   GREGORY, HORACE. "Vanity Fair, Latter-Day Version." <u>New York
      Herald Tribune Book Review</u> (6 June), p. 1.
          <u>The World in the Evening</u>, "a novel without a villain,"
      describes a modern-day "Vanity Fair" through the latest of
      Isherwood's "dispassionate pilgrims," Stephen Monk, who
      "bears a likeness to Gide's immoral moralist, and is the
      thoroughly protestant pilgrim of the story."

19   GUNN, THOM. "Book Reviews." <u>London Magazine</u>, 1 (October),
      81-85.
          In <u>The World in the Evening</u>, "Isherwood is venturing
      something far more serious, far more complex than before,
      and if its local failures are more frequent, its successes
      are more impressive, because this time we are not just in-
      terested, we are involved."

20   H., B. "A Pretentious Soap Opera." <u>Raleigh Observer</u> [NC]
      (4 July).
          "A central point of [<u>The World in the Evening</u>] is a plea
      for sympathy for homosexuals. While this may be a worthy
      aim, it is no excuse for the disappointment [the novel] will
      cause readers who remember Isherwood's earlier books...."

21   HABICH, WILLIAM. "Modern Life Put in Strong Prose." <u>Louis-
      ville Courier-Journal</u> (18 July).
          In <u>The World in the Evening</u> the "Isherwood writing per-
      forms like a Cadillac in perfect condition; and further-
      more, everything with which it concerns itself is time-
      lessly true yet painfully contemporary."

22   HAMILTON, GERALD. "The Importance of Not Being Norris."
      <u>Punch</u>, 227 (17 November), 639.
          Letter to the editor in which Hamilton disclaims any
      close identification with "Mr. Norris who has changed
      trains."

23   HAYES, RICHARD. "Private Pity." <u>Commonweal</u>, 60 (30 July),
      421-423.
          In <u>The World in the Evening</u> "the authentic tone of Mr.
      Isherwood's voice" is still present: "in the unmistakable
      accents of humane sympathy; in the note of private feeling
      which suddenly, surprisingly reverberates; in the occa-
      sional echo of raillery, and the delicious sound of vanity
      expiring upon wit."

24   HEINEY, DONALD W. "Christopher Isherwood," in his <u>Essentials
      of Contemporary Literature</u>. Woodbury, N.Y.: Barron's
      Educational Series, Inc., pp. 201, 452.
          "Since [Isherwood] was primarily interested in charac-
      ter, ...he turned to prose fiction rather than verse. His

association with the poets Spender and Auden is nevertheless apparent in the finished precision of his prose, in his careful choice of words, and in his feeling for concrete imagery." [Reprinted in 1974.6.]

25 HILL, HARRIET. "Search for Maturity." Montreal Gazette
      (14 August).
        "What makes 'The World in the Evening' so interesting is
      Elizabeth's insight, her complete lack of prudery and her
      spirituality which, not linked to any formal religion, is
      a source of strength to all who come in contact with her."

26 HODGART, PATRICIA. Review of The World in the Evening. Manchester Guardian (29 June), p. 6.
        In The World in the Evening, "Mr. Isherwood still writes
      with the unsparing honesty that marks all his work, and he
      is still a master of narrative, but he shows for the first
      time an emotional unsureness in filling out his characters."

27 JACKSON, KATHERINE GAUSS. "Books in Brief." Harper's, 209
      (July), 99-100.
        In The World in the Evening, "the always exciting prose,
      the over-all philosophy, the probing and learning from...
      the Quaker attitude, the growth of personality and ideas all
      through the book add up to a rewarding experience."

28 JONES, HOWARD MUMFORD. "Ambivalent Trio." Saturday Review of
      Literature, 37 (5 June), 14-15.
        The World in the Evening "does not seem to me satisfactory, but I cannot trace its unsatisfactoriness to the homosexual theme. Rather, it seems to me, the trouble lies in
      the mechanism of the story and in the main characters."
      Stephen "is neither attractive nor unattractive, he is a
      mere shadow, a part of the mechanism of the plot."

29 KALB, BERNARD. "The Author." Saturday Review of Literature,
      37 (5 June), 14.
        Isherwood talks about his life in California and how he
      wrote The World in the Evening.

30 LAGARD, GARALD. "A Promise at Ebbtide." Long Beach Independent Press Telegram (22 August).
        Review of The World in the Evening: "[T]he reader will
      meet a most perceptive woman in Stephen's dead first wife."

31 LUDWIG, J. B. "Fear and Trembling." New Republic, 131
      (5 July), 19-20.
        "[T]he old Isherwood world in which fear dominated the
      feelings of his characters is still present in The World in
      the Evening." Although the novel appears to end happily,

"the same man who seeks human and spiritual love is a prey
to sensuality; and though individuality is a means of sal-
vation, the ego is a force for destruction."

32 M., N. B. "Steers Course without Rudder." <u>Oakland Tribune</u>,
(18 July).
In <u>The World in the Evening</u>, "Isherwood is such a beguiling and adept writer that the reader will be lured
into going along with him until...he thinks it over after-
wards and finds that all this rich hollandaise sauce covers
spinach, not broccoli."

33 M., P. "A Camera on the U.S.--Mr. Isherwood's Latest."
<u>Toronto Telegram</u> (14 August).
"If [<u>The World in the Evening</u>] is disappointing (and it
is) it is because the sensitive recording machine that
caught the foibles of post-World-War-I Germany is working
on material that is not quite suitable. The camera itself
has become involved; and while it cannot lie, it can dis-
tort."

34 McLAUGHLIN, RICHARD. "'World in the Evening' of Two Marriages." <u>Springfield Republican</u> [MA] (1 August), p. 4C.
<u>The World in the Evening</u> "is the lugubrious tale of
Stephen Monk...whose emotional insecurity and inability to
achieve a comfortable sexual relationship ruins both his
marriages."

35 PARSONS, MARGARET. "This Game with Words." <u>Worcester Tele-
gram</u> [MA] (20 June).
The letters of Elizabeth Rydal are "the most stimulating
part" of <u>The World in the Evening</u>. Her "simplicity and her
moral sense" are refreshing.

36 PRITCHETT, V. S. "Books in General." <u>New Statesman and Na-
tion</u>, 47 (19 June), 803.
"The <u>World in the Evening</u> is simply the Berlin stories,
resown in America and coming up as a poor thin crop of
lowered vitality. Since Mr. Isherwood is a clever man and
an ingenious story-teller, he is not negligible; but I did
not for a moment believe in his lapsed and worried Quaker
or his two dreary wives and his hysterical boy-friend."

37 PUTZEL, NELL CONVERSE. "The Camera Turned Inward." <u>St. Louis
Post-Dispatch</u> (21 July), p. 2C.
The protagonist of <u>The World in the Evening</u> "seems as
inverted, self-interested, pseudo-intellectual at the end
of the book as he was in the beginning." In this novel
"the camera is focused inward, and the resulting image is
blurred and somewhat dull."

38 QUINN, PATRICK F. Review of The World in the Evening. Hudson
      Review, 7 (Autumn), 461–462.
         "In The World in the Evening, Isherwood has attempted...
      to endorse (tentatively) the Quakerism of John Woodman by
      means of a novel in the manner (vaguely) of John O'Hara...."

39 RAINER, DACHINE. Review of The World in the Evening. Santa
      Ana Register [CA] (13 June).
         The World in the Evening is "a superb novel," although
      Stephen is a "nebulous" central character.

40 RAYMOND, JOHN. "Isherwood and Powell." Listener, 52 (16 De-
      cember), 1067.
         The World in the Evening is "an extremely courageous and
      immensely readable novel which is yet full of an underlying
      and unconscious silliness. It is the silliness that at-
      taches to any novel that attempts to deal with homosexual-
      ity without that element of the comic that necessarily at-
      tends the subject in the present condition of western
      society."

41 ROGERS, W. G. Review of The World in the Evening. Everett
      Herald [WA] (14 June).
         "The thing I like about this novel...is not so much its
      immediate foreground but rather, what lies just beyond,
      what lies around the edges. It's the physical and mental
      setting that Isherwood handles well...." [This review also
      appeared in the Vancouver Daily Province (4 September).]

42 ROLO, CHARLES J. Review of The World in the Evening. Atlan-
      tic, 194 (July), 84.
         The World in the Evening "is a rather mushy chronicle of
      a man's awakening to the truth that, at thirty-six, he is
      an arrested adolescent.... Mr. Isherwood has sagged to a
      level not greatly above that of the more earnest-minded
      best sellers serialized in the women's mass magazines."

43 ROSENFELD, ISAAC. "Quaker Oats." Nation, 179 (3 July), 15.
         "In 'The World in the Evening' Christopher Isherwood
      tries to go beyond 'The Berlin Stories' and 'Prater Violet'
      by giving full character to his observer and keeping him in
      the center of the action, but he largely makes a mess of it.
      ... [O]nly the style is right...."

44 SCHORER, MARK. "Paths of Betrayal." New York Times Book Re-
      view (6 June), pp. 6, 16.
         The World in the Evening "is a novel of contrasting per-
      sons and types, and seems ultimately to rest on the juxta-
      position of contrasting worlds. One is the world of selfish
      love, the other of selfless love, and the fact that these
      cannot always be surely separated is one of Mr. Isherwood's
      ironic enigmas...."

1954

45   WAIN, JOHN. "Bergmann's Masterpiece." Spectator, 192
      (18 June), 742-743.
           In The World in the Evening, the narrator or "I," for
      the first time in an Isherwood book, "is a real, suffering,
      developing human being. This suffering and development are
      vividly brought before the reader, so that the book is con-
      tinuously interesting and often moving...."

46   WALKER, PEREGRINE. "Love Declined." The Tablet: A Weekly
      Newspaper and Review, 203 (19 June), 595.
           "If a novel need be no more than a perceptive analysis
      of a human situation, descriptively valid and sensitively
      written, then The World in the Evening will deserve the
      tributes it will doubtless receive. But if it should have
      something to say about the night that follows evening, and
      the tragic yet redeeming knowledge it may bring, then Mr.
      Isherwood has failed...."

47   WILSON, ANGUS. "The New and Old Isherwood." Encounter, 3
      (August), 62-68.
           Despite Isherwood's "extraordinary powers of entertain-
      ment and high technical achievement," there is a "failure
      in central purpose" to The World in the Evening. "A great
      deal of the novel is highly entertaining, much of it is
      percipient, some of it very moving, but is not important at
      the level to which it aspires."

*48   WINGATE, GIFFORD W. "Poetic Drama in the 1930's: A Study of
      the Plays of T. S. Eliot and W. H. Auden." Ph.D. disserta-
      tion, Cornell University.
      Cited in Doctoral Dissertations, 21 (1954), 260.

49   WORSLEY, T. C. "Aunt Edna in Berlin." New Statesman and Na-
      tion, 47 (20 March), 355.
           In I Am a Camera, "the image of the camera which Mr.
      Isherwood originally used...has been retained by Mr. Van
      Druten. But the pictures he produces with it are very much
      more comforting and good natured than the originals."

50   YORK, CHARLES MARSHALL. "Lightweight Summer Novel." Greens-
      boro News [NC] (11 July).
           In The World in the Evening, "Mr. Isherwood has written
      a good, second-rate novel that will be adequate for light,
      summer reading."

51   YOUNG, WAYLAND. "Isherwood in the Afternoon." Kenyon Review
      16 (Autumn), 637-640.
           In The World in the Evening, Isherwood is at last a com-
      mitted novelist. The "savagely antiseptic neutrality" of
      the Berlin books has been replaced by "more compassion,
      more immediacy." But the new vision is not universally
      perceptive.

1955

1 FRIEDMAN, NORMAN. "Point of View in Fiction: The Development
   of a Critical Concept." Publications of the Modern Language Association, 70 (December), 1160-1184.
        Conclues a survey of kinds of points of view with a com-
   ment on "The Camera"--sees Isherwood's "camera eye" as "the
   ultimate in authorial exclusion." [Reprinted in 1967.29.]

2 GREENWOOD, ORMEROD. "It Was Something Like This...." Ark:
   The Journal of the Royal College of Art, no. 15, pp. 35-38.
        The first organizer of the Group Theatre recalls the
   early days (1932-1937). Photograph of the Group Theatre
   production of The Ascent of F6 is included.

3 [HAMILTON, GERALD.] "Guy Burgess as I Knew Him." Spectator,
   195 (4 November), 578-580.
        Imaginary letter from "Mr. Norris" to Christopher Isher-
   wood. Alleges to be about "the only real spy" that Norris
   introduced to Isherwood--Guy Burgess.

4 KUNITZ, STANLEY and VINETA COLBY, eds. Twentieth Century
   Authors: A Biographical Dictionary of Modern Literature,
   1st Supplement. New York: H. W. Wilson Co., p. 480.
        Supplements 1942.1 with quotations from Isherwood on his
   activities in the 40s and with brief excerpts of reviews
   of The World in the Evening.

5 LEHMANN, JOHN. The Whispering Gallery: Autobiography I.
   London: Longsmans, Green, pp. 176, 179-180, 181-182, 199,
   201, 209-210, 212-213, 223-225, 231, 232, 234, 235, 237,
   242-244, 257, 262, 263, 266, 280, 287, 302, 304, 307-309,
   327, 328.
        "It was impossible not to be drawn to [Isherwood]: I
   was attracted by the warmth of his nature, and by the
   quality which appealed to me so much in The Memorial, an
   exact feeling for the deeper moods of our generation...;
   his capacity...to invent the most extravagant dream-
   situations of comedy for everyone he knew, evoked a response at once in that part of me that had produced the
   dotty fantasy plays at Eton; and at the same time I had
   fallen under the spell of his Berlin legend." [Reprinted
   in 1969.14.]

6 STEINBERG, ERWIN R. "Poetic Drama in General and Auden and
   Isherwood in Particular." Carnegie Series in English, No.
   2. Pittsburgh: Carnegie Institute of Technology, pp. 43-
   58.
        The plays of Auden and Isherwood have some serious
   flaws, but their attempt to bring poetry and drama together
   to focus on twentieth-century issues is admirable,

especially in contrast to the verse drama of T. S. Eliot,
which "was still largely looking backward to earlier days."

1956

1   BREIT, HARRY. "Talks with Mr. Isherwood," in his The Writer
     Observed. Cleveland: World Publishing, pp. 215-217.
         Reprint of 1951.1.

2   HAMILTON, GERALD. Mr. Norris and I, an Autobiographical
     Sketch. London: A. Wingate, pp. 120-143.
         "[I]t must be fairly admitted that there is so much of
     me in the character of Mr. Norris (not, I hasten to say,
     in the sex life of that worthy), and in his manner of
     speech, his reluctance to face the issue, his love of in-
     trigue and scheming, which unfortunately, would fit a de-
     scription of me at that distant epoch."

3   LUMLEY, FREDERICK. Trends in 20th Century Drama: A Survey
     Since Ibsen and Shaw. Fair Lawn, N.J.: Essential Books,
     pp. 92, 216.
         The Auden/Isherwood plays "were products of their time
     and for immediate consumption; they reflected the disil-
     lusionment and despair of man, whom they did not believe
     could survive the horrors which in fact he did." [Re-
     printed: 1967.42; revised: 1972.38.]

4   TINDALL, WILLIAM YORK. Forces in Modern British Literature,
     1885-1956. New York: Vintage Books, pp. 46-47, 48, 50,
     72, 175, 220, 233, 244.
         Reprint of 1947.27.

5   WILLIAMSON, AUDREY. Contemporary Theatre, 1953-1956. London:
     Rockliffe, Publishing, pp. 78-80.
         In I Am a Camera, John Van Druten's technique uses
     "Isherwood himself on stage as part-narrator, part-actor,
     physically within and yet spiritually outside events, re-
     cording them without moral judgment and with something of
     the detached visual clarity of a camera lens." But the
     center of the play is Sally Bowles: "Van Druten and Isher-
     wood have drawn her in microscopic detail."

1957

1   BEACH, JOSEPH WARREN. The Making of the Auden Canon. Minne-
     apolis: University of Minnesota Press, pp. 5, 10, 37, 65,
     69, 90, 98, 103-104, 114, 124, 143, 148, 150, 155, 166,
     167, 185, 187, 189, 197, 215, 226, 247, 248, 273-274, 278,
     301, 303.

"Isherwood was evidently more interested in the satirical and comic modes in propagandist drama, while Auden
wished to emphasize the moral and affirmative elements in
their social faith."

2   GUNTHER, CHARLES. "Celebrating a Poet's Centenary." St.
      Louis Post-Dispatch (15 September), p. 4B.
         "There have been many translations of Baudelaire's verse.
      Perhaps too many.... But even Baudelaire's prose is still
      not completely translated and these 'Intimate Journals'
      form a small but attractive collection of his most charac-
      teristic work in this form."

3   HOGGART, RICHARD. W. H. Auden. Writers and Their Work, No.
      93. London: Longmans, Green, pp. 15, 22.
         All of the Auden/Isherwood plays "have some good lyrics
      and choruses, but only The Ascent of F.6 is now worth close
      attention. In this play the 'Quest' theme, because it is
      more deeply probed, inspires some scenes much more search-
      ing and eloquent than any in The Dog Beneath the Skin."

4   LEVIN, HARRY. Contexts of Criticism. Cambridge: Harvard
      University Press, p. 238.
         Isherwood, like Aldous Huxley, is an example of "the
      British novelist in residence, who oscillates between Hol-
      lywood and theosophy, therby enjoying the worst of both
      worlds...."

5   McCOLLOM, WILLIAM G. Tragedy. New York: Macmillan, pp. 242-
      245.
         "In spite of its occasional preciosity and even absurd-
      ity, The Ascent of F6 is an authentic contribution to the
      art of tragedy. Few recent dramatists have equaled this
      collaboration of Auden and Isherwood...."

6   WYNDHAM, FRANCIS. "Twenty-five Years of the Novel," in The
      Craft of Letters in England. Edited by John Lehmann.
      Boston: Houghton-Mifflin, pp. 44-59.
         Isherwood is included in the survey of English fiction
      from the thirties to the mid-fifties. Brief mentions of
      All the Conspirators, Prater Violet, and The World in the
      Evening. [Reprinted: 1974.15.]

1958

1   AMIS, KINGSLEY. "Socialism and the Intellectuals," in The
      Beat Generation and the Angry Young Men. Edited by Gene
      Feldman and Max Gertenberg. New York: Citadel Press,
      pp. 299-315.

Examines the fallacy of writers like Auden, Spender,
Isherwood, and Orwell, who make politics the basis of their
thought.

2   DAICHES, DAVID. The Present Age, After 1920. Introduction to
English Literature, Vol. 5, edited by Bonamy Dobrée. London: Cresset Press; Bloomington: Indiana University
Press, pp. 159-162. [American title: The Present Age in
British Literature.]
    The comic irony and parody of The Dog Beneath the Skin
are more memorable than the serious passages. The Ascent
of F6 is "a carefully organized symbolic play of considerable power...." On the Frontier is more successful than
the more ambitious and complex Ascent.

3   GERSTENBERGER, DONNA. "Formal Experiments in Modern Verse
Drama." Ph.D. dissertation, University of Oklahoma, chapter IV.
    "[T]he Auden-Isherwood plays are of interest in their
own right in the development of modern verse drama, because
in them there is an attempt to convey wholly modern content
in the most immediately relevant terms...." [Reprinted,
somewhat revised: 1973.11.]

4   MERCIER, VIVIAN. "Baudelaire Revisited." Kenyon Review, 20
(Spring), 336.
    "I should like to welcome the reissue of Christopher
Isherwood's accurate translation of [Baudelaire's] Fusées,
Mon Coeur mis à nu, and Choix de maximes."

5   PLOMER, WILLIAM C. F. At Home: Memoirs. London: Jonathan
Cape, pp. 73, 101, 106, 120.
    "Another of our visitors at Canning Place was Christopher
Isherwood. He was a letter writer of exceptional brilliance.... If, as he pretended, he was a sort of camera
eye, then the eye of no camera can ever have had a more
diamond-like twinkle in it." [Same material included in
1975.12.]

6   WEISGERBER, JEAN. "Les Romans et Récits de Christopher Isherwood." Revue de 1'Université de Bruxelles, 10 (July-
September), 360-380.
    All the Conspirators and The Memorial are the kind of
books that one likes because one can meet himself again in
them. Among the later works, Prater Violet seems intended
more for the illustrated weeklies. This leaves the Berlin
books, whose quality accounts for the faults of The World
in the Evening. A comparison of these clearly reveals the
dangers to which Isherwood exposes himself when he abandons
the depiction of manners and falls into abstractions. [In
French]

<u>1959</u>

1   BRØGGER, NIELS C. "Timer som aldri var [Time that never was]."
    <u>Vinduet</u>, 15, no. 1, 56-61.
        On the use of time in fantasy fiction: In "I Am Wait-
    ing" Isherwood describes how the tiniest remove from
    "normal time" can have incalculable consequences. [In
    Danish]

2   BULLOUGH, GEOFFREY. "Poetry in Modern English Drama." <u>Cairo</u>
    <u>Studies in English</u>, 1: 26-42.
        <u>The Ascent of F6</u> was an "ambitious play on the social
    and psychological implications of the craze for explora-
    tion...." It contained "some clever diagnosis of the Brit-
    ish middle-class diseases of the spirit, but ended with an
    obscure vision on the mountain-top which puzzled spectators
    and readers alike."

3   CORBETT, HUGH. Review of <u>All the Conspirators</u>. <u>Books Abroad</u>,
    33 (Autumn), 464.
        Isherwood's first novel "is written with remarkable per-
    ception and clarity. However, it is dull, and the charac-
    ters, though authentic, are bores." The main interest in
    the book "lies in comparison between the angry young man of
    the Twenties and his counterpart today."

4   DONOGHUE, DENIS. "Drame à thèse: Auden and Cummings," in his
    <u>Third Voice: Modern British and American Verse Drama</u>.
    Princeton: Princeton University Press, pp. 62-70.
        <u>The Ascent of F6</u> is more concerned with "thesis" than
    with "drama." The conceptions are not realized in dramatic
    terms; there is no vital theatrical form to carry those
    conceptions without strain.

5   LEHMANN, JOHN. "Foreword." <u>London Magazine</u>, 6 (October), 7,
    9.
        "Nobody in the future is going to worry about the 'Auden-
    Isherwood affair.' Nobody will be much interested in any-
    thing except what they have given the world as artists."

6   ROBINSON, ROBERT. "Domestic Occasion." <u>Spectator</u>, 203
    (23 October), 544.
        Account of a TV interview given by Isherwood at the home
    of Stephen Spender. Isherwood is described and quoted on
    several topics, including his film writing and his associ-
    ates in the thirties.

7   SPENDER, STEPHEN. "The Auden-Isherwood Collaboration." <u>New</u>
    <u>Republic</u>, 141 (23 November), 16-17.
        Review of <u>Two Great Plays</u> (<u>The Dog Beneath the Skin</u> and
    <u>The Ascent of F6</u>): "This seems to have been not so much a

1959

collaboration as a pooling of talents, assumed to be complementary..., and an acceptance of rather facile compro-
mises whenever the plays demanded a real fusion of Auden's
fantasy with Isherwood's ironic realism."

8   WOOD, NEAL. Communism and the British Intellectuals. New
York: Columbia University Press, pp. 38-40, 79n. 80, 97-
98, 104, 112.
"From about 1925 until the beginning of the Second World
War, a new group of writers emerged: Auden, Day Lewis,
Spender, Isherwood, and MacNeice. Like their predecessors
they were tower-dwellers, but there was a difference in the
tower, and what was seen from it. All that the new writers
saw was change and revolution...."

1960

1   BEACH, JOSEPH WARREN. Obsessive Images: Symbolism in Poetry
of the 1930's and 1940's. Edited by William Van O'Connor.
Minneapolis: University of Minnesota Press, pp. 27, 48,
50, 51, 76, 99, 109, 115, 125, 127, 133, 137, 200, 235,
289, 294, 310, 344.
The comments that relate to Isherwood are primarily
about the major themes and images in the Auden-Isherwood
plays--such as "The Formless Terror" in The Ascent of F6,
or the geographic symbolism of The Dog Beneath the Skin
and On the Frontier.

2   BOULTON, MARJORIE. The Anatomy of Drama. London: Routledge
& Kegan Paul, pp. 8, 85, 94, 155.
Random comments on themes as well as structural and
theatrical features, such as the mountain in The Ascent of
F6 or the numerous episodes of The Dog Beneath the Skin,
in the Auden-Isherwood plays.

3   GASSNER, JOHN. Theatre at the Crossroads: Plays and Playwrights of the Mid-Century American Stage. New York:
Holt, Rinehart and Winston, pp. 144-146.
In I Am a Camera, "John Van Druten made it quite evident that the I-am-a-camera attitude of young Isherwood
was essentially as unproductive as it was egotistical, and
that the irresponsible behavior of the other expatriates
on whom the would-be writer trained his camera was no less
deplorable."

4   GERSTENBERGER, DONNA. "Perspectives on Modern Verse Drama."
Modern Drama, 3 (May), 24-29.
"The modern playwrights who undertook, by use of verse,
to gain for the drama a formal coherence of both language

and structure did not create a school or issue manifestoes."
Auden and Isherwood are among the "foremost" poets and
playwrights in "influence" and "awareness."

5   JONES, DAVID EDWARD. The Plays of T. S. Eliot. London:
    Routledge & Kegan Paul, p. 22.
        "Apart from the plays of Auden and Isherwood, all the
    important poetic drama of the last thirty years in England
    has been religious in basis. And the drama of Auden and
    Isherwood may in the long run reveal itself as no more than
    an interesting phenomenon of the thirties because it has no
    such basis."

6   KERMODE, FRANK. "The Interpretation of the Times." Encounter,
    15 (September), 71-76.
        Analyzes Isherwood's "jocular desperation"; compares The
    World in the Evening, which is "decadent Camp," with The
    Memorial, which is "pre- or proto-Camp." Calls The Memorial
    "the best completed novel of a most distinguished writer:
    a genuine interpretation of the times." [Reprinted:
    1962.56.]

7   LEHMANN, JOHN. I Am My Brother: Autobiography II. London:
    Longmans, Green; New York: Reynal & Co., pp. 14-15, 18,
    31, 33, 64-65, 68, 102, 153-154, 180, 185, 195, 219-220,
    285, 289, 303.
        "Christopher Isherwood's case was, I thought, the most
    spectacular example of an experience that was typical. Mr.
    Norris Changes Trains and the stories of Goodbye to Berlin
    seemed to me far too inadequate an oeuvre for someone who
    had been tipped, for every kind of good reason, as the most
    promising novelist of his generation." [Reprinted:
    1969.14.]

8   MAES-JELINEK, HENA. "The Knowledge of Man in the Works of
    Christopher Isherwood." Revue des Langues Vivantes, 26,
    no. 5, 341-360.
        "The Berlin stories and Isherwood's association with the
    literary movement of the thirties have induced people to
    think of him as a portrayer of that epoch. But it is ob-
    vious that the background of his novels interests him only
    temporarily and that his choice of it depends on the char-
    acters because it is part of their experience."

9   NICHOLSON, NORMAN. "Modern Verse-Drama and the Folk Tradi-
    tion." Critical Quarterly, 2 (Summer), 166-170.
        The resemblance between Murder in the Cathedral and The
    Ascent of F6 is deeper than the commonality of their pur-
    pose and intended audience: "Beckett, approaching martyr-
    dom and sainthood, or Ransom (the name has theological im-
    plications) approaching F6, are both facing the same moral
    problem: 'the right deed for the wrong reason.'"

1960

10   PRYCE-JONES, DAVID. "Isherwood Reassessed." <u>Time and Tide</u>,
     41 (1 October), 1162-1163.
        "Love in Isherwood's novels tends to be an ostentatious
     perversion, often described with a slightly ludicrous
     care.... Self-awareness takes priority for Isherwood over
     other people's feelings and the danger of a totalitarian
     system is that it will be a threat to self-expression and
     development."

11   REPLOGLE, JUSTIN. "Social Philosophy in Auden's Early Poetry."
     <u>Criticism</u>, 2 (Fall), 351-361.
        "In <u>Dog Beneath the Skin</u> Auden's changing [social]
     themes become quite clear. The new emphasis is on action.
     Concern for the individual begins to look like irresponsi-
     ble escapism."

12   SYMONS, JULIAN. <u>The Thirties: A Dream Revolved</u>. London:
     Cresset Press, pp. 23, 59-64, 82-84.
        "<u>Lions and Shadows</u> is a key that at first glance seems
     to unlock some doors that most people keep firmly shut.
     We turn the key, the door opens. It is disconcerting to
     find that we are not in a room at all, but in a long corri-
     dor.... We hurry along the corridor...to find another door
     at the end of it. And this door resists our key."

13   WEATHERBY, W. J. "W. J. Weatherby Meets Christopher Isher-
     wood." <u>Manchester Guardian</u> (17 November), p. 8.
        Interview in which Isherwood points out that he writes
     "fundamentally about foreigners, about exiles, about odd-
     balls, the excluded and so forth."

                              <u>1961</u>

1   BRADBURY, RAY, ed. "Introduction," in <u>Timeless Stories for</u>
     <u>Today and Tomorrow</u>. New York: Bantam Books, pp. vii-xiii.
        Comment on "I Am Waiting": "Mr. Isherwood's theme is
     immensely human and touching because we realize that his
     attic-bound hero symbolizes any of us who, trying to divine
     the future, even if it were placed before us to be examined,
     would, through circumstance or lack of imagination, be un-
     able to profit or grow from the experience."

2   CAVANAUGH, WILLIAM C. "<u>Coriolanus</u> and <u>The Ascent of F-6</u>:
     Similarity in Theme and Supporting Detail." <u>Drama Critique</u>,
     4 (February), 9-17.
        The major similarities between <u>The Ascent of F6</u> and
     <u>Coriolanus</u> are the mother-son theme, the difficulties of
     the heroes in acting according to principle (rather than
     according to attachment), and the theme of power.

*3   HART, DENIS. "Here on a Visit." <u>Manchester Guardian</u> (22 September), p. 11.
Cited: <u>Subject Index to Periodicals</u> 1961, p. 132.

4   McLEOD, STUART R. "Problems of Poetry and Dramaturgy in Modern Verse Drama." Ph.D. dissertation, University of Florida.
"W. H. Auden and Christopher Isherwood in <u>The Dog Beneath the Skin</u>...cast a propagandistic message in an atmosphere of surrealism and revealed truth." The play demonstrates a compromise between art and utility, since the "ultimate concern" of the Auden-Isherwood plays is with the social and political problems of the thirties. [Reprinted, somewhat revised: 1972.39.]

5   MANDER, JOHN. <u>The Writer and Commitment</u>. London: Secker & Warburg, pp. 32-37, 55-56, 58, 81, 129, 209.
"<u>The Dog Beneath the Skin</u> is a satire on the England of 1935. It is written, as satire must be, from a definitely committed point of view; a point of view that makes the whole business of Charity fêtes, Boys' Brigades, and Vicar's teas appear a ridiculous mummery." The other Auden-Isherwood plays are discussed; Isherwood is mentioned in three other sections.

6   POSS, STANLEY. "A Conversation on Tape." <u>London Magazine</u>, NS 1 (June), 41-58.
Isherwood answers questions about his work habits, the organization of his novels, his writing for the movies, his life in California, his latest novel (<u>Down There on a Visit</u>), writers who influenced his style, his Vedantic beliefs, various of his fictional creatons (Mr. Norris, Elizabeth Rydal, Stephen Monk), his collaborations with Auden, the young writers he finds most interesting, his pacifism, and his involvement in other political actions.

7   STEBNER, GERHARD W. "Auden, The Ascent of F6: Interpretation eines Dramas." <u>Die Neuren Sprachen</u>, 10 (September), 397-413.
Auden did not get from Marx the idea of class struggle, but the idea of a utopian-socialist humanism. In <u>The Ascent of F-6</u>, the most important collaboration of Auden and Isherwood, the moralizing nature is developed. The propagandistic quality of the play prevents deep audience involvement. Auden lacked understanding of the average person, despite his own fervid beliefs, whereas Brecht combined his beliefs with his knowledge of common people. [In German] [Reprinted, slightly revised: 1963.7.]

1962

1 AMIS, KINGSLEY. "A Bit Glassy." Spectator, 208 (9 March),
   309.
   "On the evidence of [Down There on a Visit] and of its
   predecessor, The World in the Evening (1954), there is
   reason for suspecting that glassiness may have become
   chronic.... I don't mean to be smart, let alone patron-
   ising, in calling this book promising. There's just about
   enough in it to foster the hope that that old glassiness
   may turn out not to be chronic after all."

2 ANGELIDES, JOHN. "Between Book Ends." St. Louis Post-Dispatch
   (18 April), p. 2B.
   "Christopher Isherwood has used a deft pen, an observant
   eye and a great deal of imagination in [Down There on a
   Visit].... He has attempted to show his characters as
   people shut up in private hells of their own making, self-
   dedicated to a lifelong feud with The Others."

3 ANON. "Apologia for a Myth." Times Literary Supplement
   (9 March), p. 151.
   Down There on a Visit is not merely "a series of de-
   scents into the underworld by an Orpheus whose most sinis-
   ter charm has rendered him immune to the deterioration he
   encounters, but may also be read as an apologia for the
   whole Herr Issyvoo myth, the myth of the poseur, the maso-
   chist challenging his puppets to make him feel their de-
   sires and fears."

4 ANON. "Be This Fact or Fiction It's Boring Just the Same."
   Washington Evening Star (4 March).
   In Down There on a Visit, "each succeeding episode is a
   bit more melodramatic and loosely written than the last....
   [I]t expires in all-too-boring melodramatics."

5 ANON. "The Changes in Isherwood." Miami Herald (22 April).
   Review of Down There on a Visit: "If you like writing
   for its own sake, Isherwood is for you. His style is as
   delicate and complex as a cameo. And somewhere there is a
   moral. But try and find it."

6 ANON. "Dilettante of the Depths." Time, 79 (23 March), 90.
   Down There on a Visit "sometimes seems little else than
   a portrait of the artist as aging adolescent," yet Isherwood knows "the world of respectability and the underworld
   of self-indulgence.... He is a dilettante of the higher
   depths, a kind of demi-Virgil leading the reader through a
   hop-skip-and-jump tour of Hell."

7   ANON. "Four Men, Four Periods and 'I.'" Detroit News
      (25 March).
          "There is no element of self-pity in 'Down There on a
      Visit,' but we feel that we have been permitted to see
      glimpses of a personal purgatory and we are grateful for
      such sensitively expressed insight."

8   ANON. "Isherwood, Christopher," in The Reader's Encyclopedia
      of American Literature. Edited by Max J. Herzberg. New
      York: Thomas Y. Crowell, p. 521.
          Summary of Isherwood's writing career.

9   ANON. "New Fiction." London Times (8 March), p. 15.
          Down There on a Visit is an "elegant and serious produc-
      tion." The second and fourth sections "are beautifully
      balanced and observed. And the writing is, as always, very
      clear, very moving, and, sometimes, very funny."

10   ANON. Review of Down There on a Visit. Boulder Sentinel [CO]
      (1 April).
          In Down There on a Visit, "Isherwood is the observer as
      he probes rather listlessly into the hates, tensions and
      undercurrents of his former selves. I think the average
      onlooker will hardly be ruffled, surprised or even partic-
      ularly gripped."

11   ANON. Review of Down There on a Visit. Dallas Times-Herald
      (22 April).
          "Sex mixes with a sort of Oriental religious atmosphere;
      the best thing about the book is the expert dialogue, the
      worst is the people. The reader's final reaction: why?"

12   ANON. Review of Down There on a Visit. Long Beach Press-
      Telegram (18 March).
          "There are no dull moments in a novel by Christopher
      Isherwood. Down There on a Visit...is not top-grade Isher-
      wood..., but it still is a superior novel."

13   ANON. Review of Down There on a Visit. New York Post
      (4 March).
          "Anecdotes and honest and penetrating character por-
      traits are loosely tied into [Down There on a Visit] by the
      recurrent theme of homosexuality and by the role of the
      observer-writer who does not really involve himself...."

14   ANON. Review of Down There on a Visit. Virginia Kirkus'
      Service, 30 (15 January), p. 97.
          "The homosexual's fantastic but slanted awareness of
      people, the bitchery, jealousy, loneliness and Everyman's
      desperate search for a way out, all combine to make [Down
      There on a Visit] a frantic, fascinating, unsettling book--
      in spite of its skill and sophistication."

1962

15 BARNER, W. G. "Isherwood Novel Called Delightful." Charleston News and Courier [SC] (15 April).
  "'Down There' refers to another world within all individuals, and in this case the author laughs at the private hells of these individuals' own making. He takes the reader on a delightful tour and shows a strong introspect into what makes people tick."

16 BARRETT, WILLIAM. "Hollywood and Vina." Atlantic, 209 (April), 156-157.
  "Down There on a Visit is Mr. Isherwood's best work of fiction since The Berlin Stories.... For robust realism this book cannot match the earlier stories, but the author has gained in depth, reflectiveness, and compassion...."

17 BAUER, MALCOLM. "Authors' Lives Reflected in New Novels." Portland Oregonian (11 March).
  In Down There on a Visit, "Mr. Isherwood, as urbane as ever and sometimes a bit too precious, has succeeded in subordinating his fictional self to the role of a mirror..., and the result is a piercing portrayal of four extraordinary characters who have left their marks on his life."

18 BISCHOFF, BARBARA. Review of Down There on a Visit. Portland Journal [OR] (26 May).
  "All of the people encountered, their private hells and feuds, are viewed with compassion, which is made part of the writer's own common scheme of things."

19 BLIVEN, NAOMI. "The Rueful Cameraman." New Yorker, 38 (1 September), 77-80.
  Most of Down There on a Visit "is written sharply, with honest, flat wit, and is joined by suitably invisible seams." Isherwood seems to be answering the question "What have you done with your youth?"--in a "reserved mood of despair."

20 BOWER, HELEN. "This One's Not for Aunt Minnie." Detroit Free Press (11 March).
  Review of Down There on a Visit: "In this saga of Isherwood in search of himself, the first half has some titillation and more 'tedious naughtiness.' In the concluding visit Isherwood's devotion to yoga changes and somewhat slows the pace."

21 BRADBURY, MALCOLM. "New Novels." Punch, 242 (4 April), 549-550.
  Down There on a Visit "acquires a singular force from its power to evoke tension, corruption and falsity; yet the sharpest falsity and in a curious way the largest corruption seems to lie within Isherwood himself."

22 BRADY, CHARLES A. "Isherwood Adopts Pre-War Posturing in
    Novel on Himself." Buffalo Evening News (3 March).
        Down There on a Visit "provides an accurate enough mir-
    roring of the pastel half-world of the '30s and '40s, the
    'gay' world that is without gaiety, the womanless world
    that is so hideous a parody of the world of mimic emotion
    wherein everything, even vice, gets turned 'to favor and to
    prettiness. "

23 BRANCHE, BILL. "New Novel Is Seen Among Year's Best." Nia-
    gara Falls Gazette [NY] (11 March).
        Down There on a Visit "is hardly as introspective as its
    theme--in fact, it is deceptively light and interesting.
    Its principal assets are excellent characterizations of
    some most unusual people, a polished style, a well-organized
    but not over-powering plot and a fine feeling for the effect
    of environment on character."

24 BRANDT, G. W. "Realism and Parables: From Brecht to Auden,"
    in Contemporary Theatre. Stratford-upon-Avon Studies 4.
    Edited by John Russell Brown and Bernard Harris. New York:
    St. Martin's Press, pp. 33-55.
        The message of the parable in The Ascent of F.6 is "far
    from clear": "Auden and Isherwood's plot fails to pro-
    vide...an objective correlative for their message."

25 BROWN, LOUISE FIELDING. Review of Down There on a Visit.
    Book-of-the-Month Club News (June), pp. 10-11.
        "Mr. Isherwood examines himself with the same wide-
    ranging, gently sardonic eye he turns upon others. [Down
    There on a Visit] is uneven in quality, passages of lyrical
    beauty and true psychological insight alternating with
    shallow passages of personal prejudice and some thoroughly
    dull dross, but it is clearly an honest report of human
    experience...."

26 CARBERRY, EDWARD. "Christopher's Eye." Cincinnati Post and
    Times-Star (24 March).
        Down There on a Visit "is a kind of tour of the small
    hells of those who try to make a life of sex, usually de-
    viate...or ambiguous, alcohol and drugs, and are sometimes
    drawn finally to Oriental mysticism.... Love is on perma-
    nent leave in this world and the taste of dusty death comes
    early."

27 COFFEY, WARREN. Review of Down There on a Visit. Ramparts, 1
    (September), 88-90.
        "I had the feeling that I was listening to a 'Fantasy on
    an Air by Jack Kerouac.' But it was only Isherwood after
    all and predictable Isherwood at that. As Auden was shrewd
    enough to see, a spectacularly irrational conversion had

1962

long been in the offing for Isherwood. It has come and
has proved an even greater bore than all the years of
fashionable naughtiness."

28   COOLEY, FRANKLIN D. "Isherwood Looks Back on His Life."
     Richmond Times Dispatch (1 July).
         In Down There on a Visit, "scenes are sharp and vivid;
     persons are acutely analyzed and evoked. But I must con-
     fess that I found the book, fascinating as it is, unpleas-
     ant, largely because of the atmosphere of ambiguous sexual-
     ity...."

29   COULBOURN, KEITH. "Isherwood's New Novel: Exercise in Char-
     acters." Tampa Tribune (15 April).
         "Despite the 'chunky' makeup of [Down There on a Visit],
     it doesn't have a stop-and-go quality about it for the most
     part. Possibly because the four individuals he centers his
     tale about are either so shallow or--more likely--such
     purposeful monomaniacs that one cares to read no more about
     them than what is written."

30   CRONIN, JOAN. "World Is Just One Big Sodom to Him." Miami
     Daily News (25 March).
         "Isherwood is a master at conjuring up that urbane,
     languishing society where men call each other 'lovey' and
     are likely to give 'coquettish wriggles.' If you can en-
     dure the faint, sick-sweet odor of its corruption (and
     there is, in fact, much wittiness and funniness and good
     talk), you may wish to follow Christopher in his rather
     titillating pursuit of his Atman" in Down There on a Visit.

31   D., E. J. "Strangers in Worlds Not Theirs." New Bedford
     Standard [MA] (11 March).
         "No synopsis [of Down There on a Visit] can do full jus-
     tice to the excellent dialogue, the amusing situations, the
     satire.... What Isherwood seems to be saying...is that
     there is a nether world within each individual: a place of
     loneliness, alienation, and hatred of 'others.'"

32   DAVIS, REV. CHARLES E. "Dunghill Eruption." Omaha World Her-
     ald (15 April), p. 24.
         "One does not doubt that the disciples of the 'That's
     the way life is' school whose knowledge of Man seems to
     come solely from madhouses and Port Said brothels, will
     hail [Down There on a Visit] as a new Dante's Inferno, but
     Dante's work...had its capstone, Paradise. This book be-
     gins in a compost heap and ends in a dunghill."

33   DAWKINS, CECIL. "'Down There' with Isherwood..." <u>Milwaukee</u>
      <u>Journal</u> (25 March).
          <u>Down There on a Visit</u> "treats alienation with humor and
      pathos. But there remain bewildering ambiguities. There
      is always an uncertainty about whether the narrator is
      merely a sympathetic witness..., or whether his is a per-
      sonal involvement."

34   DIENSTFREY, HARRIS. "Personal, Secret Journey." <u>Commentary</u>,
      34 (October), 360-363.
          "Despite all that Christopher Isherwood achieves in his
      new work--with its lucid, barely tense prose and its com-
      plex structure--<u>Down There on a Visit</u> is a curiously thin
      and, in a sense, even an unfinished book."

35   DOLBIER, MAURICE. "Out of a Certain Foreignness: An Inter-
      view with Christopher Isherwood." <u>New York Herald Tribune</u>
      <u>Books</u> (11 March), p. 5.
          Primarily a discussion of Isherwood's coming to the
      United States and his life in California, with one comment
      on his "new novel" (<u>Down There on a Visit</u>).

36   DOUGLAS, ROBIN. "An Alter Ego in Deep Blue." <u>Chicago Sun</u>
      <u>Times</u> (4 March), section 3, p. 4.
          <u>Down There on a Visit</u> "may shock some, but all who read
      it will recognize the fact that Isherwood knows his way
      around the demimondaine world of queer people. There are
      some interesting perversions not touched upon: I wonder
      why not?"

37   E., J. "Author Observes Several Selves in This Novel." <u>Des</u>
      <u>Moines Sunday Register</u> (11 March), section G, p. 15.
          In <u>Down There on a Visit</u> "only the author's virtuosity...
      saves the reader a feeling which at times borders on revul-
      sion."

38   EAKINS, ROSEMARY. "Christopher Isherwood and 'The Hells Be-
      neath.'" <u>Montreal Daily Star</u> (17 March).
          Isherwood "now appears to have succumbed to the excesses
      of Southern California, to the great detriment of his tal-
      ent as a novelist. <u>Down There on a Visit</u>, despite its
      seeming sensationalism, is dull and tasteless."

39   EIMERL, SAREL. "A Portable Hell." <u>Reporter</u>, 26 (29 March),
      48.
          In <u>Down There on a Visit</u> the "operative word in the title
      is <u>Down,</u> for the stories are threaded together not by the
      narrator but by a common theme, which is despair, and by a
      common condition, which is homosexuality. The humor and
      frivolity that occasionally lightened Isherwood's early
      books have gone, but he still possesses the writer's su-
      preme gift of compelling attention...."

1962

40 ELSON, JANET. "New Fiction by Isherwood." <u>Tulsa World</u>
    (22 April).
    "There are several questions that come to mind when one
    finishes [<u>Down There on a Visit</u>]. Is Isherwood asking so-
    ciety to accept the deviate more sympathetically? Does he
    have a design in mind, some way of looking at life?"

41 ENGLE, PAUL. "World of Broken Values." <u>Chicago Tribune Maga-</u>
    <u>zine of Books</u> (4 March), p. 8.
    "The stories [in <u>Down There on a Visit</u>] are joined not
    only by the part which the narrator plays in each but by
    their common preoccupation with the worst of each individ-
    ual. Essentially, this is the account of a world in which
    all decent values, save occasional personal loyalties, are
    shattered. It is a fascinating account."

42 GENTRY, CURT. "Interview with Isherwood--On Censorship and
    Literature." <u>San Francisco Chronicle</u> (23 September), "This
    World" magazine section, pp. 26-27.
    Isherwood responds to questions about what is wrong with
    America, what the writer's function in such a society is,
    what the differences between modern American and British
    writing are, which younger American writers he admires,
    what solutions Vedantic philosophy offers to the West, and
    what his responses are to the complaints that <u>Down There on</u>
    <u>a Visit</u> is an offensive work.

43 GERSTENBERGER, DONNA. "Poetry and Politics: The Verse Drama
    of Auden and Isherwood." <u>Modern Drama</u>, 5 (September), 123-
    132.
    "Whatever the original reasons for the interest of Auden
    and Isherwood in the stage, their experiments with the
    verse play have the value which extreme manifestations of
    any genre always have. They aid in defining limits and in
    exploring possibilities as well as in objectifying an in-
    herent dissatisfaction...with the conventionally established
    products of the past."

44 GRANSDEN, K. W. <u>E. M. Forster</u>. New York: Grove Press, pp. 8-
    9, 24-25, 30, 113, 117.
    The influence of <u>The Way of all Flesh</u> is traced through
    Forster's <u>The Longest Journey</u> to Isherwood's first novel,
    <u>All the Conspirators</u>. Other echoes of Forsterian technique
    are noted. [Revised: 1970.8.]

45 H., A. C. "An Excursion into Self." <u>Savannah News</u> [GA]
    (11 March).
    In <u>Down There on a Visit</u>, "[l]ife appears to be a game
    in which one must play by rules by 'the Others.' The in-
    dividual must conform, escape or rebel, and the rebel as
    pictured here is not prepossessing."

46   HALE, BOB. "More Than a Month in the Country." <u>Deep River</u>
     <u>New Era</u> [CT] (15 March).
         In <u>Down There on a Visit</u>, Isherwood regards his charac-
     ters "not as objects of scorn or pity or derision, but of
     affection.... He reports, he does not judge. This is the
     seed of the book's charm and of its value...."

47   HAMPSHIRE, STUART. "Isherwood's Hell." <u>Encounter</u>, 19 (Novem-
     ber), 86-88.
         "All four episodes [of <u>Down There on a Visit</u>] seemed to
     me like visits to hell; but they are lightly and humorously
     described by the narrator, who, exercising his professional
     powers as observer, evidently enjoyed himself.... But the
     exact recording of voices and manners and moods makes up
     for everything else and silences disapproval...."

48   HOGAN, WILLIAM. "Isherwood Again Plays the 'Camera.'" <u>San</u>
     <u>Francisco Chronicle</u> (9 March), p. 33.
         <u>Down There on a Visit</u> "is brilliantly written, morbid
     and disturbing.... But Isherwood, it seems to me, ap-
     proaches his laboratory as a victim of the malaise he at-
     tempts to describe rather than a healer."

49   HOLMESLY, STERLIN. "Four Men in One." <u>San Antonio Express</u>
     [TX] (11 March).
         <u>Down There on a Visit</u> "is filled with lively incidents
     and vivid writing. But the current underneath is one of
     self-study and the changes which evolve as one grows
     older."

50   HOPE, FRANCIS. "Photographing the Cameraman." <u>Time and Tide</u>,
     43 (8 March), 26.
         The flaw of <u>Down There on a Visit</u> is that "fiction dis-
     guised as documentary truth leads one, eventually, to ig-
     nore the line between truth and fiction altogether." Al-
     though "the fabulous ease of style and lightness of touch,
     and the <u>rightness</u> of so many minor incidents are still
     there," Isherwood is not the novelist his narrator poses
     as--he is, instead, "the uncreative visitor snooping among
     his diaries."

51   J., U. G. "Lacks Many Elements That Make Good Novel." <u>Durham</u>
     <u>Herald</u> [NC] (26 August).
         In <u>Down There on a Visit</u> "the fifth Christopher Isher-
     wood retains his lofty spot looking down on his characters,
     telling their story, and thereby claiming to be apart from
     them.... It is cleverly done, yet lacks many of the ele-
     ments that could make this a good novel."

1962

52 JEBB, JULIAN. Review of Down There on a Visit. London Maga-
    zine, NS 2 (April), 87-89.
       "The greatest single success of Down There on a Visit is
    the vindication of Christopher Isherwood's 'method.' While
    keeping exactly within the territory where his inquisitive-
    ness and sympathy can best wander, he has...grown taller:
    the country is the same but he surveys it now from an Olym-
    pian but always human maturity."

53 KARL, FREDERICK R. The Contemporary English Novel. New York:
    Farrar, Straus & Cudahy, pp. 9, 274, 290-292.
       "Perhaps no novelist of the last thirty years seemed
    better equipped than Christopher Isherwood to catch the
    peculiar tone of his times; he had verbal facility, inven-
    tive ability, and a sense of form and movement.... Instead
    of maturing into a novelist, however, Isherwood demonstrated
    that his real skill lay in the short sketch.... [His tal-
    ents] were placed at the service of basically trivial char-
    acters." [Revised: 1972.31.]

54 KEESE, PARTON. "Private Hell Self-Made." Worcester Telegram
    [MA] (18 March).
       "Autobiographical, aimless and meditative, Down There on
    a Visit is a sort of Person to Person divided into four
    abstract parts.... Each visit is to a different world--a
    nether world of the individual. Christopher himself is
    changed in each instance."

55 KENNEY, MICHAEL. "Fields for Insight." Hartford Courant [CT]
    (18 March).
       "The best that one person can do for another, an Anglo-
    Oriental mystic tells the character Isherwood, is to create
    a field in which all kinds of insight can occur. It is
    such a field, or series of fields, that the writer Isher-
    wood sets up in [Down There on a Visit]."

56 KERMODE, FRANK. "The Interpretation of the Times," in his
    Puzzles and Epiphanies. London: Routledge and Kegan Paul,
    pp. 121-130.
       Reprint of 1960.6.

57 KERR, WALTER. "Making a Cult of Confusion." Horizon, 5 (Sep-
    tember), 41.
       "Twenty-five years ago W. H. Auden and Christopher Isher-
    wood wrote a stage direction for their Ascent of F-6 asking
    that the principals 'jump on each other's shoulders...and
    behave in general like the Marx brothers.' It was at this
    moment that the play fell apart. For the parallel is simply
    not acceptable."

58   KHAN, B. A. The English Poetic Drama. Aligarh, India: Mus-
     lim University, pp. 47-51.
          In their theatrical collaboration, Auden and Isherwood
     "created a new genre that was lively and influential."
     The plays, however, never achieved a satisfactory "drama-
     tic integration."

59   LAMPORT, SARA. "An Isherwood Novel of a Wanderer." Baltimore
     Sun (14 March).
          In Down There on a Visit the writing is "spare and
     sparkling. There are also poignant moments. Toward the
     end, the focus shifts inward, to the alienation and intense
     loneliness of the individual's struggle against the formid-
     able 'others' of life."

60   LANCOUR, HAROLD. Review of Down There on a Visit. Library
     Journal, 87 (15 March), 1150.
          "The four parts [of Down There on a Visit] are effective
     personality studies of four diverse, unconventional male
     characters.... Characteristically well-handled dialogue,
     bizarre situations, and homosexual overtones."

61   LINDAU, BETSY. "The Substratum of Men's Souls." Winston-
     Salem Journal and Sentinel [NC] (4 March).
          "Supposedly the great revelation [of Down There on a
     Visit] is that each man makes his own hell, the author in-
     cluded. This is true enough, but it seems to me Isherwood
     goes a step further"--in his projection of the uninvolved
     narrator.

62   LONG, THEODORE. "Isherwood Novel Paints Vivid Characteriza-
     tion." Salt Lake City Tribune (8 July), p. W15.
          In Down There on a Visit, "the characters are not nice
     people. They are, however, interesting to read about and
     difficult to forget."

63   LOPEZ, SANDRA. "A Proclivity for Rebels." Bridgeport Sunday
     Post [CT] (8 April).
          Down There on a Visit concerns "individuals whose lives
     and pursuits are socially unacceptable.... [Isherwood's]
     proclivity for people in revolt against convention provides
     the two most colorful episodes, on a Greek island and in
     Hollywood."

64   McALEER, JOHN J. Review of Down There on a Visit. Best Sell-
     ers, 22 (15 April), 35-36.
          In Down There on a Visit "only Paul, with his strange
     hardness of will, argues that there is for man some loftier
     destiny than the fleshpots. Quite possibly this is the
     point of the whole book. Most of the time, however, the

1962

author seems merely desirous of proving that the English
find it difficult to be either moral or immoral spontane-
ously...."

65 M'CAFFERY, LAURA. "Isherwood Christopher Plays Visitor in
    Novel." <u>Fort Wayne News Sentinel</u> [IN] (17 March).
        <u>Down There on a Visit</u>, "however earthy, still has poetic
    moments. It also has moments of pure comedy.... The nar-
    rator shows up as a person whose life has touched the lives
    of many, but who has never really involved himself with any
    of them."

66 McLARN, JACK. "This Visit Holds No Happy Memories." <u>Char-
    lotte Observer</u> [NC] (11 March).
        <u>Down There on a Visit</u> "is a study in composition, a
    study in characterization, a study in contrasts. Everything
    in life cannot be good and clean and beautiful; the book is
    a slice of life, well-written, well done."

67 MADDOCKS, MELVIN. "Isherwood Novel." <u>Christian Science Moni-
    tor</u> (24 May), p. 7.
        "Mr. Isherwood's gifts have always been special.... But
    now he appears to have reached a dead end. The charming
    eccentrics whom he once cherished have turned self-destruc-
    tive and the only thing he has left to admire in 'Down There
    on a Visit' is the logic of their suicides."

68 MALIN, IRVING. "Delightfully Unpleasant." <u>Louisville Courier-
    Journal</u> (4 March).
        <u>Down There on a Visit</u> "contains many juxtapositions:
    flippancy combats seriousness; pastoral fights realism; and
    recollection injures reality. The novel is delightfully
    unpleasant because like any important book, it makes us
    face ourselves."

69 MARTIN, DONALD F. "'Down There on a Visit.'" <u>Montgomery Ad-
    vertiser Journal</u> [AL] (27 May).
        "'Down There on a Visit' is a well-written, weirdly con-
    structed novel.... [It] is almost a snarl at the world in-
    side the individual, a hell filled with the feuding damna-
    tions of loneliness, alienation and hatred."

70 MAYNE, RICHARD. "Herr Issyvoo Changes Trains." <u>New States-
    man</u>, 63 (9 March), 337-338.
        "For anyone interested in Isherwood...<u>Down There on a
    Visit</u> is recommended reading, since in some respects it
    takes up the thread of <u>Lions and Shadows</u>, and is a further
    apologia for the Vedantist and 'high camp' manifestations
    that startled some admirers of the Berlin books after their
    author had settled in America...."

71 MEEKER, JOSEPH W. "Guided Tour of the Inner Man." <u>Los Ange-
    les Times</u> (8 April), "Calendar" Sunday magazine section,
    p. 20.
        In <u>Down There on a Visit</u>, "the inevitable mystic sermon-
    izing is sharply undercut by deliberate ridicule and honest
    vulgarity. A provocative balance is struck between soul-
    fulness and sex, thanks largely to Paul, the dominant char-
    acter of this fourth chapter."

72 MITGANG, HERBERT. "Books of the Times." <u>New York Times</u>
    (23 March), p. 31.
        In <u>Down There on a Visit</u>, "Isherwood writes with cool-
    ness and purpose. As a social critic of these crucial
    times, however, he has turned out only a minor work....
    He has turned the camera on himself this time, and the
    image is frightening."

73 MORSE, J. MITCHELL. "Fiction Chronicle." <u>Hudson Review</u>, 15
    (Summer), 294-295.
        "<u>Down There on a Visit</u> retains its urbanity throughout.
    That it does so without any suggestion of superciliousness
    or moral indifference is a cheering reminder that honesty
    and taste are quite compatible."

74 N., W. E. "Visit Inside Christopher Isherwood." <u>Birmingham
    News</u> [AL] (6 May).
        "The substance [of <u>Down There on a Visit</u>] is just weird
    enough to keep your attention and the style is that ultra-
    dry, understated English dialect that hints at rather than
    nails down specifics. Isherwood gives you a chance to go
    'down there' with yourself as you follow his trip through
    the labyrinth of ego."

75 PARKER, DOROTHY. Review of <u>Down There on a Visit</u>. <u>Esquire</u>,
    57 (May), 33-34.
        "The words have not come to me to speak about this re-
    markable book [<u>Down There on a Visit</u>].... Oh, it is beau-
    tifully written of course--well, why not, it's by Isher-
    wood.... I wish I could say what I think about this book.
    I cannot without going into words like superb and so forth."

76 PAULDING, GOUVERNEUR. "Journey to Many Places--and to No-
    where." <u>New York Herald Tribune Books</u> (11 March), p. 14.
        <u>Down There on a Visit</u> "could be described simply as un-
    pleasant but entertaining. The fact is, however, that Mr.
    Isherwood has chosen to present these episodes as marking
    steps in his own progress through the years. To lay such
    a weight on such emptiness is no doubt courageous; but in
    view of the author's past achievement, it is also sad and
    disquieting."

1962

77   PEDEN, WILLIAM. "Odyssey to Inner Beings." <u>Saturday Review</u>
      <u>of Literature</u>, 45 (24 March), 25-26.
      "Few writers have so unsparingly scrutinized their
      worlds. 'Down There on a Visit' is outrageous, bitter,
      bleak, angry, wry, revealing, infuriating, and at times
      marvellously comic...."

78   PICKREL, PAUL. Review of <u>Down There on a Visit</u>. <u>Harper's</u>
      <u>Magazine</u>, 224 (April), 90.
      "Isherwood is a brilliant writer, and in <u>Down There on a</u>
      <u>Visit</u> he repeatedly shows the power of characterization
      that made immortals of...Mr. Norris and Sally Bowles....
      At the same time he is less willing to stand aside and let
      his characters operate independently of him than he once
      was; there is a little too much of the author in the book."

79   PIERCY, ESTHER J. "The Depths Within Us." <u>Baltimore Sun</u>
      (12 March).
      "In spite of himself, the reader of [<u>Down There on a</u>
      <u>Visit</u>] is amused at times, but he is also shocked, repelled,
      and discouraged. Over all, he is fascinated by the perform-
      ance of this virtuoso writer."

80   POWERS, DENNIS. "Christopher Isherwood: 'Up Here on a Visit.'"
      <u>Oakland Tribune</u> (3 September).
      Report of an informal press conference in which Isher-
      wood comments on life in the United States, the social pur-
      poses of writers, contemporary writing and writers in Brit-
      ain and America, and his current work with Vedanta and a
      biography of Ramakrishna.

81   RAVEN, SIMON. "New Maps of Hell." <u>Listener</u>, 67 (8 March),
      438-439.
      <u>Down There on a Visit</u> contains "tours of inspection
      through the private hells of four different acquaintances."
      These four studies "are not so much of others' unhappiness
      as of Isherwood's own reactions to that unhappiness...."

82   REPLOGLE, JUSTIN. "The Gang Myth in Auden's Early Poetry."
      <u>Journal of English and Germanic Philology</u>, 61 (July), 481-
      495.
      Auden draws upon a private myth in his early poetry,
      which began with the schoolboy life of Isherwood and the
      manufacture of a schoolboy-saga.

83   RIDER, COWL. "Downhill Isherwood." <u>Wall Street Journal</u>
      (5 March), p. 12.
      In <u>Down There on a Visit</u>, Mr. Lancaster is the "only
      sympathetic character"; the rest of the book is "peopled
      with an extraordinarily depressing assortment of deviates,
      perverts, and alcoholics...."

84   ROGERS, W. G. "Rare Novel Woven from Author's Life." Phila-
      delphia Evening Bulletin (4 March), section 2, p. 3.
           Down There on a Visit "is more an experience than a nov-
      el, reads in fact like a journal.... Above all, it reads
      excellently; Isherwood's writing is unfailingly expressive,
      evocative and challenging." [This review also appeared in
      the Youngstown Vindicator [OH] (4 March), the Hartford
      Times [CT] (19 May), and the St. Petersburg Times [FL]
      (4 March).]

85   ROSENFELD, ISAAC. "Isherwood's Master Theme," in his An Age
      of Enormity: Life and Writing in the Forties and Fifties.
      Cleveland: World Publishing, pp. 149-154.
           Reprint of 1946.30.

86   RUMLEY, LARRY. "Isherwood Gives Intimate Look into Lives of
      Himself, Others." Baton Rouge Advocate [LA] (15 April).
           In Down There on a Visit, Isherwood is "sympathetic to a
      high degree, probing for the answers to problems of person-
      ality and character, to problems of interrelationships; yet
      never forgetting that he is a writer with a story to tell,
      a story to catch and hold the reader's interest."

87   SCHOTT, WEBSTER. "But Sometimes Brilliance Is Bewildering."
      Kansas City Star [MO] (15 July), p. 12D.
           "One finishes [Down There on a Visit] with a mass of
      disorganized impressions. The stories are sad, as all must
      be that deal with homosexuality; the world is not ready for
      these people.... Isherwood's great strength lies in devel-
      oping characters, yet he cannot fix them in space because
      he is one of them himself...."

88   SCOTT, JAMES. "Expatriate's Dilemma." Toronto Telegram
      (7 April), p. 12.
           "A good deal of modern psychological thought will ap-
      plaud the message of [Down There on a Visit]. All the mys-
      tics, crackpot and genuine alike, will like it too. For
      the more pedestrian reader, equally beset by problems from
      within and without, it may be a bit disturbing and defeat-
      ist but it will certainly be thought-provoking and stimulat-
      ing."

89   SHRAPNEL, NORMAN. Review of Down There on a Visit. Manchester
      Guardian (9 March), p. 7.
           "Irritating, amusing, restlessly perceptive, [Isherwood]
      is fascinated by people...and moves among their darkest
      problems with vigour and wit and a kind of understanding."

1962

90 SLOAT, WARREN. "Religious Symphony." Newark News (6 May).
    "In his symphony with its slowly-revealed integrity,
    Isherwood the author encounters the problem of all who
    write of religious experience. What can only be responded
    to, what can only be lived, escapes words.... [Down There
    on a Visit] is a heady, disgusting, sometimes shocking
    book, but it is, make no mistake, a religious book."

91 SMITH, WILLIAM JAMES. "The Lotus Kick." Commonweal, 76
    (18 May), 214.
    "Down There on a Visit does have its message after all:
    a lifetime spent in the company of effeminate bores and
    professional brutes is apt to end up in California in the
    lotus position."

92 SPENDER, STEPHEN. "Isherwood's Heroes." New Republic, 146
    (16 April), 24-25.
    Down There on a Visit may be "a preliminary for a novel
    which will really visit Hell": "I feel that despite his
    almost compulsive pulling of punches, Isherwood may one day
    write such a novel, and perhaps it is the involvement of
    the projected Isherwood character with the portraits of
    semi-real people, which has here prevented him from going
    much further into the abyss than he does...."

93 STAHL, MARTIN. "A Self-Portrait in Four Different Takes."
    Fayetteville Observer [NC] (8 April).
    Down There on a Visit is "well written" and "told in a
    conversational style. Mr. Isherwood's ramblings and char-
    acter sketches are an off-beat success."

94 SYKES, GERALD. "Compulsively Detached." New York Times Book
    Review (18 March), pp. 4, 37.
    Down There on a Visit may be the best novel Isherwood
    has written--it "deepens and reinforces his extraordinary
    narrative talents with the philosophic disciplines he has
    pursued for the past two decades."

95 TAZEWELL, WILLIAM L. "Isherwood 'Not for Nannies.'" Norfolk
    Pilot [VA] (18 March).
    Down There on a Visit "is extraordinary and just a lit-
    tle overripe, like a mango. It is a guided tour through a
    number of intimate infernos, disconnected hells of exclu-
    sion, loneliness and the severed self."

96 TRILLING, LIONEL. "The Wheel." The Mid-Century (July),
    pp. 5-10.
    "Down There on a Visit is actually not anything else
    than a simple book. It is about one of the simplest, as it
    is one of the oldest, subjects, the Wheel of Life, the
    pain, disgust, and shame that follows on the attachment to

self. The great novelists have always known about the
Wheel, but they have always been uncertain in their response to it because they have so much loved the self;
from this uncertainty comes their power. Down There on
a Visit is not a great novel, but it is a curiously affecting one for the same reason."

97   V. de G., E. "'The Others' within One's Self." Columbia
     State and Record [SC] (12 July).
         Down There on a Visit "is a good example of the current
     trend of the novel. There is an excessive preoccupation
     with psychological and sexual interpretations of life and
     its problems."

98   WHEILDON, L. "A Visit to Dark World." Boston Herald
     (25 March).
         Down There on a Visit "is not a particularly pretty
     book, but it is well and sensitively written. It is a book
     you will remember."

99   YEISER, FREDERICK, "From New Crop of Spring Novels." Cin-
     cinnati Enquirer (25 March), p. 12-D.
         The four episodes in Down There on a Visit are uneven in
     quality: the first is "rather dull"; the second is the
     "best in the book" because it is "the truest artistically";
     the third is "transitional and topical"; while the last is
     the one that Isherwood has given his best to, it is not
     totally successful perhaps because the author tried to make
     Paul "too much of a sinner--or too much of a saint."

100 YODER, JANE. "The Same Old Christopher." Greensboro News
     [NC] (16 September).
         "Down There on a Visit is a brilliantly related tour of
     a world of unhappy, persecuted people.... Isherwood is
     filing a brief for his characters. But its effect...is to
     confirm the thought of thee and me that these are queer
     folk indeed."

1963

1   G[ENTRY], C[URT]. Review of An Approach to Vedanta. San
     Francisco Chronicle (14 July), "This World" magazine sec-
     tion, p. 29.
         An Approach to Vedanta "is a fascinating piece, personal
     in its details and philosophy, yet reflecting the broad
     background of a generation of writers, each seeking his own
     explanations for such events of his time as the rise of
     Fascism, the Spanish Civil War, the Chinese Communist Revo-
     lution, World War II and Hiroshima."

1963

2 NICOLL, ALLARDYCE. <u>British Drama</u>. Fifth edition. New York: Barnes & Noble, p. 321.
    Reprint, slightly revised, of 1947.20.

3 POWERS, DENNIS. "Isherwood Discusses His Life and Work." <u>Oakland Tribune</u> (2 May).
    Report on and summary of the second in a series of three lectures, given at the University of California, on the subject "The Autobiography of My Books"; Isherwood was regents' lecturer at the university for the spring semester.

4 SELLERS, W. H. "Edward Upward: An Introduction." <u>The Dalhousie Review</u>, 43 (Summer), 162-178.
    Discusses Upward's associations with Auden, Spender, and Isherwood; comments on the Mortmere stories. [Reprinted: 1969.20.]

5 SHERIDAN, PHILIP. Review of <u>Down There on a Visit</u>. <u>Carleton Miscellany</u>, 4 (Winter), 106-109.
    "Talented homosexuals are likely to have a different set of experiences from those of most people, though therefore they need not be interesting. Those of Mr. Isherwood <u>are</u> interesting (we may as well regard the novel <u>Down There on a Visit</u> as autobiographical) though neither because of the homosexuality nor quite in spite of it...."

6 SPEARS, MONROE K. <u>The Poetry of W. H. Auden: The Disenchanted Island</u>. New York: Oxford University Press, passim.
    Isherwood is consistently used to comment upon and explain Auden's poetry. Their collaborations are all discussed briefly.

7 STEBNER, GERHARD. "Wystan H. Auden and Christopher Isherwood: The Ascent of F6," in <u>Das Moderne Englische Drama: Interpretationen</u>. Edited by Horst Oppel. Berlin: Erich Schmidt, pp. 201-218.
    Reprint, slightly revised, of 1961.7.

8 STRAVINSKY, IGOR and ROBERT CRAFT. <u>Dialogues and a Diary</u>. Garden City, N.Y.: Doubleday, pp. 37, 38, 39-40, 156.
    "Later, when I knew Isherwood, I was astonished by how exactly like the 'Chris' of the stories he was. The question of 1) "my art" and 2) "my life" did not exist for him. His books were himself, and he stepped in and out of them without so much as zipping a zipper."

9 WEST, PAUL. <u>The Modern Novel</u>. Vol. 1. London: Hutchison University Library, pp. 77-79.
    Isherwood "has done for pre-war Berlin not what Joyce did for Dublin or Mann for Lübeck but has typified the urban microcosm in sexual renegades." Isherwood and

Somerset Maugham are authors who "collect the facts, the fascinating copy, and hinge it all carefully into non-committal albums." [Reprinted, in second edition, 1965.38.]

10   WILEY, PAUL. "Book Reviews." Wisconsin Studies in Contemporary Literature, 4 (Spring-Summer), 225-228.
        Down There on a Visit "has all the sophistication of full maturity; and although the grin of the young Isherwood of the Sally Bowles days is by no means lost, it is now sealed in an amber of ripe self-knowledge never quite contemptuous...."

11   WOOD, FREDERICK T. "Current Literature 1962." English Studies, 44 (June), 224.
        Down There on a Visit "is very readable, yet somehow one remains unimpressed by it. The characters are not particularly interesting, the general atmosphere seems rather unreal, one is never certain whether the author is in earnest or whether he is writing ironically, and all the time one feels that much ado is being made about trivialities."

1964

1   ADAMS, PHOEBE. "Prisoner of the Perverse." Atlantic, 214 (September), 122-123.
        A Single Man is "a grim, witty novel about an aging homosexual professor of literature and his battle with the normal world."

2   ALLEN, WALTER. The Modern Novel in Britain and the United States. New York: E. P. Dutton, pp. 42, 234-240. (British title: Tradition and Dream: The English and American Novel from the Twenties to Our Time. London: Phoenix House.)
        "In one respect, Isherwood is the greatest disappointment in the history of contemporary fiction. It seems clear, after his most recent novels,...that his best work is essentially of the thirties. It is certainly one of the most considerable achievements of that time...."

3   ANON. "Also Current." Time, 84 (4 September), 107E-108.
        Review of A Single Man: "George is only a faint thickening in the midst of the world's loneliness. The expression of his isolation is this fictional record of a day.... It is not a plea, only a series of impressions on the silvered surface of a film."

1964

4   ANON. "George and Jim." <u>Times Literary Supplement</u> (10 September), p. 837.
     <u>A Single Man</u> contains a "romantic fallacy" at its "core":
     "The final test which must be applied is whether nostalgia
     about a <u>heterosexual</u> marriage such as George's and Jim's, a
     description of heterosexual leching..., or of a heterosexual
     flirtation...would be rewarding. Offered plain, as Mr.
     Isherwood offers them, with a wide-eyed confidence that such
     revelations must arouse sympathy once revealed, they seem
     strangely commonplace."

5   ANON. "New Fiction." <u>London Times</u> (10 September), p. 15.
     Review of <u>A Single Man</u>: "Lucid and lightly elegant
     though the prose is, there is something here like Joyce's
     <u>Ulysses</u>, and not only in time scheme: it is in the feel-
     ing...that a man can be quite insignificant to the world at
     large, and beset by all the sins and ills of humanity, yet
     still live an intensely acceptable life."

6   ANON. "One Day in the Life of a Lonesome Man." <u>Washington
     Evening Star</u> (23 August).
     <u>A Single Man</u> is "articulate and engaging. It has the
     stamp of truth. Perhaps it is too direct, too simplified,
     too lacking in overtones."

7   ANON. Review of <u>A Single Man</u>. <u>Chicago Herald-American</u>
     (30 August).
     "Isherwood is at his best in [<u>A Single Man</u>]; the story
     has a haunting quality that never seems to leave the read-
     er.... The style--one moment sheer gossamer, the next
     graphic earthiness--is flawless."

8   ANON. Review of <u>A Single Man</u>. <u>Pasadena Star News</u> (6 August).
     "Stifling one's outrage at mores which differ from our
     own and are therefore evil (because after all, we hetero-
     sexuals are, by God, in the majority), one must still admit
     that Isherwood has written with candor, bravery, and elec-
     tric insights."

9   ANON. "Time Exposure." <u>Newsweek</u>, 64 (31 August), 76-77.
     Review of <u>A Single Man</u>: "Here, in the famous brilliantly
     clear and natural style, is the self-confrontation of a man
     who, quite simply, does not want to die. Yet his calm but
     merciless empiricism offers no consolation."

10   ARCHER, WILLIAM K. "A Numb Man Alone." <u>Quincy Patriot-Ledger</u>
     [MA] (29 August).
     Review of <u>A Single Man</u>: "Many people, of course, are
     trapped in their private hells here and now, and it's not
     because they're homosexuals. Homosexuality doesn't seem to
     be the crux of George's problems, either. The loss of love
     is."

98

11   BARKHAM, JOHN. "Isherwood Novel Evokes Admiration and Dis-
         taste." New York World Telegram and Sun (25 August).
         A Single Man "is likely to leave readers with mixed
      feelings of admiration and distaste. Isherwood's gifts
      are so protean--his mastery of style, his insights into
      the human mind--that they command applause. In the new
      book, however, they are lavished on an unsympathetic char-
      acter not worthy of them."

12   BEDFORD, SYBILLE. "Poor Old Chap." Spectator, 213 (11 Sep-
         tember), 343.
         Some of the parts of A Single Man are poignant and
      stirring. "The protagonist's homosexuality is, in my opin-
      ion, the book's main artistic flaw because it impairs what
      might have been the august universality of the theme."

13   BLOOMFIELD, BARRY C. W. H. Auden, A Bibliography: The Early
         Years through 1955. Charlottesville: University Press of
         Virginia, pp. 1, 3, 12-15, 16-19, 24, 27-28, 29-32, 43, 54,
         55, 74, 80, 98, 125, 137, 141.
         Detailed bibliographical descriptions, including notes
      about composition, productions of plays, later additions,
      and reviews. Dedications to Isherwood are also noted.
      Cites works by Isherwood which comment on Auden (such as
      Lions and Shadows). Includes bibliographical data on
      Auden/Isherwood contributions to periodicals. [Revised
      and expanded: 1972.11.]

14   BLYTHE, RONALD. The Age of Illusion: England in the Twenties
         and Thirties 1919-1940. Boston: Houghton, Mifflin,
         pp. 105, 106, 117-118.
         Comments on the three plays of the Auden-Isherwood col-
      laboration.

15   BURGESS, ANTHONY. "Why, This Is Hell." Listener, 72 (10 Oc-
         tober), 514.
         Isherwood "wants to demonstrate that hell, like love, is
      not hereafter; it is a portable void that exists in time....
      In A Single Man Mr. Isherwood concentrates openly on this
      hell and calls on the unities of time and space to help
      hold the lamp."

16   CALDWELL, DAVID S. "Ulysses' Return." Pittsburgh Press
         (13 September).
         "A novel such as [A Single Man] easily lends itself to
      vulgarity, because so much of our lives when seen bit by
      bit under a microscope is rather unpleasant. In Isher-
      wood's artistic hands, however, this every-moment-counts
      gambol becomes a poignant accumulation of the 'stuffs' of
      life."

1964

17 CAPOUYA, EMILE. "Twilight Man with Sorrow." Saturday Review
    of Literature, 47 (5 September), 31.
        "A Single Man is a sober portrait of an aging homosex-
    ual, about as childish as the rest of us, and no more mon-
    strous.... I am here to state that one male American,
    formerly touchy as most on the question of homosexuality,
    found George sympathetic, and only intermittently offen-
    sive--when he reminded me of what I most dislike in my-
    self...."

18 CASSILL, R. V. "Under Froth--the Tragedy." Chicago Sun
    Times (6 September).
        "Spinning out a deceptively simple story in a charmingly
    candid and casual fashion, Christopher Isherwood's new
    novel [A Single Man] has the underlying toughness of the
    classical view. Under the impudence and froth of gay man-
    nerisms and attitudes there is the tough articulation of
    tragedy."

19 COMANS, GRACE P. "Study in Loneliness." Hartford Courant
    [CT] (16 August).
        A Single Man "is a study in loneliness and in man's
    desperate need for love.... Isherwood, by the force of
    his writing, compels the reader to become involved, to
    feel, to react to George, to identify with him, or to say,
    'there but for the grace of God, go I.'"

20 COOK, BRUCE. "The Trouble with George." Critic, 23 (October/
    November), 65-66.
        A Single Man "has to do with death. From the first page
    until the last, we detect a fatal quality that informs the
    action of the book and gives authority to its every inci-
    dent."

21 COOLEY, FRANKLIN D. Review of A Single Man. Richmond Times
    Dispatch [VA] (27 September).
        "I cannot say [A Single Man] is entertaining; it is too
    close to life for that. It is as if one were eavesdropping
    on the privacy of another person. The result is fascination
    and a kind of embarrassment...."

22 DAICHES, DAVID. "Life without Jim." New York Times Book Re-
    view (30 August), pp. 5, 16.
        The intention of A Single Man "seems to be to illus-
    trate--wryly, ironically, fatalistically--that a man is
    what he is, physiologically and psychologically, and we'd
    better accept it because--well, because a man is what he
    is." The novel is "a sad, sly report on the predicament of
    the human animal."

23 DAVID, DIANE. "Face to the Mirror." <u>Chicago Daily News</u>
       (12 September), "Panorama" section, p. 6.
          In <u>A Single Man</u>, "George is no heroically tragic figure,
       he's not even particularly likeable. Yet there is tragedy
       here. In disclosing George so intimately to us, Mr. Isher-
       wood forces, yes, even drives each of us up to the mirror."

24 DAVIS, PAXTON. "The Unique Place of Mr. Isherwood." <u>Roanoke</u>
       <u>Times</u> [VA] (4 October).
          <u>A Single Man</u> "is a petulant, peevish and ultimately self-
       pitying book. The dirty world that George sees exists, to
       be sure, but are there no clean spots at all? Isherwood
       suggests not."

25 DeMOTT, BENJAMIN. "Hard Times." <u>Harper's Magazine</u>, 229
       (September), 109-110.
          "The reality of the single man, as presented in this
       tale, consists not only of the man's nature as he under-
       stands it but the man's nature as it might appear to exist-
       ence itself."

26 DERRICKSON, HOWARD. "The Professor's Last Day." <u>St. Louis</u>
       <u>Globe Democrat</u> (13 August).
          Isherwood "seems at the crest of his undoubted powers"
       in <u>A Single Man.</u> This absorbing novel rings completely
       true in its presentation of dialogue and classroom ex-
       changes.

27 EMERSON, DONALD. "Isherwood as Before." <u>Milwaukee Journal</u>
       (23 August).
          <u>A Single Man</u> represents "Isherwood as before, now beached
       on the California coast and teaching under the name of
       George.... There are passing reflections on the mores,
       freeways and folkways of California, of the kind we have
       come to expect of this British born author."

28 EVERETT, BARBARA. <u>Auden</u>. Writers and Critics series. Edin-
       burgh: Oliver & Boyd, pp. 52-65.
          In <u>On the Frontier</u>, "[t]he optimism has...dwindled to a
       use of bold slogans, strikingly in contrast to the lyrical
       certainties of <u>The Dog Beneath the Skin</u>, and to the involve-
       ment of personal sympathies in <u>The Ascent of F6</u>."

29 FORD, BORIS, ed. <u>The Modern Age: A Guide to English Litera-</u>
       <u>ture 7</u>. London: Cassell & Co., pp. 217, 378, 380-381,
       476, 499, 543-544.
          Isherwood is mentioned in several essays, especially his
       collaborations with Auden. <u>The World in the Evening</u> is in-
       cluded. A brief biographical summary is given.

1964

30   FRASER, GEORGE S. The Modern Writer and His World. Revised
      edition. Baltimore: Penguin Books, pp. 29, 90, 133, 137-
      139, 199, 209, 212, 224-225, 298, 301.
          Revised version of 1953.1. "I would have said in the
      1930s that Isherwood was the most exciting of the younger
      English novelists. He is still a writer of great attrac-
      tiveness, but one cannot say that the promise was ful-
      filled."

31   FRESHWATER, PHILLIP C. "Isherwood Catches a Life as It Teeters
      on Edge of Existence." Sacramento Bee (23 August).
          A Single Man is not a gloomy book despite the protagon-
      ist's concern with death. "It is in excellent taste; it
      has flashes of high comedy...and a great deal of biting
      wit."

32   GAINES, ERVIN J. Review of A Single Man. Library Journal,
      89 (1 September), 3184.
          A Single Man "will appeal most to readers who wish to
      follow the sad, unhappy career of a sexual deviate. Isher-
      woods' clarity, wit and lean style serve him well, but this
      reviewer wishes he could put his talents to use on more
      universal material."

33   GEESLIN, CAMPBELL. "Too Much about Too Little." Houston Post
      (19 July).
          "In spite of Mr. Isherwood's skill in handling the pres-
      ent tense and the book's admirable construction, [A Single
      Man] repells [sic] because George is just about the most
      unattractive deviate one can imagine. He is petty, totally
      selfish, peevish, disgustingly precious and, in his own
      words, 'positively flirty.'"

34   G[ENTRY], C[CURT]. "Seven Ages in a Day." San Francisco Sun-
      day Chronicle (30 August), "This World Magazine," p. 36.
          "By night fall, [George] has lived all the seven ages
      multiple times, behaving more childishly than any of his
      students, acting with regretful maturity; and by book's
      end, we know George with an intimacy rarely experienced in
      fiction. 'A Single Man' is a beautifully wrought, very
      special book...."

35   GREENE. A. C. "One Day, One Man: Two Natures." Dallas Times
      Herald (23 August), p. E5.
          Review of A Single Man: "It might be said that a better
      book could have been made of the same story without the
      homosexuality. Perhaps. But Isherwood had this one idea
      in mind...he created something which we may validly suppose
      was very close to what he started out to do--to show the
      hopelessness but the humanness of all such single men."

36   GREENE, GEORGE. "Crying for Help." <u>Commonweal</u>, 81 (2 Octo-
         ber), 51-53.
            "One grows tired of the sentimental assumption that in-
         version is an absolute prerequisite for any sense of--and
         share in--the nightmare of mortality. It is not George's
         bitchy asides and sensual reveries which make him moving
         as well as irritating. It is those moments when he es-
         capes from the tyranny of self."

37   GROSS, ALFRED A. "An Ineluctable Fact." <u>Christian Century</u>,
         81 (30 September), 1214.
            <u>A Single Man</u> "speaks to the conditions of men whose
         existence society professed to ignore until only yesterday.
         It speaks feelingly and objectively about recognizable
         human beings."

38   GROSS, JOHN. "Civil Monsters." <u>New Statesman</u>, 68 (11 Septem-
         ber), 360-361.
            "The treatment of homosexuality in <u>A Single Man</u> is hon-
         est but mercifully not 'frank.' Yet the final section
         does provoke a few squirms--not on account of the realism,
         but because of anti-climax. We have been led precisely
         nowhere; all the life and wit runs out of the book, and it
         simply caves in."

39   HADDAD, BARBARA. Review of <u>A Single Man</u>. <u>Denver Post</u>
         (23 August).
            "Subtle enough to please the no-punctuation set, [<u>A
         Single Man</u>] also provides a sufficiently lucid structure
         to satisfy addicts of 'a good story.' The major reward of
         the book...is the presentation of a very complex character
         clearly and cogently, to the point where the reader feels
         an identification in spite of himself."

40   HARDWICK, ELIZABETH. "Sex and the Single Man." <u>New York Re-
         view of Books</u>, 2 (20 August), 4.
            "If <u>A Single Man</u> seems tired, it is also true in feel-
         ing. It is a sad book, with biological melancholy running
         through it, a sense of relentless reduction, daily diminish-
         ment."

41   HAZARD, FORREST EARL. "The Auden Group and the Group Theatre:
         The Dramatic Theories and Practices of Rupert Doone, W. H.
         Auden, Christopher Isherwood, Louis McNeice, Stephen Spen-
         der and Cecil Day Lewis." Ph.D. dissertation, University
         of Wisconsin, pp. 118-177.
            The "archetypal quest pattern" is made evident through
         the "numerous mythological images" in <u>The Dog Beneath the
         Skin</u> and <u>The Ascent of F6</u>. <u>On the Frontier</u> contains fewer
         mythological images, but the play is built on archetypal
         patterns nevertheless. These patterns were used, apparently,

103

1964

because "they offered a timeless criterion for judging
moral behavior regardless of the current social mores and
because they gave [the] plays the parabolic quality...art
needs in order to teach lessons without telling one, in
the manner of propaganda, specifically what to do."

42 HILL, WILLIAM B., S.J. Review of A Single Man. Best Sellers
    (1 September), p. 201.
        A Single Man "is an eloquent little novel about a most
    unpleasant individual. As a good novelist, Mr. Isherwood
    is intent upon putting the man down, not evaluating him--
    the distaste which the protagonist evokes arises slowly,
    inevitably, out of the character itself...."

43 HUBLER, RICHARD G. "Disjointed Limp Wrist Saga." Los Angeles
    Times (2 August).
        In A Single Man the "defense mechanism built up for the
    homosexual is, of course, both feeble and disgusting. But
    the tasteless fatuity of the book is not its most unfortu-
    nate aspect. It is simply a poor work."

44 IRVING, MAGGIE. "Disturbing Book Hard to Forget." Worcester
    Telegram [MA] (23 August).
        A Single Man "is a disturbing novel; and it arises from
    a subsurface destructiveness, a searing, hopeless contempt
    for self and humanity implicit in each relentlessly cruel
    detail of George's day, down to curious, nasty little func-
    tion obsessions which hint at strange child-like antagonism
    to the mother."

45 JARKA, HORST. "Pre-War Austria as Seen by Spender, Isherwood
    and Lehmann." Proceedings of the Pacific Northwest Confer-
    ence on Foreign Languages, 15: 231-240.
        "The best known English book in which the events of Feb-
    ruary 1934 are reflected is undoubtedly Christopher Isher-
    wood's short novel Prater Violet.... The most bitter irony
    about Prater Violet is one that Isherwood did not have to
    make explicit: he wrote and published the book at the end
    of the war, when every reader knew that Bergmann's anxiety
    had not been unfounded, when Isherwood's friend, Berthold
    Viertel, had become an exile, when exile had become one of
    the literary metaphors for man's existence."

46 KAUFFMANN, STANLEY. "Death in Venice, Cal." New Republic,
    151 (5 September), 23-25.
        A Single Man is "a sad story, kept from being a thor-
    oughly moving one because...we have a consciousness of its
    intent to be sad." The protagonist's tragedy "is that he
    knows himself so bitterly well that he knows his life is no
    tragedy: just one more intelligent, unfulfilled life."

47   LEWIS, GROVER. "'Single Man' Exceptional in Treatment." <u>Fort Worth Star</u> (30 August).
     "As much a carefully enunciated social document as it is a novel, 'A Single Man' is a memorable and absorbing work that should be widely read, both for its flawless narrative technique and its author's unerringly on-target perceptions."

48   LITTLER, FRANK. Review of <u>A Single Man</u>. <u>Chicago Tribune Books Today</u> (6 September), p. 5.
     "There may be old Isherwood hands who will plumb oceanic depths of significance in 'A Single Man,' but it is a straightforward story, told with foreseeable polish. To interject short travelog and sidelong social commentary into California fiction is no novelty, but I doubt whether it has been better done than it is here."

49   LONGSTREET, STEPHEN. "Among the Publishers." <u>Hollywood Canyon Crier</u> (6 August).
     Review of <u>A Single Man</u>: "Mr. Isherwood's habit of undressing in public is now a literary must, and his last two books are frankly a plea for a homosexual world.... He writes well as usual, but it is the saddest of all his texts."

50   M[ADDOCKS], M[ELVIN]. "Outsiders, Insiders and Other Victims." <u>Christian Science Monitor</u> (24 September), p. 7.
     "The particulars of [<u>A Single Man</u>]--a British writer teaching at a California college grieves the violent end of a homosexual affair--finally seem less vivid than the overwhelming atmosphere of panic that surrounds it. Mr. Isherwood has become that special case of anguish, the aging writer who looks into his mirror and sees nothing but the spastic grin of Yorick's skull."

51   MAKEN, RONALD. "Power and Conflict in <u>The Ascent of F.6</u>." <u>Discourse: A Review of Liberal Arts</u>, 7 (Summer), 277-282.
     The central, concrete symbol in <u>The Ascent of F6</u> is the mountain, a symbol of power: "Just as F.6 looms large and central in the play, so power becomes its central, dominant image."

52   MAY, CARL. "Best Yet? Might Be--." <u>Nashville Tennessean</u> (6 September).
     In <u>A Single Man</u>, Isherwood "has provided a sharp contrast with the normal man and yet he has been able to show that all people experience the same emotions and face similar crises, no matter how they may differ in normality or perspective."

1964

53 MOORE, HARRY T. "New Fiction in Brief." St. Louis Post-
    Dispatch (16 August), p. 4B.
        "Readers who don't know the writings of Christopher Ish-
    erwood may not be attracted by this rather torpid novel,
    while those familiar with 'The Berlin Stories' and 'Prater
    Violet' will find 'A Single Man' singularly lacking in the
    Isherwood flavor. Now and then, a wry observation brings
    the story to life...but mostly this chronicle of a man's
    day is commonplace."

54 MORGAN, MIKE. "Bitterlonely Portrait." Miami Herald (6 Sep-
    tember).
        A Single Man is "closely detailed with the skill and
    fine simplicity that is the merit of the author. It is
    not a story of homosexuality so much as the unfolding
    tragedy of a middle-aged, intelligent, mildly ironic
    gentleman who has the capacity of playing many roles and
    presenting many façades."

55 OSTERMANN, ROBERT. "'George' Is Really Mr. Isherwood in the
    Oppressive 'A Single Man.'" National Observer, 3 (7 Sep-
    tember), 17.
        In A Single Man "a reader can't escape the oppressive
    conviction that he is tracking not George but Christopher
    Isherwood to the lair where he will nurse his hurts until
    death reprieves him. This is art that is almost too pain-
    ful to watch...."

56 PIERCY, ESTHER. "Bitter, Artful, Exquisite." Baltimore Sun
    (30 August).
        A Single Man "is near perfection in its skillful plot-
    ting, its spare and selective action, its painful mirror-
    ing of life, its vivid profiles of people, its biting wit,
    its realistic conversations, and its singing prose."

57 PINE, GEORGE J. "One Day's Life." Boston Herald (30 August).
        In A Single Man, "George has a wry humor, and his ob-
    servations are sometimes amusing to read, but there's no
    deep excitement in the story--the reader doesn't really
    care very much, one way or another--and the air of gentle,
    cynical melancholy isn't enough to carry the thin tale
    along."

58 POWERS, DENNIS. "Isherwood's 'A Single Man.'" Oakland Trib-
    une (23 August).
        "Like a good deal of Isherwood's fiction, 'A Single
    Man' is brave and ambitious. George's thoughts, his ob-
    servations and his conversation become vehicles for im-
    portant (and familiar) ideas about man, our society, and
    life itself."

59 PRYCE-JONES, ALAN. "Masterful Use of a Close-Up Lens." <u>Book Week</u> (30 August), p. 5.
In <u>A Single Man</u>, "Isherwood has caught with extreme brilliance and economy...the texture of life itself.... The only false note which intrudes from time to time is when his stream of consciousness elevates homosexuality to a doctrine."

60 REPLOGLE, JUSTIN. "The Auden Group." <u>Wisconsin Studies in Contemporary Literature</u>, 5 (Summer), 133-150.
Describes the formation and development of the so-called Auden Group, especially its later move toward Marxism, which did not include Isherwood. Contains some comments on the Auden-Isherwood collaborations.

61 SAUNDERS, NICHOLAS. "Disappointing Novel of Ennui." <u>Nashville Banner</u> (4 September).
<u>A Single Man</u> "is not vintage Isherwood, but there are occasional moments of good writing, although there are not enough to sustain the mood.... Tragedy was obviously the goal, but self-pity was the second-best result."

62 SCHLESINGER, TOM. "For a Single Man: A Lonely Day." <u>Norfolk Pilot</u> [VA] (23 August).
Review of <u>A Single Man</u>: "Isherwood, a proven master of the written word, has obviously undergone a profound experience and in fictionalizing it attempts to give it meaning while exploring its relationship to himself, his fellowman and life itself. At times, the result is oddly touching in its naïvete; but more often, it is embarrassing in its intimacy and depth of torment and revelation."

63 SHERMAN, JOHN K. "Isherwood Is Older, But Still Sharp." <u>Minneapolis Tribune</u> (13 September).
<u>A Single Man</u> "has the bite of satire in its view of such things as middle-class suburbia and modern education" but it is primarily "a study of loneliness in the late middle years, sensitive, often amusing.... It also provides insight, a rather queasy one for normal readers, into the feelings and viewpoints of homosexuals."

64 SMITH, MILES A. "Isherwood Tells a Strange Story with Compassion." <u>Charlotte Observer</u> [NC] (30 August).
In <u>A Single Man</u>, "Isherwood has written a novel of mood, of kaleidoscopic inner thoughts. Despite its sustained sense of haunting melancholy and rue, it is not morbid. It is an eerily compassionate book...." [This same review appeared, anonymously, in the <u>Monroe World</u> [LA], the <u>Lansing State Journal</u> [MI], and the <u>Waterbury Republican</u> [CT], all on the same date--30 August.]

1964

65 STANLEY, DONALD. "Lonely View at 58." San Francisco Examiner
    (26 August).
        A Single Man "is a most ambitious little book and...
    tries gallantly to utilize all that Isherwood has learned.
    It fails, I think, because of a crankiness, an unforgiving-
    ness that makes George's individuality become a kind of
    assertion that 'Everybody's out of step but him.'"

66 TORKELSON, DICK. "One Day's Experience for a Lonely Profes-
    sor." Santa Rosa Press Democrat [CA] (30 August).
        In A Single Man "the familiarity with the environment is
    masterly, the dialogue, the subjective thoughts, the minor
    ironies, the faces, the classrooms, the bars hold the pages
    with total believability."

67 W., H. A. "Intriguing Novel." Trenton Times [NJ] (11 October).
        A Single Man "is a novel of quality and perhaps of con-
    troversy but it is a first-rate piece of writing.... It is
    a sad book with some ironic overtones, but a book that is
    much better than the writing that is coming out today."

68 WEST, WILLIAM C. "Concepts of Reality in the Poetic Drama of
    W. B. Yeats, W. H. Auden, and T. S. Eliot." Ph.D. disser-
    tation, Stanford University, pp. 116-144.
        "When he joined with Christopher Isherwood, Auden made
    an artistic alliance which promised at first more than it
    was ultimately able to realize.... It is interesting to
    note...how a poet such as Auden can be brought by steps
    from an esoteric allegorical expression...to the brink of
    dramatic realism...and with each step be forced to compro-
    mise his poetry in the cause of coherent theatrical expres-
    sion." Isherwood's influence probably contributed a great
    deal to this development.

69 WILLIAMS, RUSSELL. "Was George Killed for His Sins?" Cleve-
    land Plain Dealer (27 September).
        Review of A Single Man: "Isherwood has little to say,
    but he says it well.... Was George killed for his sins,
    which are slight? Not likely. More probably, Isherwood
    could figure no way out of the friendless dilemma without
    inviting the reader deeper into the psychic swamps."

                                1965

1   ALLSOP, KENNETH. "Everywhere on a Visit," in his Scan. Lon-
    don: Hodder and Stoughton, pp. 34-37.
        "[T]he personal dissociation in [Down There on a Visit
    and A Single Man], the viewpoint and meaning, make sense
    only if recognised as that of the homosexual closed order.

The world is that of the homosexual demi-monde, isolated in exclusion, surrounded by alienation...." [Reprinted: 1966.1.]

2   ANDERSON, PATRICK. "Some Lives." Spectator, 214 (4 June), 726.
        Ramakrishna and His Disciples "is so humbly and cosily written, so sweet and equable in tone, that it reads like an act of self-abasement."

3   ANON. "All Paths Lead to God." Times Literary Supplement (29 April), p. 334.
        Ramakrishna and His Disciples is reviewed with two other religious books. Little comment is made about Isherwood's book beyond the summary of the facts about Ramakrishna's life, drawn, presumably, from Isherwood's biography.

4   ANON. "Holy Casebook." London Times (13 May), p. 15.
        "There is nothing aridly dogmatic about [Ramakrishna and His Disciples]. It is an easy, unassertive, gently argued casebook of the phenomena in a holy man's life."

5   ANON. Review of Ramakrishna and His Disciples. Booklist, 61 (15 July), 1053.
        "A well-known novelist...dispassionately and somewhat disorganizedly narrates the major events and spiritual crises in the life of this nineteenth-century Indian Hindu mystic."

6   ANON. Review of Ramakrishna and His Disciples. Choice, 2 (September), 399.
        Praises the book's "readability and comprehensiveness" but faults it for its lack of footnotes and Isherwood's tendency to generalize about Indian philosophy and intellectual history.

7   ANON. Review of Ramakrishna and His Disciples. Los Angeles Times (20 June).
        Ramakrishna and His Disciples "is a book which, shot through with elements of Hindu mysticism and religion, at once intrigues the reader with its rare material and startles and challenges with its extraordinary approach."

8   ANON. Review of Ramakrishna and His Disciples. New Yorker, 41 (17 July), 110.
        In Ramakrishna and His Disciples, Isherwood "clearly and sympathetically expounds religious customs, behavior, and concepts that are unfamiliar to most Westerners, and if he can relate them to Christian beliefs or practices, he does, but he never seeks to convince or convert by blurring theological distinctions."

9   ANON. Review of <u>Ramakrishna and His Disciples</u>. <u>Virginia</u>
     <u>Kirkus' Service Bulletin</u>, 33 (1 January), 50.
         "Isherwood calls Ramakrishna a phenomenon, and tells
     his story with simplicity and charm; almost as phenomenal
     is the journey the author of <u>Goodbye to Berlin</u> has taken
     from the fashionably perverse to the ascetic and holy."

10   BLAIR, JOHN G. <u>The Poetic Art of W. H. Auden</u>. Princeton:
     Princeton University Press, pp. 17, 18, 27, 67, 96, 98,
     99-103.
         Contains essentially the same analysis of the Auden/
     Isherwood plays that appears in 1965.11.

11   BLAIR, JOHN G. "W. H. Auden: The Poem as Performance."
     <u>Shenandoah</u>, 16 (Spring), 55-66.
         The "schematic construction" of the last scene of <u>The</u>
     <u>Ascent of F6</u> "is typical of the Auden-Isherwood plays. <u>On</u>
     <u>the Frontier</u> and especially <u>The Dog Beneath the Skin</u> move
     from one set piece to another without even the limited
     dramatic momentum that is set up in the early part of <u>F6</u>.
     In their movement these plays resemble a collection of
     slides more than a movie film." [This analysis is also
     contained in 1965.10.]

12   CONNOLLY, CYRIL. <u>The Modern Movement: One Hundred Key Books</u>
     <u>from England, France and America 1880-1950</u>. London: Andre
     Deutsch and Hamish Hamilton, p. 80.
         No. 86: <u>Goodbye to Berlin</u>. Comment: "A serene Marxist
     who later gravitated into the Vedanta movement round Heard
     and Huxley, and the most gifted novelist since Greene and
     Waugh..., [Isherwood's] is an unexpected weakness, a desire
     to please amounting to ingratiation."

13   CURLEY, DAVID. "The Reality of Love." <u>New Leader</u>, 48 (18 Jan-
     uary), 22-33.
         "<u>A Single Man</u> is a book sharply divided against itself.
     It is in part another example of the silly kind of book
     about America by an Englishman, delivered in a prose that
     would be embarrassing in an undergraduate writing class;
     and it is in part an extremely moving and beautifully pre-
     sented account of the inner life of a man who has refused
     to give up his belief that love is a distinct possibility
     among human beings."

14   CURTIS, JEAN-LOUIS. "Pétrone à la recherche de Dieu."
     <u>Cahiers des Saisons</u>, no. 40, pp. 594-595.
         Isherwood's narrator gives a double perspective on a
     singular life and on the times. [In French]

15   DILLON, RICHARD H.   Review of Ramakrishna and His Disciples.
     Library Journal, 90 (15 March), 1330.
          "[T]he general reader, at whom Isherwood is aiming this
     introduction to Vedanta, may find it dull going, for the
     low-keyed approach together with the lack of outward drama
     in the Swami's life can be tedious."

16   ETHRIDGE, JAMES M. and BARBARA KOPALA, eds.   Contemporary
     Authors: A Bio-Bibliographical Guide to Current Authors
     and Their Works.   Vols. 13-14. Detroit: Gale Research,
     p. 228.
          Brief summary of biographical and bibliographical data.
     [Revised and updated: 1969.9 and 1975.8.]

17   GENTRY, CURT.   "A Religious Influence Who Became a Happening."
     San Francisco Sunday Chronicle (11 July), "This World Maga-
     zine," p. 33.
          In Ramakrishna and His Disciples, Isherwood avoids the
     temptation to explain and justify Ramakrishna in terms of
     his own time. "Instead he writes simply, convincingly,
     beautifully, and well of a person with whom he feels a
     personal involvement."

18   GHOSH, PRABODH CHANDRA.   "The Ascent of F6 and Fry," in his
     Poetry and Religion as Drama.   Calcutta: World Press
     Private, pp. 185-196.
          "As a thesis play, The Ascent of F6 has a partisan so-
     cial message, especially for the countries which believe
     in Imperialism and Colonialism. But it also tries to trace
     the struggle for Power, as opposed to Virtue and Knowledge,
     to its origin in a deeper plane of metaphysical implica-
     tion, and seeks to link it even with spiritual and reli-
     gious issues."

19   HART, JAMES.   "Isherwood, Christopher," in his The Oxford Com-
     panion to American Literature.   Fourth edition. New York:
     The Oxford University Press, pp. 411-412.
          Summary of Isherwood's writing career.

20   HARTLEY, LOIS.   Review of Ramakrishna and His Disciples.
     America, 113 (17 July), 82.
          In Ramakrishna and His Disciples, "Isherwood has invited
     us to judge, not merely acknowledge. In judging, most
     Westerners will reject much.... The book will, however,
     entirely hold the attention and exercise the judgment."
     [A somewhat shortened version of this review appeared in
     the Boston Herald (6 June).]

21   HENGIST, PHILIP.   "An Especial Fad." Punch, 248 (5 May), 676.
          In Ramakrishna and His Disciples "the style is decep-
     tively easy, the presentation limpid and synoptic.

Gradually the personality of Ramakrishna...imposes itself.
This is largely due to the lucid and simple manner in which
the writer explains and clarifies features of the Hindu
religion that the West still finds obscure."

22 HOPE, FRANCIS. "Guru and Swamis." New Statesman, 69 (16
April), 616.
"Mr. Isherwood's simplicity has always suited narrative
better than argument"; Ramakrishna and His Disciples "is
more likely to interest than to shatter most materialist or
Christian readers...."

23 JAMES, BARRY. "Isherwood's God." Quincy Patriot-Ledger [MA]
(21 July).
Isherwood, "a latter day disciple of Ramakrishna, attempts to tell the story of his deity in terms acceptable
to all but the most skeptical. He asks no exceptional
charity of his readers, except the notion that 'this, too,
is humanly possible.'"

24 KERMODE, FRANK. "The Old Amalaki." New York Review of Books,
4 (17 June), 18-20.
"As an outsider considering [Ramakrishna and His Disci-
ples], I have not only to register a certain repugnance but
also a conviction that it matters less as an account of the
saint than as a hint of what it is that comes over Hindu
thought when it moves west."

25 KUEHN, ROBERT W. "Fiction Chronicle." Wisconsin Studies in
Contemporary Literature, 6 (Winter-Spring), 134-135.
"A Single Man is philosophically exhausted..., but the
writing is precise and alert. However distasteful one may
find Isherwood's nihilism, one cannot deny that his craft
is as impressive as ever."

26 LIDDELL, ROBERT. A Treatise on the Novel. London: Jonathan
Cape, pp. 33, 39-40, 44, 45-46.
Compares Isherwood with Somerset Maugham: both have
limited range, both are extremely ingenious, both constantly overreach. [Reprinted: 1969.15.]

27 LITTLER, FRANK. Review of Ramakrishna and His Disciples.
Chicago Tribune Books Today (30 May), p. 10.
Isherwood does not "use biography to proselytize. Once
he has acquainted us with his own views, which are not
bigoted, he tells the life story of the great Hindu mystic
as simply and directly as he can."

*28 McNEELY, JAMES T. "W. H. Auden and the Drama." Master's
thesis, University of Alberta.
Cited: Bloomfield and Mendelson, 1972.11, p. 363.

29   MUGGERIDGE, MALCOLM. "Swamis Go West." London Observer
      (11 April), p. 30.
           Review of Ramakrishna and His Disciples: "With the ex-
      ception of Mr. Waugh at his best, Mr. Isherwood is about
      the most elegant of contemporary English prose writers.
      It may be contended (in my opinion rightly) that the enor-
      mous promise of 'Mr. Norris Changes Trains' and 'Goodbye
      to Berlin' has not been fully realised. Yet it is still a
      pleasure to read him even on this out-of-the-way subject,
      whose treatment has obliged him to accept more or less at
      their face value the pious reminiscences of Ramakrishna's
      disciples, no other material being readily available."

30   REPLOGLE, JUSTIN. "Auden's Marxism." Publications of the
      Modern Language Association, 80 (December), 584-595.
           Except for incidental satiric material, the Auden-Isher-
      wood plays contain little Marxist thought.

31   ROSS, NANCY WILSON. "Madman or Saint?" New York Times Book
      Review (14 November), pp. 22, 24.
           Ramakrishna and His Disciples is "a fresh and important
      contribution to the history of religious mysticism, a sub-
      ject of ever-increasing interest in a psychology-conscious
      age."

32   SCRATCH, PATTY. Review of Ramakrishna and His Disciples. Van
      Nuys Valley News and Green Sheet [CA] (12 August).
           "This is a fascinating study of an unusual man....
      [Isherwood] writes with great sympathy for the man whom he
      considers an avatar, a divine incarnation."

33   SMITH, STEVIE. Review of Ramakrishna and His Disciples.
      Listener, 73 (22 April), 607-608.
           "[I]t is a wonderfully sweet-tempered, loving, modest,
      really innocent picture Mr. Isherwood gives us of the
      Hindu world. And in the background, not unsympathetically
      drawn, are those peculiar love-hate objects, the English...
      who, like the Romans, interfere with religion only if law
      and order are threatened...."

34   SPENDER, STEPHEN. "Must There Always Be a Red Brick England?"
      in The Great Ideas Today 1965. Edited by Robert M. Hutch-
      ins and Mortimer J. Adler. Chicago: Encyclopedia Britan-
      nica, pp. 184-186.
           "A Single Man is about missing Jim, about being middle-
      aged and a homosexual with feelings of persecution in a
      society where it is important to conform.... Isherwood
      has a gift for describing a sense of human behavior as
      though it were something different, intenser, more spec-
      tacular, like the gyrations of tropical birds in a vast,
      golden cage."

1965

35   THORPE, DAY. "An Isherwood Biography of the Mystic Rama-
         krishna." Washington Star (6 June).
         "Mr. Isherwood's sober and entertaining book [Rama-
         krishna and His Disciples] may win converts to Ramakrishna.
         It certainly will arouse interest in the great Hindu lead-
         er."

36   WATTS, ALAN. "One for All, All for One." Book Week (4 July),
         p. 3.
         In Ramakrishna and His Disciples, "Isherwood has...pre-
         sented us with a biography which tries, valiantly, to in-
         terpret this fantastic paradox of a person to our own
         culture. He has written a thoroughly absorbing and pro-
         found book, although there are points at which one might
         wish to engage him in very serious debate."

37   WEINTRAUB, STANLEY. Review of A Single Man. Books Abroad,
         39 (Summer), 351.
         Although handled with "great sensitivity," A Single Man
         does not gain "reader empathy" because "the subject [homo-
         sexuality] cannot rise to it." Isherwood is attempting
         the impossible in trying to present a "'romantic' concep-
         tion of a homosexual relationship."

38   WEST,. PAUL. The Modern Novel. Second edition. Vol. 1.
         London: Hutchison University Library, pp. 77-79.
         Reprint, without change, of 1963.9.

39   WHITEHEAD, JOHN. "Christophananda Isherwood at Sixty."
         London Magazine, NS 5 (July), 90-100.
         "Thirty years separate the appearance of Mr. Norris and
         the publication of Christopher Isherwood's hagiographical
         study of Ramakrishna.... In order to find some common de-
         nominator in two such dissimilar books, it is necessary--
         and, to mark the occasion of Isherwood's sixtieth birthday
         last year, appropriate--to review his work as a whole
         and...to relate it to the main, published events of his
         life."

40   WICKES, GEORGE. "An Interview with Christopher Isherwood."
         Sheanandoah, 16 (Spring), 22-52.
         After a brief introduction and description of Isherwood,
         the interview ranges over a wide variety of topics: Isher-
         wood's work-in-progress, plans for future projects, methods
         of working, his admiration of Forster, coming to America,
         his associations with Huxley, his interest in Vedanta, the
         collaborations with Auden, his work on films, teaching and
         lecturing, his use of himself as narrator, the creation of
         Friedrich Bergmann, and his reactions to the reviews of
         A Single Man.

41   WOODCOCK, GEORGE. Review of Ramakrishna and His Disciples.
      Commonweal, 82 (24 September), 702-704.
         In Ramakrishna and His Disciples, Isherwood writes as
      "an avowed devotee," but "the great flaw" in his treatment
      of the subject is "that he accepts uncritically the most
      extreme views of Ramakrishna as divine incarnation.... As
      a consequence he has written a one-sided biography, and an
      unconvincing apologia, which stimulates one's interest in
      Ramakrishna but never fully satisfies it."

                              1966

1   ALLSOP, KENNETH. "'Everywhere on a Visit': Christopher
      Isherwood Talks Shop to Kenneth Allsop." Books and Bookmen,
      11 (March), 5, 81.
         Reprint of 1965.1.

*2   ANANTHA MURTHY, U. R. "Politics and Fiction in the 1930s,
      Studies in Christopher Isherwood and Edward Upward."
      Ph.D. dissertation, Birmingham University [England].
         Cited: Laurence McNamee, Dissertations in English and
      American Literature: Supplement One, 1964-1968, p. 255.

3   ANON. "Quick Guide." London Times (7 April), p. 15.
         In Exhumations, Isherwood "has done 'absolutely no re-
      writing' and this gives extra value to a lively selection."

4   ANON. Review of Exhumations. Booklist, 62 (15 June), 987.
         "An uneven but never dull collection."

5   ANON. Review of Exhumations. Virginia Kirkus' Service Bulle-
      tin, 34 (15 March), 363.
         "Among the best of Isherwood's exhumations: I Am Wait-
      ing, a short story of abortive prescience and an essay
      about early Los Angeles in burgeoning abundance.... [T]he
      book is dandy for the initiated but those new to Chris-
      topher Isherwood's work had best look elsewhere."

6   ANON. "Tourist and Camera." Times Literary Supplement
      (7 April), p. 296.
         "Mr. Isherwood's work offers no real answers but it
      constantly raises the question [about why he became an
      'exile']. In this sense Exhumations, with its collected
      scraps from his literary past, might have provided at least
      a broad hint. But the stories and the verse and most of
      the articles are at his chattiest, least revealing level;
      only the religious articles have an independent life apart
      from Mr. Isherwood's literary legend."

1966

7   ANON. "Where Are They Now?" <u>Newsweek</u>, 68 (15 December), 20.
Quotes Isherwood's reactions to the Broadway production
of "Cabaret"--"I wouldn't suppose I'll go to see it"; relates information on the "Cabaret" originals; and reports
on Isherwood's present life.

8   BEDFORD, SYBILLE. "Personal Collection." <u>New York Times Book
Review</u> (19 June), pp. 4-5.
<u>Exhumations</u> "is a collection that does the writer proud;
it is also a portrait of the writer as a man...a series of
touches for an unselfconscious sketch."

9   BENDER, EILEEN. "Happy Sampling of Christopher Isherwood."
<u>Pasadena Star News</u> (15 May).
"After reading [<u>Exhumations</u>], one is doubtlessly tempted
to read more of Isherwood. The choice is varied, and in-
dicates the wide range of this urbane and sensitive author."

10   BORKLUND, ELMER W. "What Happened to Isherwood." <u>Book Week</u>
(15 May), p. 3.
<u>Exhumations</u> should impress on the reader "the realization
that Isherwood is one of the very few writers of his generation who has had the endurance to live and work at the
dead center of his time." It demonstrates Isherwood's
"awareness of the universal elements in the particular
crimes which surround us."

11   BRUEHL, WILLIAM J. "The Auden/Isherwood Plays." Ph.D. dissertation, University of Pennsylvania, 286 pp.
The Auden/Isherwood plays are not "primarily motivated"
by Marxist doctrine or by concepts of the social protest
movement of the thirties. To appreciate the plays fully,
they must be seen "as pleas for the revival of the human
spirit, for the individual's commitment, not merely to society but to his own personal fulfillment."

12   BURGESS, ANTHONY. "Candid Camera." <u>Spectator</u>, 216 (18 February), 201.
Review of <u>Exhumations</u>: Isherwood "is good on anything
that approaches the fiction-writer's job--the encapsula-
tion of atmosphere, the observation of faces and bodies.
But, instead of giving us these bits and pieces, Isherwood
could have worked them up into another <u>Down There on a
Visit</u>, common cormorant and all."

13   DAVIS, PAXTON. "'Exhibits A & B' Artfully Ordered." <u>Roanoke
Times</u> [VA] (8 May).
"Like Forster's 'Abinger Harvest,' which in many ways it
resembles, 'Exhumations' is cunningly arranged to reveal
this or that about Isherwood--but always, as with Forster,
a step or so removed."

116

14   HARRIS, HENRY. "The Symbol of Frontier in the Social Allegory
     of the 'Thirties." Zeitschrift für Anglistik und Amerikan-
     istik, 14 (April), 127-140.
          Discusses the symbols of frontier, border, and mountains
     and the traditional use they were put to by various writers
     of the 30s. On the Frontier and The Ascent of F6 are both
     referred to several times.

15   HINDUS, MILTON. "A Critic without Superfluous Barbs." Boston
     Globe (8 May).
          The reviews in Exhumations communicate Isherwood's "en-
     thusiasm for a book" at the same time indicating "unerring-
     ly its limitations and shortcomings." One of the best sec-
     tions, "People," contains "touching evocations which...
     manage subtly to imply that human beings can never be good
     enough to each other."

16   KING, FRANCIS. "Down There for the Harvest." Listener, 75
     (17 March), 407.
          "[A]nyone who has no interest in [Isherwood], so un-
     justly neglected or minimized in his country of origin, has
     only to read Exhumations to be at once fascinated by the
     character revealed of a man not merely highly talented,
     perceptive, and intelligent, but also touching, oddly inno-
     cent and, in the last analysis, lovable."

17   LAMBERT, GAVIN. "Christopher Isherwood," in Double Exposure.
     Edited by Roddy McDowell. New York: Delacorte, pp. 106-
     107.
          "The most obvious connection between the legendary Ber-
     lin Stories and A Single Man is that the latter, given a
     little time..., will become equally legendary. The gift of
     sharing people in a society at a particular vivid moment of
     change, the way they celebrate and squirm and walk the
     tight rope and wait, is uniquely [Isherwood's]."

18   LANCOUR, HAROLD. Review of Exhumations. Library Journal, 91
     (1 June), 2845.
          "Isherwood is not everyone's cup of tea but many readers
     will find [Exhumations] interesting and entertaining."

19   LEHMANN, JOHN. The Ample Proposition: Autobiography III.
     London: Eyre & Spottiswoode, pp. 28-32, 74, 81, 102, 126,
     142, 172, 179-180, 197-198, 199, 200, 225, 247, 250.
          "One event of the winter of 1946-7 brought the contrast
     between past and present into sharp focus: Christopher
     Isherwood's first visit to England since he had left with
     Wystan Auden almost exactly eight years before. It made
     me, and I think his other friends, suddenly see the dis-
     tance we had travelled since before the war...." [Re-
     printed: 1969.14.]

1966

20 LEWIS, KAREN. "Eclectic Isherwood Collection." Louisville
 Courier-Journal (12 June).
 Exhumations "is the first time many of these articles
 and stories have been published in this country. Mr. Isherwood's reputation is borne out by them."

21 LONG, THEODORE. "Author Pools Past Items." Salt Lake City
 Tribune (22 May).
 In Exhumations "the autobiography and some of the criticism are particularly welcome.... But Isherwood is a better
 observer than critic and analyst...."

22 MILOARD. "Sur deux traductions d'Isherwood." Cahiers des
 Saisons, no. 45, pp. 550-552.
 Mr. Norris Changes Trains and Prater Violet are presented
 in the same fashion: as a series of souvenirs. [In French]

23 MITCHELL, BREON. "W. H. Auden and Christopher Isherwood: The
 'German Influence.'" Oxford German Studies, 1:163-172.
 The so-called "German influence" on the Auden-Isherwood
 plays is based on a false assumption: "The fact is that
 the entire evidence for Brecht's influence in the 1930's
 boils down to one play Auden saw before he was fluent in
 German, and what he had read of the poetry...."

24 NAIPAUL, V. S. "The Writer." New Statesman, 71 (18 March),
 381-382.
 In Exhumations, "Isherwood admits the reader to a proc-
 ess of writing, but the reader does in the end feel exclud-
 ed. He misses...the big end-product which he feels he has
 been led to expect; it is as though Isherwood's exposure to
 experiences has been for purely private purpose."

25 PANGBORN, CYRUS R. Review of Ramakrishna and His Disciples.
 Journal of Asian Studies, 25 (February), 356.
 "Isherwood's wish to commend Ramakrishna, without setting
 to one side the unnecessary surplus love, for critical ap-
 praisal, suggests to a reader that the movement inspired by
 Ramakrishna must require gullibility when it asks for devotion."

26 POORE, CHARLES. "Two Generations This Side of Queen Victoria."
 New York Times (5 May), p. 45.
 "Christopher Isherwood and Auberon Waugh are brilliant
 members of two contrasting British postwar generations.
 Their new books [Exhumations and Who Are the Violets Now?]
 iconoclastically suggest that the more things change, the
 more they grow very different indeed."

27   PROCTOR, PATRICK. Review of The World in the Evening. Books
      and Bookmen, 11 (March), 79-80.
          Notice of the paperback reprint of The World in the
      Evening: The letters of Elizabeth Rydal "contain some of
      Isherwood's finest writing and bear an uncanny insight into
      the working of a woman's mind...."

28   PROCTOR, PATRICK. "On a Giant Bestriding the Years." Books
      and Bookmen, 11 (April), 30.
          "The figure of Isherwood the man that emerges from his
      novels is one of diffidence and wayward brilliance. But
      this is no more a definite judgement than 'Exhumations' is
      an accurate register of the contents of this collection.
      For as we wait in the wings watching the unfolding of these
      tableaux vivants, it is a giant who bestrides the years.
      The vision is unclouded, the friends distinguished and the
      judgement impeccable."

29   RETLEW, THOMAS M. "Isherwood Collection." Wilmington News
      [DE] (4 May).
          Exhumations is a rewarding collection. "The wry title
      of the compilation is an example of the tone, and so are
      the comments Isherwood prefixes to each category of work."

30   SHRAPNEL, NORMAN. "The Confessor." Manchester Guardian
      Weekly, 94 (24 March), 11.
          Review of Exhumations: "To anyone formed or malformed
      by the 1930s, these bits and pieces of Isherwood's...are
      likely to be entirely fascinating.... [Isherwood] is
      shrewd and enlightening about this so-near-so-far past, his
      own and others'."

31   SOLWAY, CLIFFORD. "An Interview with Christopher Isherwood."
      Tamarack Review, no. 39 (Spring), pp. 22-35.
          Transcript of an interview filmed by the Canadian Broad-
      casting Corporation TV network on 30 May 1965. The discus-
      sion focuses on A Single Man, homosexuality, and the meaning
      of "Camp."

32   STACTON, DAVID. "Isherwood Book His 'Best' Pieces." Denver
      Post (12 June).
          Exhumations "is just what it says it is, a collection of
      table scraps. Such books are seldom, however, either so
      tasty or so nourishing. There is even a touching little
      fable called 'The Wishing Tree.'"

33   STARRETT, VINCENT. "Sherlockian Point in Dispute." Chicago
      Tribune Books Today (10 July), p. 7.
          Exhumations is "one of the most provocative gatherings
      of a writer's fugitive pieces" that has come out in recent
      years. Concentrates almost entirely on the suppressed

1966

introduction, written for a collection of stories, in which Isherwood calls Sherlock Holmes a comic character; and takes issue with it.

34　STEELE, RICHARD. "Isherwood Collection." <u>Pittsburgh Press</u> (19 June).

"While the general reader may regard some of the exhumations as a trifle unfortunate, a considerable portion of the material makes excellent reading." The discussions of Stevenson, Mansfield, Santayana, Woolf, and Spender are "extremely good" and the article on Ernest Toller "is especially moving."

35　S[TRENG], F. J. "Along the Bookshelf: Miscellaneous." <u>The Personalist</u>, 47 (Summer), 454-455.

<u>Ramakrishna and His Disciples</u> is "a readable and interesting introduction to the historical events that incited the Ramakrishna Mission. Understandably, though unfortunately, the author's comments include a stereotyped portrayal of Christianity..., taking British Protestant ecclesiastical expression of the late nineteenth century as a normative expression."

36　TAUBMAN, ROBERT. "Uncles' War." <u>New Statesman</u>, 72 (16 September), 401.

Reviewed with five other books, <u>All the Conspirators</u> is seen as "innocently dated" but a "highly accomplished first novel."

37　WILSON, ANGUS. "Insights into Isherwood." <u>London Observer</u> (20 March), p. 26.

Review of <u>Exhumations</u>: "There are those for whom Mr. Isherwood's fiction and the self-presentation so integral to it are without interest; there are those for whom his work is sometimes a disappointment; but I do not believe that there are any whose interest has remained slight. Once you care about what he writes, you care strongly enough to read everything that he produces. His fictional life is one of the important Anglo-Saxon literary legends of our time and everything that he writes relates to that legend."

38　WILSON, ANGUS. "Vues sur Isherwood." <u>Cahiers des Saisons</u>, no. 46, pp. 33-35.

Isherwood's work presents one of the most significant literary legends of our time. His acceptance of amorality may be an adolescent view, but it may also be adult compassion. He sees all types of vanity as the greatest obstacle to spiritual progress. [In French]

1967

1   ANON. "Bookstack: Fiction Reprints." Books and Bookmen, 12
    (February), 57.
        All the Conspirators "survives as lively and readable,
    though its health depends to some extent on artificial
    stimulants such as curiosity about the 20's and Isherwood's
    beginnings."

2   ANON. "Briefly Noted: Fiction." New Yorker, 43 (15 April),
    193.
        In A Meeting by the River, the confrontation between the
    two brothers is contrived and does not settle anything.
    Patrick, however, is "large enough and sinister enough to
    sustain a much longer and fuller novel than this."

3   ANON. "Brothers & Others." Time, 89 (21 April), 104, 107.
        In A Meeting by the River, it "seems to be Isherwood's
    intention to show the spirit of Vedanta triumphant against...
    corruption, but it is the evil Patrick who runs away with
    the book.... The disappointment, though, is that Isherwood
    stints...."

4   ANON. "A Fine New Novel from Christopher Isherwood." Newsday
    (8 April).
        A Meeting by the River "has a deceptive simplicity that,
    along with its sheer charm of style, makes it certainly the
    best of [Isherwood's] recent books.... This is probably the
    best use of letters to forward a story I have ever seen."

5   ANON. "Naked, Not Unashamed." Times Literary Supplement
    (15 June), p. 525.
        "If you blushed at A Single Man, you will writhe at A
    Meeting by the River.... To explain saintliness without
    smugness is difficult even for a very gifted novelist.
    Desperate honesty can be embarrassing not only because it
    is honest, but also because it is desperate." [Reprinted:
    1968.1.]

6   ANON. Review of Exhumations. Choice, 4 (March), 40.
        "Isherwood writes in a facile style and offers some
    minor but interesting views of such literary personages as
    W. H. Auden and Virginia Woolf."

7   ANON. Review of A Meeting by the River. Booklist, 63
    (1 June), 1033-1034.
        The conflict is "not without dramatic tension" but the
    narrative is "unemotive" and "limited" in appeal to Western
    readers.

1967

8   ANON. Review of <u>A Meeting by the River</u>. <u>Choice</u>, 4 (November), 982.
"Light Isherwood, but better than none at all."

9   ANON. Review of <u>A Meeting by the River</u>. <u>Hollywood Canyon Crier</u> (11 May).
Isherwood's theme "is again the homosexual (and how dull it all is now the boys have won the right to go drag and camp) and the Hindu Yoga bit (which LSD has made pretty much a waste of time).... This is not the early Isherwood..., but in a minor key, of a man troubled by age, the world as it is."

10   ANON. Review of <u>A Meeting by the River</u>. <u>Kirkus Service Bulletin</u>, 35 (1 February), 156.
<u>A Meeting by the River</u> "is by no means as peckishly unpleasant as <u>A Single Man</u>; it is expectedly well-written and well-informed.... [I]t is sufficiently skillful to invite curiosity even though it may not prompt any deeper speculation."

11   B., C. A. "Isherwood Novel Divides His Ego into 2 Brothers." <u>Buffalo Evening News</u> (8 April).
<u>A Meeting by the River</u> fails artistically but is "psychologically interesting." Isherwood "divides himself into two brothers who represent what he apparently conceived of as the two halves of his nature."

12   BAIL, JAY. "A Keeper of Brothers." <u>Quincy Patriot-Ledger</u> [MA] (7 April), p. 32.
"Even when Patrick and Oliver despise each other the most, there is still that gentleness, that fiery, argumentative, vain, hate-filled feeling between two people who also know that they are both human beings and both brothers."

13   BANNON, BARBARA A. Review of <u>A Meeting by the River</u>. <u>Publisher's Weekly</u>, 191 (13 February), 73.
"Nothing very much in the way of a story develops [in <u>A Meeting by the River</u>].... Neither brother is really very interesting."

14   BARKER, PAUL. "New Fiction." <u>London Times</u> (1 June), p. 7.
"<u>A Meeting by the River</u> is the latest example of late Isherwood. His postwar work is as much a special taste as...(fill in the missing word, and justify calling it 'special' in not more than 25 words).... <u>A Meeting by the River</u> is three times as saccharine as I can take."

15   BLOOM, ROBERT. "Auden's Essays at Man: Long Views in the
      Early Poetry." Shenandoah, 18 (Winter), 36-38.
          The Dog Beneath the Skin and The Ascent of F6 convey a
      "similar sense of insurmountable limitation." In F6 Auden
      and Isherwood are "concerned with the spiritual and psycho-
      logical problems that beset the exceptional man...."

16   BRUEHL, WILLIAM J. "Polus Naufrangia: A Key Symbol in The
      Ascent of F6." Modern Drama, 10 (September), 161-164.
          The invented botanical speciman is a "symbol of both the
      play's action (the attempt to gain knowledge, power, and
      honor through the conquest of the mountain) and the theme
      (the dilemma of the exceptionally gifted man)."

17   BUNKE, JOAN. "In a Tense War It Is Hedonist Versus Ascetic."
      Des Moines Register (23 April), p. 19-G.
          In A Meeting by the River, Isherwood "achieves...the
      creation of two vivid, strong-minded characters, skillfully
      played off against each other in a tense exercise in per-
      sonal psychological warfare."

18   BURGESS, ANTHONY. "Hindu Crush." Spectator, 218 (16 June),
      714.
          Writing in letter form, in imitation of the epistolary
      style of A Meeting by the River, Burgess calls the novel a
      "very nice little book" but too much like a moral tract for
      "the Beauties of Hindu Contemplation."

19   BURGESS, ANTHONY. The Novel Now: A Student's Guide to Con-
      temporary Fiction. London: Faber and Faber; New York:
      W. W. Norton, pp. 98, 112-114, 118.
          Isherwood is best known for his novels about Berlin in
      the 1930s, but his later works show a steady development
      beyond those early successes: the approach to persona in
      Down There on a Visit is "much more involved than in the
      earlier books"; A Single Man is "a brief, taut novel, funny
      and pathetic, a manifesto of loneliness." [Reprinted:
      1971.8.]

20   CAZAMIAN, LOUIS and RAYMOND LAS VERGNAS. "Modern Times (1660-
      1967)" in A History of English Literature. Revised edition.
      New York: Macmillan, pp. 1402-1403, 4134.
          Isherwood is "chiefly interesting to-day as an authori-
      tative witness of the Age [the thirties]." But A Single
      Man "is evidence of an obvious renewal." The Auden-Isher-
      wood plays are also mentioned.

21   CHATURVEDI, B. N. English Poetic Drama of the Twentieth Cen-
      tury. Gwalior: Kitab Ghar, pp. 76-85.
          "The most cogent criticism of the plays of Auden and
      Isherwood would be that they tried to condense too much

1967

> into them.... The diverse elements...are not fused to-
> gether by any singleness of purpose...."

22   COMANS, GRACE P. "Parting of the Ways." Hartford Courant
      [CT] (16 April).
          Review of A Meeting by the River: "The confrontation of
      the brothers, serious yet with overtones of comedy and hu-
      mor, affects them both. When they say goodbye, each has
      been changed by their meeting."

23   COOK, BRUCE. "Even Meticulous Mr. Isherwood Can Come a
      Cropper." National Observer, 6 (17 April), 21.
          A Meeting by the River returns to Isherwood's "two ob-
      sessive themes"--homosexuality and religious experience--
      and presents a moral confrontation which is "more than a
      bit too neat." The epistolary form is "perilously catech-
      tical: the believing half of the dialog is always moved
      to excessive zeal."

24   COOK, RODERICK. "Books in Brief." Harper's Magazine, 234
      (May), 118-119.
          A Meeting by the River presents "an interesting confron-
      tation of the mystic and the worldly, at a time when both
      are forced to find the courage of their convictions."

25   DAVIS, PAXTON. "2 Brothers, 2 Viewpoints." Roanoke Times
      [VA] (7 May).
          A Meeting by the River presents "the two faces of Chris-
      topher Isherwood": the "worldy bohemian" and the mystic.
      The dual between the brothers "is the vehicle through which
      Isherwood raises the two currents of his life to objective
      reality."

26   DOYLE, PAUL A. Review of A Meeting by the River. Best Sel-
      lers, 27 (15 April), 24-25.
          Although the epistolary technique is bothersome and the
      development of the conflict too brief, Isherwood can still
      be credited with "producing a mature, thought-provoking
      and extremely well-written novel."

27   EBBITT, DAVID R. "Pure Isherwood." Boston Herald (4 June).
          In A Meeting by the River, Patrick "represents the total,
      amoral indulgence of the ego, as opposed to the death of
      self that Oliver seeks to achieve."

28   FRENCH, WARREN. Review of A Meeting by the River. Kansas
      City Star [MO] (24 April).
          "What [Isherwood] has to say is always worth hearing,
      but should not necessarily be accepted. People who don't
      like jazz masses may thrill to this attempt to make the

ancient debate between body and soul of contemporary interest, but most readers are likely to find both the novel and
the issue inert."

29 FRIEDMAN, NORMAN. "Point of View in Fiction: The Development
of a Critical Concept," in The Theory of the Novel. Edited
by Philip Stevick. New York: The Free Press, pp. 108-137.
Reprint of 1955.1.

30 GAINES, ERVIN J. Review of A Meeting by the River. Library
Journal, 92 (15 March), 1178.
A Meeting by the River is "rather artificial and precious"--"Isherwood does not achieve the necessary distance
between himself and his material." [Reprinted: 1969.7.]

31 GARIS, ROBERT. "Varieties of the Will." Hudson Review, 20
(Summer), 330-331.
In A Meeting by the River, Isherwood attempts to enlist
sympathy for both brothers, but the "comic double perspective" fails and a "frank distaste" develops for Patrick.
Thus, a contrast between "pure bad faith and pure good
faith" emerges, an opposition for which comedy cannot provide a "tolerant perspective."

32 GATHORNE-HARDY, JONATHAN. "Selected Books." London Magazine,
NS 7 (August), 93-94.
In A Meeting by the River, Isherwood has failed "in the
recreation of one of the major moral struggles of our time"
because he is "dishonest" in presenting the conflict: "So
overwhelming is the impression left by Patrick, so obsessive and skilful his creation, that it seems likely that
this was in fact the real intention of the book."

33 GROSS, JOHN. "A Question of Upbringing." New York Review of
Books, 8 (18 May), 34-36.
"As a study in complementary and conflicting tempera-
ments..., [A Meeting by the River] has its undoubted
point.... But at the heart of the book there is a blur:
the underlying religious assumptions are insufficiently
dramatized...and have to be taken too much on trust."

34 GRUTZMACHER, HAROLD. "3 Hits and a Miss." Chicago Tribune
Books Today (23 April), p. 13.
The style of A Meeting by the River is its strongest
point; the story is thin but satisfactory.

35 HOFMANN, FRANK. "Isherwood on Honesty, Even for Brothers."
Dayton Daily News [OH] (7 May).
In A Meeting by the River, Isherwood is "as usual, a
writer sensitive to all nuances of the human personality
and a writer capable of weaving descriptions of them into
a fascinating tale."

36   HOWELL, BRENT. "The Reader Gets in Novel 'Sack.'" <u>Pasadena</u>
       <u>Star News</u> (9 April).
            <u>A Meeting by the River</u> "is a good novel by a master of
       the English language and Hindu thought, and it is to [his]
       credit...that he does not try to impress us with one mas-
       tery while trying to sell us on the other."

37   HOYT, ELIZABETH N. "A Brother's Vows." <u>Cedar Rapids Gazette</u>
       [IA] (18 June), pp. 2C, 6C.
            "When reality confronts mysticism..., it is difficult
       to ascertain which element wins. However, the realist,
       Patrick, is by far the more interesting character in 'A
       Meeting by the River.'"

38   JOHNSTON, VANCE. "Down by the River." <u>Tampa Tribune</u>
       (30 April).
            In <u>A Meeting by the River</u>, the confrontation "has many
       interesting complications which will at times baffle the
       reader but at all times keep him interested in what is to
       follow...."

*39   JURAK, MIRKO. "Angleska poeticuo-politicna drama v leith
       1930-1940." Ph.D. dissertation, Ljubljana University.
            Cited: Bloomfield and Mendelson, 1972.11, p. 364.
            [Reprinted: 1968.10.].

40   KAUFFMANN, STANLEY. "Passages to India." <u>New Republic</u>, 156
       (15 April), 22, 37.
            <u>A Meeting by the River</u> "makes its way to a rewarding
       complexity through the addition of simplicities.... [N]ot
       compromising his beliefs in the slightest, Isherwood has
       made a novel that is credible, moving and ultimately
       ironic."

41   LEE, DONALD. "East, West Collide in 'Meeting' Novel." <u>Fay-</u>
       <u>etteville Observer</u> [NC] (9 April).
            "It is the attitude of the narrator that makes <u>A Meeting</u>
       <u>by the River</u> read so much more interesting than most of the
       season's other novels. He is a real adept, capable of gen-
       uine compassion in the face of most of the contemporary
       World conflicts and psychological duresses."

42   LUMLEY, FREDERICK. <u>New Trends in 20th Century Drama: A Sur-</u>
       <u>vey Since Ibsen and Shaw</u>. New York: Oxford University,
       pp. 81, 310-311.
            Reprint of 1956.3. [Revised: 1972.38.]

43   McCORMICK, JAY. "Two Brothers, Two Paths." <u>Detroit News</u>
       (9 April).
            <u>A Meeting by the River</u> is a "lesson in brevity." Isher-
       wood deals amusingly with the issues of love, God, and
       souls.

44   MADDOCKS, MELVIN. "Isherwood's Interior Debate." Christian
      Science Monitor (11 May), p. 13.
          A Meeting by the River is the "best novel Isherwood has
      written in a long time.... [He] is no Dostoyevsky; he is
      a cool writer, a man of wit rather than passion, a great
      observer rather than a great feeler. But at his own quiet
      level he has set up his own small classic drama between
      Dmitri and Alyosha."

45   MAY, DERWENT. "Fiction: Self-Deceivers Ever." Listener, 77
      (22 June), 829.
          A Meeting by the River is about false expectations and
      their dispersion. The attention to the main characters is
      so close that too little of the atmosphere of the Ganges
      and the monastery comes through.

46   MORTIMER, JOHN. "No Gurus Is Good Gurus." New Statesman, 74
      (29 September), 397-398.
          "When Auden and Isherwood turned their attention from
      the shambles of Europe in 1937 and wrote The Ascent of F6,
      it became clear that the artists were also in search of
      their guru."

47   NEWQUIST, ROY. "Christopher Isherwood," in his Conversations.
      Chicago: Rand McNally, pp. 169-181.
          After a brief autobiographical summary, Isherwood re-
      sponds to questions about living in California, his inter-
      est in Hindu philosophies, his life in Berlin, and his
      opinions about literary criticism and contemporary writing.
      He also makes a comment on the composition of A Single Man.

*48   NOWELL, ROBERT. Review of A Meeting by the River. The Tab-
      let: A Weekly Newspaper and Review, 221 (10 June), 641.
          Cited: Index to Book Reviews in the Humanities, 8
      (1967), 180.

49   OLSON, IVAN. "Meeting in Monastery." Fresno Bee [CA]
      (9 April).
          Review of A Meeting by the River: "The intense but
      often comical struggle between the two men...makes a sus-
      penseful and unusual novel. Much of the virtue of the book
      results from Isherwood's simple, seemingly effortless han-
      dling."

50   PRICE, R. G. G. "New Fiction." Punch, 253 (5 July), 32.
          "[T]hough the absence of communicable religious emotion
      may be responsible for the general effect of well-mannered
      slightness, [A Meeting by the River] is far more enjoyable
      than it may sound. Perhaps the comedy travels across re-
      ligious frontiers while the tragedy doesn't."

1967

51 PRYCE-JONES, ALAN. "New Isherwood Novel a Delight, But It Presents a Credibility Gap." New York World Journal Tribune, 1 (13 April), 30.
    In A Meeting by the River there is "a credibility gap between the world of Indian mysticism which is designed to provide the attractive force in Isherwood's scheme of things and the pair of suburban-minded Westerners who are exposed to it."

52 ROGERS, THOMAS. "Isherwood in India." Book Week (16 April), 6, 12.
    The "product of a lifetime consciousness of exile and foreignness," A Meeting by the River "is compounded from all the different strands of feeling" in Isherwood's earlier books.

53 SCRATCH, PATTY. Review of A Meeting by the River. Van Nuys Valley News and Green Sheet [CA] (27 April).
    A Meeting by the River "is a beautiful and sensitive novel, going deeply into the feelings of one who feels a religious urge."

54 SELLERS, W. H. "New Light on Auden's The Orators." Publications of the Modern Language Association, 82 (October), 455-464.
    An understanding of the concept of the Test, as defined by Isherwood (in Lions and Shadows), helps to comprehend the central concern of The Orators.

55 SEWARD, WILLIAM W., JR. "2 Brothers Take a Spiritual Journey." Norfolk Pilot [VA] (14 May).
    A Meeting by the River implies "that these two [brothers] can never be brought together permanently nor can they be separated forever.... Who knows, they may represent the two halves of Isherwood's experience as exile and tourist."

56 SHERMAN, JOHN K. "Virtue vs. Carnality Leads to a Tenacious Devotion." Minneapolis Tribune (23 April).
    In A Meeting by the River, "Christopher Isherwood...has fleshed out, in the persons of two brothers of opposing views of the conduct of life, a dialogue between virtue and contemplation, on the one hand, and practicality and carnality on the other."

57 SIGGINS, CLARA M. "Two in Search of a Soul." Boston Globe (30 April).
    Review of A Meeting by the River: "Isherwood, one of the most detached of writers, in a matchless style draws heavily upon the reader's imagination for the story's sentimental and sensual inflections. The letters unfold innuendo after innuendo which the reader snatches at eagerly."

58 STELLA, CHARLES. "New Isherwood Novel a Bit on the Slow Side."
    Cleveland Press (14 April).
        In A Meeting by the River, "the meeting of the two
    brothers forces each to think through his own motives and
    what life is all about. Isherwood, a facile writer, is
    always a pleasure to read, especially as he makes the mys-
    teries of the Oriental mind scrutable."

59 STEVENSON, LIONEL. Yesterday and After. History of the Eng-
    lish Novel, Vol. 11. New York: Barnes & Noble, pp. 369-
    370, 372.
        "Isherwood is unquestionably a man of acute sensibility
    and civilised intelligence, but these qualities are not
    robust enough to sustain full-length novels about the vio-
    lent and chaotic contemporary world."

60 SYKES, GERALD. "Tom Spilled the Beans." New York Times Book
    Review (25 June), p. 41.
        A Meeting by the River "invites comparison" with Hesse's
    Siddhartha: "Isherwood's book is by comparison narrowly
    observed, uncritical of its enthusiasms, narcissistic, and
    esthetically unwise.... On the other hand, it is far more
    authentic than Somerset Maugham's comparable novel, The
    Razor's Edge."

61 TAYLOR, WILL. "Isherwood Novel Candidly Studies East-West
    Views." Albuquerque Journal (20 November).
        "While [A Meeting by the River] is certainly provocative
    in its candid and apparently sincere delineation of East
    versus West values it does not come up to the dramatic or
    literary quality of some of Isherwood's earlier novels."

62 THOMAS, SIDNEY. "Angry Clash of Butterflies." Atlanta Con-
    stitution and Journal (23 April).
        A Meeting by the River "has all the excitement of a
    clash between angry butterflies.... This book might be of
    interest to those who are following, with dismay or other-
    wise, the deterioration of Christopher Isherwood's talent."

63 THOMPSON, DON. "Tired Technique Given New Spark." Denver
    Rocky Mountain News (23 April).
        In A Meeting by the River, the tired epistolary tech-
    nique "becomes fresh and effective, revealing the inner
    person far more concisely than narration or stream of con-
    sciousness could do."

64 TREVOR, WILLIAM. "Shapely Fragment." Books and Bookmen, 12
    (June), 42-43.
        "Had A Meeting by the River been written in any other
    form I doubt that it would have been nearly as successful
    as it is. The essential economy of letters and diary-

entries reduces the size of the theme to a petit-point pattern that's quietly rich in suggestion and shadow and overtone."

65 W., B. "This One Never Quite Gets There." Miami Herald (9 April).
    In A Meeting by the River, "Isherwood, as always, writes well and gracefully, but in 191 pages he is unable to interpret the true story of why an educated young Englishman should leave his own country and background and defect to the philosophy of the East."

66 W., L. G. "Novel of Two Brothers." Worcester Telegram [MA] (23 April).
    "The talented Christopher Isherwood has written [A Meeting by the River] in the form of letters, notes from diary and recorded thoughts. His style is quiet, almost understated; his story is poignant. And he tells it beautifully."

67 WOLFF, GEOFFREY A. "A Novel by Isherwood." Washington Post (16 April).
    A Meeting by the River "is muscular and precise; there is no fat on it, it wastes no motion.... What first engrosses us--reading other people's mail and diaries--finally persuades and teaches us: there are conditions attached to our various meddling. We are obliged to try to understand."

68 WOODCOCK, GEORGE. Review of A Meeting by the River. Commonweal, 86 (12 May), 241-242.
    "Clumsy in its psychology, [A Meeting by the River] does not carry enough conviction as a portrayal of real human agony to touch the emotions."

69 WOOLF, LEONARD. Downhill All the Way: An Autobiography of the Years 1919-1939. New York: Harcourt, Brace, and World, p. 176.
    Tells of the publication of Mr. Norris Changes Trains by the Hogarth Press.

70 WOOLF, VIRGINIA. "The Leaning Tower," in her Collected Essays. Vol. 2. New York: Harcourt, Brace, and World, pp. 162-181.
    Reprinted from 1948.16.

71 WORDSWORTH, CHRISTOPHER. "The Swami and the Publisher." Manchester Guardian Weekly, 96 (8 June), 11.
    "At the heart of A Meeting by the River is an enigma variation on the difficult theme of the Bhagavad Gita, Maya

and the world imprisoned in its own activity. It is presented at novella length and, it goes without saying, is
clinker-built with sharpness and wit...."

1968

1   ANON. "Naked, Not Unashamed," in <u>T.L.S.: Essays and Reviews</u>
    <u>from the Times Literary Supplement, 1967</u>. Vol. 6. London:
    Oxford University Press, pp. 112-114.
        Reprint of 1967.5.

2   ARNOLD, LESLIE E. "The Motif of the 'Quest' in the Early Works
    of W. H. Auden." Ph.D. dissertation, Simon Fraser Univer-
    sity, passim.
        The "Quest" is the only unifying image in Auden's early
    work, including the three plays that he wrote with Isher-
    wood. This quest concept, which holds that an individual
    must discover his own order in a chaotic and decadent
    world, relates to Auden's own search for identity but is
    also drawn from the early schoolboy fantasies that were
    part of the poet's association with Isherwood.

3   ASHLEY, LEONARD R. N. and STUART L. ASTOR, comps. <u>British</u>
    <u>Short Stories: Classics and Criticism</u>. Englewood Cliffs,
    N.J.: Prentice Hall, pp. 297-309, 394-396.
        Introduction gives publication history and a brief crit-
    ical review for "I Am Waiting," which is included in the
    anthology. Biographical notes add some little-known de-
    tails, such as the fact that Isherwood's first novel sold
    only five copies.

4   CRAFT, ROBERT. "Stravinsky and Some Writers." <u>Harper's</u>, 237
    (December), 101-108.
        Informal exchanges with Auden, Evelyn Waugh, Aldous
    Huxley, and Isherwood about literature, music, religion,
    etc.

5   DRAPER, R. P. Review of <u>Exhumations</u>. <u>Modern Language Review</u>,
    63 (January), 234-235.
        "[I]n the miscellaneous collection which constitutes
    <u>Exhumations</u> there are several hints that [Isherwood's]
    progress has been from a liberal, but immature atheism,
    dallying with the serious things of life, to the discovery
    of his true spiritual self and a new kind of honest con-
    cern."

6   GREENBERG, HERBERT. <u>Quest for the Necessary: W. H. Auden and</u>
    <u>the Dilemma of Divided Consciousness</u>. Cambridge: Harvard
    University Press, pp. 17, 23, 31, 38-39, 48, 51, 59-60, 61,
    66, 75, 78, 81, 83-84, 85, 86, 198.

1968

"Auden's catharsis was one shared with contemporaries," and his interest in "spies and such types as the neurotic hero and his opposite, the 'truly strong man,' and the notion of a war between the younger generation and their oppressors" came from a common "fund of schoolboy fantasy" that Auden shared with Spender, Day Lewis, Upward, and especially Isherwood, "who had constructed their rebellious attitude toward established authority into a private mythology of opposition."

7 HIGHAM, CHARLES. "Isherwood on Hollywood." London Magazine, NS 8 (April), 31-38.
Interview: Isherwood answers questions about his work in cinema and his life in California.

8 JARKA, HORST. "British Writers and Austria of the Thirties," in Österreich un die Angelsächsische Welt: Kulturbegegnungen und Vergleiche. Vol. 2. Edited by Otto Hietsch. Vienna: Wilhelm Barumüller, pp. 453-462.
"Perhaps the most restless spirit of a restless generation was Christopher Isherwood.... He was keenly sensitive to the European political drama, and although he spent only a very short period in Vienna (1933), it is not surprising that in two novels, Prater Violet and The World in the Evening, he includes Austria in his account of a world on its 'journey to a war.'"

9 JURAK, MIRKO. "English Political Verse Drama of the Thirties: Revision and Alteration." Acta Neophilologica, 1:67-68.
The revisions and alterations in the texts of six plays of the Group Theatre, including the three Auden/Isherwood plays, come from a double source: first, the author or director in preparing the play for the stage; and, second, the suggestions of the censor.

*10 JURAK, MIRKO. Glavna problemska obmocja v angleski poeticno-politicni dramatiki v letih 1930-1940: The Main Spheres of the Problems in the English Politico-Poetic Drama (1930-1940). Ljubljana: Univerza v Ljubljani, passim.
Cited: Bloomfield and Mendelson, 1972.11, p. 356. Reprint of 1967.39. [In Slovene with summary in English.]

11 LANCASTER, MARIE-JACQUELINE, ed. Brian Howard: Portrait of a Failure. London: Anthony Blond, pp. 349, 363, 365, 371, 399, 430, 508.
Isherwood's associations with Howard are randomly mentioned.

12 PEREZ MINIK, DOMINGO. "Christopher Isherwood, Un Novelista Famoso, pero Frustrado." Insula, 23 (February), 5.

Isherwood's family background, university education, and intellectual distinction did not prepare him for the uncertain, sordid, and oppressive conditions that he encountered and wrote about in Berlin of the thirties. His style, intellectual conduct, and moral attitude were out of phase with the social history of the times. Thus, Isherwood became a famous but inevitably frustrated novelist. [In Spanish.]

13 RABAN, JONATHAN. The Technique of Modern Fiction. London: Edward Arnold, pp. 18, 26-32, 56.
　　The narrative style of A Single Man is marked by "extraordinary pliancy": "There are effectively three varieties of tense and four of person, and the shifts from one to another mirror the emotional movements of the narrative."

14 SCOTT-KILVERT, IAN. "English Fiction 1967." British Book News, no. 331 (March), pp. 165-169.
　　In A Meeting by the River, "Isherwood brings off a remarkable fusion of his interest in Eastern philosophy... with his gift for social comedy and acute observation."

15 VALGEMAE, MARDI. "Auden's Collaboration with Isherwood on The Dog Beneath the Skin." Huntington Library Quarterly, 31 (August), 373-383.
　　After examination of letters, scenarios, and manuscripts of early versions of the play, "we can assure John Lehmann that the joint authorship of The Dog was in fact a genuine collaboration. For Isherwood...was an active participant in the labors of composition...."

16 WESTBY, SELMER and CLAYTON M. BROWN. Christopher Isherwood: A Bibliography 1923-1967. Los Angeles: California State College at Los Angeles Foundation, 51 pp.
　　Part I lists Isherwood's own writings, except translations into foreign languages, film scripts, and phonorecords. Part II, works about Isherwood, is selective and contains some 250 items, most of which were examined by the compilers.

17 WILLIAMS, RAYMOND. "Poets and Plays, 1935-1955," in his Drama from Ibsen to Brecht. London: Chatto & Windus, pp. 199-206.
　　Reprint, slightly revised, of 1952.11.

1969

*1 ANON. "From a Conversation with Christopher Isherwood." Performing Arts, 3 (April), 23, 31.

1969

Playbill for Isherwood's adaptation of Shaw's The Adventures of the Black Girl in Her Search for God. Cited: Orphanos, 1976.25.

2   ANON. "Paperbacks." London Observer (7 September), p. 32.
Notice of Penguin publication of A Single Man: "What there is left in life for a lonely Californian academic, a homosexual, whose friend has died..., candidly, carefully, spinterishly described." Also notes the paperback release of Exhumations.

*3   ANON. Review of The Adventures of the Black Girl in Her Search for God. Variety (21 March), p. 19.
Cited: Orphanos, 1976.25. Cannot locate.

4   BROWNING, D. C., ed. Everyman's Dictionary of Literary Biography: English and American. Revised edition. New York: E. P. Dutton, pp. 355-356.
Biographical summary.

5   CAPETANAKIS, DEMETRIOS. "Notes on Some Contemporary Writers," in his The Shores of Darkness. Freeport, N.Y.: Books for Libraries Press, pp. 135-146.
Reprint of 1949.5 and 1947.7.

6   EVANS, B[ENJAMIN] IFOR. English Literature Between the Wars. [Folcroft, Pa.]: The Folcroft Press, pp. 123, 129.
The Ascent of F6 is a "bold experiment...to use verse in a play that explored character, and was yet a comment of the values that underlay a troubled decade."

7   GAINES, ERVIN J. Review of A Meeting by the River. The Library Journal Book Review 1967. New York: R. P. Bowker, p. 659.
Reprint of 1967.30.

*8   GRAFFIN, WALTER R. "The Novels of Christopher Isherwood." Ph.D. dissertation, University of Wisconsin, 269 pp.
"Because Isherwood's novels often stress characterization rather than plot, the dissertation gives considerable attention to the kinds of characters who consistently appear in his work--the young artist, the homosexual, the outsider, and the religious convert. These figures share the alienation and despair of many modern fictional characters.... [But] Isherwood's main theme has evolved from alienation to accommodation in his books of the 'fifties and 'sixties.... [T]he dissertation shows that the later works, with their attention to the individual's involvement in the lives of others, provide a positive resolution to the problems of alienation presented in the earlier books." [Dissertation Abstracts International, 30 (1969), 1168A.]

9   HARTE, BARBARA and CAROLYN RILEY, eds. <u>200 Contemporary</u>
     <u>Authors</u>. Detroit: Gale Research Co., pp. 156-157.
          Revision of 1965.16; later updated in 1975.8.

10   HOPE, FRANCIS. "Another of the Gang." <u>New Statesman</u>, 78
     (1 August), 149.
          Review article for paperback reissues of three books by
     Edward Upward; discusses the writers of the 30s and the
     Auden group; makes several references to Isherwood.

11   HOSKINS, KATHARINE BAIL. <u>Today the Struggle: Literature and</u>
     <u>Politics in England during the Spanish Civil War</u>. Austin:
     University of Texas Press, pp. 164-182 and passim.
          Discusses the political themes and purposes of the three
     Auden-Isherwood plays.

12   JURAK, MIRKO. "The Group Theatre: Its Development and Signi-
     ficance for the Modern English Theatre." <u>Acta Neophilolo-</u>
     <u>gica</u>, 2:3-43.
          Auden, Isherwood, Spender and MacNeice "wished to find a
     proper medium for the expression of their feelings, thoughts
     and views, a medium that would connect them actively with
     the public. Out of this belief the Group Theatre was born
     and it was joined, or at least morally supported, by a num-
     ber of prominent artists."

13   KURDYS, DOUGLAS B. "Form in the Modern Verse Drama." Ph.D.
     dissertation, Stanford University.
          Chapter 5 centers on <u>The Ascent of F6</u>, which is seen as
     "one of the most popularly successful of the modern verse
     dramas. It is also the clearest example of the modern
     verse drama's most characteristic fault, the subordination
     of plot to another dramatic element...." [Reprinted, some-
     what revised: 1972.34.]

14   LEHMANN, JOHN. <u>In My Own Time: Memoirs of a Literary Life</u>.
     Boston: Little, Brown, passim.
          Single volume of Lehmann's autobiography; published orig-
     inally in three volumes: 1955.5; 1960.7; 1966.19.

15   LIDDELL, ROBERT. <u>Robert Liddell on the Novel</u>. Chicago: Uni-
     versity of Chicago Press, pp. 34-36.
          Contains a reprint of 1965.26.

16   MAXWELL, D. E. S. <u>Poets of the Thirties</u>. London: Routledge
     & Kegan Paul, pp. 3-4, 19, 34, 37, 40, 104, 156, 161-165,
     190.
          Comments on the Marxist slant of <u>Mr. Norris Changes</u>
     <u>Trains</u>: "Isherwood, like the other writers [of the thir-
     ties], felt the excitement of a new philosophy which ap-
     peared to leave nothing in doubt." The Auden/Isherwood
     plays are also discussed.

1969

17 PARKES, DAVID L. "Isherwood, Christopher," in Twentieth Cen-
    tury Writing: A Reader's Guide to Contemporary Literature.
    Edited by Kenneth Richardson. London: Newnes Books,
    pp. 315-316.
        Brief biographical and critical sketch: "Isherwood's
    best work is in his accounts of the social decay and moral
    decadence of pre-1939 Germany." Comments on the Berlin
    stories and Down There on a Visit.

18 REPLOGLE, JUSTIN. Auden's Poetry. Seattle: University of
    Washington Press, pp. 8, 13n, 16, 17, 18, 19, 27-28, 29, 32,
    36, 41, 45-47, 55n, 111, 112.
        Discusses the three Auden/Isherwood plays, especially On
    the Frontier, which is seen as largely Isherwood's work and
    also more Marxist in structure and theme than the earlier
    plays.

19 SAVAGE, DEREK S. "The Strange Case of W. H. Auden," in his
    The Personal Principle: Studies in Modern Poetry. Fol-
    croft, Pa.: The Folcroft Press, pp. 155-182.
        Reprint of 1944.1.

20 SELLERS, W. H. "Edward Upward: An Introduction," in The Rail-
    way Accident and Other Stories by Upward. London: William
    Heinemann, pp. vii-xxx.
        Reprint of 1963.4.

21 SMITH, GROVER. "Isherwood, Christopher" in Encyclopedia of
    World Literature in the 20th Century. Vol. 2. Edited by
    B. Fleischmann. New York: Frederick Ungar, pp. 151-152.
    Brief biographical sketch and bibliography.

22 SMITH, GROVER, ed. The Letters of Aldous Huxley. London:
    Chatto & Windus, pp. 474-476, 510-511, 621-622, 627, 629-
    630, 904.
        Contains six letters to Isherwood: 7 February 1942,
    28 July 1944, 10 April 1950, 19 July 1950, 11 August 1950,
    and 21 February 1961.

23 STRAVINSKY, IGOR and ROBERT CRAFT. Retrospectives and Conclu-
    sions. New York: Alfred A. Knopf, pp. 79, 152, 153, 154,
    233, 310, 335.
        "Virginia Woolf's likening Isherwood to a jockey is per-
    fect. Not the clothes, of course, though they are less
    conspicuously suited to Hollywood than those of Aldous or
    I.S. [Igor Stravinsky]..., but the stature, bantam weight,
    somewhat too short legs and disproportionately, even simi-
    anly long arms, a comparison forced on the attention because
    of their frequent employment for metrical purposes." [Re-
    printed: 1972.19.]

24 SULLIVAN, DAN. "'Black Girl': It May Be Preachy, But It's
    Shaw." Los Angeles Times (20 April), Sunday "Calendar"
    section, p. 26.
        Review of The Adventures of the Black Girl in Her Search
    for God: "Without changing the basic religious theme of
    the fable--Shaws's belief that man creates God in his own
    (improvable) image--Isherwood's translation and Lamont
    Johnson's Center Theatre Group production focuses more
    sharply than the original did on racial matters."

25 VIERTEL, SALKA. The Kindness of Strangers. New York: Holt,
    Rinehart and Winston, pp. 225, 241, 289, 290-291, 319.
        "Isherwood [is] one of the finest and most original
    writers. He observes very sharply, behind his mask of boy-
    ish charm.... [H]is Berlin Diary [is] a stylistic master-
    piece, the humor is quite devilish."

26 WARE, JAMES M. "Shaw's 'New' Play: The Black Girl." Shavian,
    4 (Summer), 11-15.
        "In an attempt to combine the literary solidity of Sha-
    vian drama with the dramaturgic freedom of the contemporary
    stage, Christopher Isherwood and the Minnesota Theare Com-
    pany...have produced a 'new' Shaw play, The Adventures of
    the Black Girl in Her Search for God. Mr. Isherwood fash-
    ioned a script from Shaw's story.... The Black Girl will
    not stand up to Saint Joan, but Mr. Isherwood and the Min-
    nesota Company are to be praised for attempting to force a
    topical and religious play from the wit of Shaw...."

27 WRIGHT, GEORGE T. W. H. Auden. New York: Twayne Publishers,
    pp. 13, 14, 22, 28, 30, 39, 42, 56, 59, 64-69, 85-86, 159,
    163, 166.
        The plays of Auden and Isherwood are heavily indebted to
    the theatrical techniques of Bertolt Brecht. Critical com-
    ments are made about each of the three plays, as well as
    about Journey to a War.

1970

1 Academy of Motion Picture Arts and Sciences and Writers Guild
    of America. Who Wrote the Movie: An Index of Screen Writ-
    ers and Their Film Works, 1936-1969. Edited by Leonard
    Spigelgass. Los Angeles: Ray Freidman & Co., p. 85.
        Lists Isherwood's screen credits.

2 ANON. "A Small, Civilised Country." Listener, 83 (2 April),
    448.
        A brief report of Isherwood's comments on his return to
    England, made in a TV interview.

1970

3   BROPHY, JAMES D. <u>W. H. Auden</u>. Columbia Essays on Modern
    Writers, No. 54. New York: Columbia University Press,
    pp. 40-42, 43.
        "Borders, divisions, and limits to personal freedom are
    central concerns of the three plays which Auden wrote in
    the middle thirties with Christopher Isherwood."

4   DAVISON, DENNIS. <u>W. H. Auden</u>. Literature in Perspective.
    London: Evans Brothers, pp. 134-140.
        The Auden-Isherwood plays "were valiant attempts to cre-
    ate a popular theatre at a time of European crisis, using
    devices borrowed from German cabaret sketches, Expression-
    ist drama, and surrealism...."

5   DEWSNAP, TERENCE. "Isherwood Couchant." <u>Critique: Studies
    in Modern Fiction</u>, 13, no. 1, 31-47.
        The "mental connection between relativity and eternality
    is at the core of Isherwood's later fiction; it is the
    source of the paradox of the saint-like sinner. The con-
    cept of character as variable helps to define a change in
    technique. The sharply defined Flaubert characters...have
    disappeared, to be replaced by a cast of vague presences
    existing in a world more maya than actuality."

6   FULLER, JOHN. <u>A Reader's Guide to W. H. Auden</u>. New York:
    Farrar, Straus, & Giroux, pp. 79-98 and passim.
        Extensive comments on the relative merits of the three
    Auden-Isherwood plays. Numerous references to Isherwood's
    associations, both personal and literary, with Auden.

7   GEHERIN, DAVID JOHN. "The Shaping of an Artist: A Study of
    the Novels of Christopher Isherwood." Ph.D. dissertation,
    Purdue University, 222 pp.
        Isherwood is an essentially serious novelist who employs
    a "comic manner" to balance the tragedy in his novels. The
    comedy does not diminish the serious intent of his work but,
    rather, it emphasizes the humanity of his themes and height-
    ens the impact of the tragedy. Entertaining as his work
    may be, Isherwood is an artist who "never strays from a
    profound concern with history and society, man and his
    world, life and death."

8   GRANSDEN, K. W. <u>E. M. Forster</u>. Revised edition. Edinburgh:
    Oliver & Boyd, pp. 8-9, 24-25, 30, 113, 117.
        Revision of 1962.44; no changes in the comments on Ish-
    erwood.

9   HAHNLOSER-INGOLD, MARGRIT. <u>Das englische Theater und Bert
    Brecht. Die Dramen von W. H. Auden, John Osborne, John
    Arden in ihrer Beziehung zum epischen Theater von Bert</u>

Brecht und den gemeinsamen elisabethanischen Quellen.
Schweizer Anglistische Arbeiten, 61. Bern: Francke Ver-
lag, pp. 101–112.
The Ascent of F6 and On the Frontier endure, not as a
kind of satirical picture and not as the unmasking of a
futureless social order, but as persuasive dramatic state-
ments that clothe the intentions of the authors in a completely plotted form which attains its own dramatic reality. [In German with English summary in back.]

10 HART, DEREK. "A Fortunate, Happy Life--Christopher Isherwood
Talks to Derek Hart." Listener, 83 (2 April), 449–450.
Isherwood responds to questions about his father, his
rejection of militarism, his writing of screen plays, his
"identification" with the main character of A Single Man,
and his life in California, including his study of Hindu
philosophy.

11 HAZARD, FORREST E. "The Ascent of F6: A New Interpretation."
Tennessee Studies in Literature, 15:165–175.
Michael Ransom was patterned after T. E. Lawrence and
was intended to be portrayed as "a modern version of the
mythical hero," not a failure and not just a victim of a
mother-fixation or a lust for power.

12 HEILBRUN, CAROLYN G. Christopher Isherwood. Columbia Essays
on Modern Writers, No. 53. New York: Columbia University
Press, 48 pp.
"Since Christopher Isherwood has been denied, or spared,
the gifts of widespread fame or fashion, it is appropriate
to begin with the pronouncement that he is the best British
novelist of his generation.... Neither as witty as Waugh's
nor as intense as Orwell's, his fictions have achieved the
integrity of art while illuminating the human tensions of
our time. Muted in tone, self-effacing in manner, his
works continue to make a quiet but persistent claim on our
attention."

*13 LEHANE, BRENDAN. "Isherwood Plays a Guessing Game." London
Daily Telegraph (7 August), colour supplement, pp. 18–20.
Cited: British Humanities Index 1970, p. 215.

14 MAES-JELINEK, HENA. Criticism of Society in the English Novel
between the Wars. Paris: Société d'Editions "Les Belles
Lettres," pp. 449–471.
"The early novels and stories of Christopher Isherwood
are, like the period they so well mirror, full of a promise
that was never fulfilled. Within their limits, however,
they are also a unique expression of the spirit and moods
of the inter-war period."

1970

15 M[ALKIN], M[ARY] A[NN] [O'BRIAN]. Review of <u>Lions and Shadows</u>.
    <u>AB Bookmans' Weekly</u>, 45 (16 March), 855.
       "A romantic trip back to London Bohemia of the Twenties."

16 ROBSON, W. W. <u>Modern English Literature</u>. London: Oxford
    University Press, pp. 126, 128, 134-135, 157.
       Review of Isherwood's work from <u>All the Conspirators</u> to
    <u>Down There on a Visit</u>; feels that "Isherwood's best work is
    neat, spare, limited" but that his later works are "col-
    oured by Californian eccentricity and religiosity."

17 THOMAS, DAVID P. "The Fiction of Christopher Isherwood: Per-
    sonality as Form." Ph.D. dissertation, State University of
    New York at Binghamton, 375 pp.
       "The subject of Isherwood's fiction from beginning to
    end has been the drama of self-consciousness. Nothing is
    served by glibly announcing that the neurotic's search for
    wholeness finds a natural haven in mysticism, that Freud
    and Ramakrishna are complementary 'cures'.... To read Ish--
    erwood for his subtlety as a psychoanalyst, political com-
    mentator, <u>guru</u>, is to be disappointed. But the continuing
    history of his neurotic hero is expressive of the changing
    modes of identity of our time: the self which is both ex-
    istentially and <u>sub specie aeternitatis</u>, stubbornly wrest-
    ling for the unitive life. It is in these terms Isherwood
    should be judged."

18 WARD, A. C. <u>Longman Companion to Twentieth Century Literature</u>.
    London: Longman Group, p. 276.
       Biographical sketch.

19 WHITE, ERIC WALTER. <u>Benjamin Britten: His Life and Operas</u>.
    Berkeley: University of California Press, pp. 23, 25, 26,
    30.
       Revised edition of 1949.18.

20 WILDE, ALAN. "Irony and Style: The Example of Christopher
    Isherwood." <u>Modern Fiction Studies</u>, 16 (Winter), 475-489.
       <u>Lions and Shadows</u> is full of irony and disguise; its
    theme is "the failure to establish contact between the self
    and the world." The book is finally a "validation of it-
    self" rather than of the life it records.

21 WILLETT, JOHN. <u>Expressionism</u>. New York: McGraw-Hill,
    pp. 215-216.
       "A growing English awareness of the 1920s in Germany is
    reflected in Auden's...plays with Christopher Isherwood and
    in Isherwood's Berlin stories.... These were early symp-
    toms of the change of temper which was to develop after the
    Second World War."

22 WOOLF, LEONARD. The Journey Not the Arrival Matters: An
    Autobiography of the Years 1939-1969. New York: Harcourt,
    Brace & World, pp. 103-105.
        Discusses Isherwood's part in the publication of New
    Writing (1938-1939).

1971

1 ALTMAN, DENNIS. Homosexual: Oppression and Liberation. New
    York: Outerbridge & Dienstfrey, pp. 13, 18, 20, 26-28, 38,
    218, 219.
        "The bitterness/irony/amusement that go to make up the
    sensibility of the homosexual who moves continually between
    a gay and a straight world is perfectly caught in...A Sin-
    gle Man, a book that is...a much finer exploration of the
    homosexual sensibility than more touted works...." Also
    mentions Kathleen and Frank, A Meeting by the River, and
    The World in the Evening.

2 ANON. "The Berlin Stories," in Survey of Contemporary Litera-
    ture. Vol. 1. Edited by Frank N. Magill. New York: Salem
    Press, pp. 374-376.
        The Berlin Stories "image realistically the rottenness,
    restlessness, and lack of direction which possessed Berlin
    in the dying days of the German republic."

3 ANON. "Isherwood in Search of His Parents." Times Literary
    Supplement (22 October), p. 1338.
        "Kathleen and Frank is a dual-purpose book: Isherwood
    in Search of his Parents, and Christopher in Search of
    Himself.... In Christopher Isherwood's books, his parents
    and families appeared not as they were, but as projections
    of his fantasy. But when his mother died and he was
    planning what he called The Autobiography of My Books on
    the relation between his own life and his literary subject
    matter, he found it necessary to study his own life and
    family in depth; and this is what he has done, with the
    result that at last there is a family reconciliation."

4 ANON. "The Isherwood Saga." Economist, 241 (6 November),
    "Autumn Books" section [after p. 58], xiv.
        In Kathleen and Frank "the relevance of [Isherwood's]
    parents, his ancestors, his heritage, to his own mature
    self came home so powerfully to the maverick son that he
    has constructed from fragments of the past a memorial that
    does justice to all concerned."

1971

5   ANON. Review of <u>Kathleen and Frank</u>. <u>Kirkus Reviews</u>, 39
      (1 November), 1193.
          In <u>Kathleen and Frank</u> "the diary entries are brief,
      perishable as they so often are, but the interpolations of
      Christopher do much to fill out their collective experi-
      ence...."

6   BAYLEY, JOHN. "The Author's Parents." <u>Manchester Guardian
      Weekly</u>, 105 (6 November), 25.
          "The sense of the past—that potent gift handed from
      mother to son—fills [<u>Kathleen and Frank</u>] with an extra-
      ordinary detail and animation, ramifying out through the
      mother's and father's families: the gaiety of 'Lions and
      Shadows' reproduces itself on an immensely spacious Ed-
      wardian scale."

7   BUCKLE, RICHARD. "The House of Isherwood." <u>Books and Book-
      men</u>, 17 (December), 36-37.
          <u>Kathleen and Frank</u> is Isherwood's "atonement" for his
      rebellion against his parents and their society. "Neither
      Kathleen nor Frank were [sic] extraordinary people—and
      yet! what is more extraordinary than an ordinary person?
      Christopher's gift is to illuminate the everyday."

8   BURGESS, ANTHONY. <u>The Novel Now: A Student's Guide to Con-
      temporary Fiction</u>. London: Faber and Faber, pp. 114-116,
      119-120.
          Reprint of 1967.19.

9   FRY, PHILLIP and JAMES W. LEE. "An Interview in Austin with
      John Lehmann." <u>Studies in the Novel</u>, 3 (Spring), 80-96.
          "I think [Isherwood] has written some absolutely bril-
      liant things since [the 1930s]. <u>Prater Violet</u> struck me as
      a very brilliant work which prefigured something new in
      Isherwood, his preoccupation with Vedanta and Eastern re-
      ligion.... I think <u>A Single Man</u> is a most remarkable book.
      I think it is a marvellously designed book."

10   FULLER, ROY. "The Making of Herr Issyvoo." <u>Listener</u>, 86
      (21 October), 545-546.
          <u>Kathleen and Frank</u> is an "unexpected and extraordinary
      book." The narrative about Isherwood's parents is strong
      and interesting. The personal revelations are equally in-
      triguing but disappointing because they indicate "a vein
      of feeling and power that [Isherwood's] fiction has not
      succeeded in fully mining."

11   HAMARD, J. "Christopher Isherwood et l'Allegmagne: Un
      itinéraine spirituel." <u>Revue de Littérature Comparée</u>, 45
      (Octobre-Décembre), 514-540.
          It is only with <u>A Single Man</u> and <u>A Meeting by the River</u>
      that Isherwood takes up localities other than Germany or

or Germanic countries for the scene (total or partial) of his novels. This German theme, not studied up to now, seems to provide us with an interesting subject for consideration, since it is almost central to the novels of Isherwood and because it is generally looked upon as the best mirror for an entire generation of British literature. [In French.]

12   [JOHNSTON, ALBERT]. Review of Kathleen and Frank. Publisher's Weekly, 200 (15 November), 69.
       While Kathleen and Frank provides a "fascinating record" of the lives of the author's parents, "the remarkable aspect of this memoir is Isherwood's own interpretations, which run counterpoint to his parents' story...."

13   OLSON, RICHARD D.   Review of Kathleen and Frank. Library Journal, 96 (1 October), 3126.
       "Although readers may feel that there are far too many minutiae here about the parents and too few facts about the author, one can derive considerable understanding of the author and his works...." [Reprinted: 1972.45.]

14   RABAN, JONATHAN. "A Born Narrator." New Statesman, 82 (22 October), 546-547.
       "Kathleen and Frank is [Isherwood's] English estate, his share of the past.... [I]t provides a place where the son can posthumously meet his parents.... It has a feline obliquity of method, and it should sit squarely beside the best of Isherwood's novels."

15   RATCLIFFE, MICHAEL. "All the Conspirators are Exorcized: Isherwood Greets His Family Ghosts." London Times (21 October), p. 12.
       "Kathleen and Frank challenges the mythology that mourning-mother and hero-father engendered in All the Conspirators and The Memorial, and shatters those dim icons with much sparkling written evidence; it enacts a rite of love and reparation...."

16   ROSS, ANGUS. "Isherwood, Christopher (William Bradshaw)," in The Penguin Companion to English Literature. Edited by David Daiches. New York: McGraw-Hill, p. 272.
       Biographical sketch and summary of literary career. Comment on the Berlin stories: "The technique of the observer ('Issyvoo'), 'I am a camera,' fits the [episodic] method of telling the story and also provides a powerful moral element in the books...."

*17   THORNE, NICOLA. "Christopher Isherwood in Conversation with Nicola Thorne." Vogue, 15, Nos. 2060-2128 (November), 154-155.
       Cited: Orphanos, 1976.25. Cannot locate.

1971

18 WEBB, W. L. "Top Shelf of the Year." Manchester Guardian
    Weekly, 105 (25 December), 18.
        List of the year's best books: In Kathleen and Frank,
    "Isherwood has produced a memoir of almost Proustian full-
    ness and intimacy."

19 WILDE, ALAN. Christopher Isherwood. Twayne's United States
    Author Series, No. 173. New York: Twayne Publishers,
    171 pp.
        "Isherwood is concerned throughout his career with the
    ego's attempts to overcome its detachment and to break
    through to the genuine forms of life." The broad spectrum
    of his work presents a "developing literary experiment in
    detecting the disguises and subterfuges of the protean
    self." While Isherwood's "most remarkable achievement has
    to do with the inventiveness and versatility of his han-
    dling of technique," the important fact is that "all of his
    techniques are carefully used to force the reader into
    discovering and constructing for himself the shape of char-
    acter and meaning."

20 WILSON, ANGUS. "Issyvoo and His Parents." London Observer
    (24 October), p. 36.
        "[T]he most delightful aspect of Kathleen and Frank is
    the degree to which the result transcends on so many levels
    the somewhat banal expectations of personnel and milieu....
    What does the book tell us about one of our best living
    novelists? Well, of course, that, although he rejected his
    mother's obsession with the past, renounced England, Cheshire
    and Kensington, they work in and through him all the time
    to his benefit."

21 WILSON, COLIN. "Detached Retina." Spectator, 227 (27 Novem-
    ber), 767-768.
        Kathleen and Frank is "in some ways...a labour of
    hate.... Isherwood's slightly hostile detachment, far from
    spoiling the story, brings out the tragedy and deepens the
    reader's involvement.... For me it also had the effect of
    pulling all Isherwood's other books into focus...."

1972

1 AMORY, CLEVELAND. "Trade Winds." Saturday Review, 55 (19 February), 10.
       Isherwood responds briefly to questions about his par-
   ents, his trip to China, his life in America, and his work
   in Hollywood.

2   ANON. "Isherwood, Christopher (William)." <u>Current Biography</u>,
      33 (October), 18-20.
          "In the guise of an unengaged observer of events around
      him, during the 1930's Christopher Isherwood narrated his
      Berlin stories. In their clarity, crispness, enduring ap-
      peal, and light-fingered grasp of an historic crisis, they
      have both rewarded and plagued him for years as the touch-
      stone for his later work." [Reprinted: 1973.1.]

3   ANON. "Isherwood, Christopher (1904)," in <u>McGraw-Hill Encyclo-
      pedia of World Drama</u>. Volume 2. New York: McGraw-Hill
      Book Co., p. 415.
          Summary of Isherwood's career; comments and summary of
      the Auden-Isherwood plays are included in the Auden entry
      (vol. 1, p. 109).

4   ANON. "Notable Nominations." <u>American Libraries</u>, 3 (June),
      681.
          Publication notice of <u>Kathleen and Frank</u>.

5   ANON. Review of <u>Kathleen and Frank</u>. <u>Booklist</u>, 68 (1 April),
      645.
          <u>Kathleen and Frank</u> "reveals the author's prolonged re-
      bellion against his past and his recently made peace with
      it.... [It is a] volume for Isherwood enthusiasts or read-
      ers interested in personal histories and the Edwardian
      years."

6   ANON. Review of <u>Kathleen and Frank</u>. <u>Choice</u>, 9 (November),
      1130.
          <u>Kathleen and Frank</u> is "awkwardly arranged, self-indul-
      gent, and rather charming to a limited audience.... [Ish-
      erwood] rather tosses his head about his homosexuality,
      and again the book indicts the educational system of
      English upper and middle classes, which seems never to
      change for the better."

7   ANON. Review of <u>Kathleen and Frank</u>. <u>New Yorker</u>, 47 (22 Jan-
      uary), 100.
          "The narrative [of <u>Kathleen and Frank</u>] is entrancing;
      its art also creates one of those confusions about time
      that are commoner in real life than in science fiction, for
      Isherwood's memories of his parents' way of life are so
      vivid that it is impossible to believe that everything...
      has vanished entirely, and equally impossible to believe
      that that life...existed within this century."

8   ANON. "A Selection of Recent Titles." <u>New York Times Book
      Review</u> (4 June), p. 16.
          <u>Kathleen and Frank</u> is listed among titles "in the main
      fields of reader interest": "Using his own mother's

1972

diaries and his own memory, a son tells, with novelistic
imagination, of the early family life that charted his own
future course, culminating in a moving reconciliation...."

9   AUDEN, W. H. "The Diary of a Diary." New York Review of
Books, 18 (27 January), 19-20.
"As I read it, Kathleen and Frank is [Isherwood's] attempt, wholly successful in my opinion, to solve his Integrity crisis." The diaries and letters are enlivened by
Christopher's trenchant comments and revealing explana-
tions. "I cannot imagine any reader, whatever his social
background and interests, not being enthralled by it."

10 BELL, PEARL K. "Isherwood Remembers Mama." New Leader, 55
(24 January), 17-18.
Review of Kathleen and Frank: "The debt Isherwood attempts to settle in this remarkably candid book is his
realization that if not for his mother's obstinate opposition, he might well have become the respectable citizen she
wanted him to be."

11 BLOOMFIELD, BARRY C. and EDWARD MENDELSON. W. H. Auden: A
Bibliography, 1924-1969. Second edition. Charlottesville:
University Press of Virginia, pp. 1, 3, 14-19, 20-24, 30,
34-36, 37-40, 52, 53, 62, 63, 95, 102, 186, 187, 225, 245,
252, 260, 269, 278, 330, 331.
Updates and expands 1964.13, adding data on paperback
editions, reviews, radio and TV productions and appear-
ances, and recordings.

12 BLYTHE, RONALD. "An Oblique Autobiography and a Lesson on How
to Handle the Family Records." New York Times Book Review
(23 January), pp. 3, 10.
"An oblique autobiography, an intriguing parade of those
confident attitudes which, not so long ago, all the best
Anglo-Saxons struck as a matter of course, a lesson on how
to handle the family records, 'Kathleen and Frank' is all
of these. Candor of the kind most of us take good care to
grow out of lights up everything."

13 BORKLUND, ELMER. "Isherwood, Christopher," in Contemporary
Novelists. Edited by James Vinson. New York: St. Martin's, pp. 662-667.
"There are a number of valid ways of describing Christopher Isherwood's achievements over the past forty years,
but it is the theme of rebellion and growth which dominates
everything he has written.... Isherwood's career has been
spent in the service of sending extraordinary, synoptic
postcards from crucial places at crucial times...." [Re-
printed: 1976.6.]

14   BOWLES, PAUL. <u>Without Stopping: An Autobiography</u>. New York:
      G. P. Putnam's Sons, pp. 109, 110, 114, 215, 331.
      "I soon found that Isherwood with Spender was a very
      different person from Isherwood by himself. Together they
      were overwhelmingly British, two members of a secret soci-
      ety constantly making references to esoteric data not
      available to outsiders."

15   CATINELLA, JOSEPH. Review of <u>Kathleen and Frank</u>. <u>Saturday
      Review</u>, 55 (22 January), 66.
      "<u>Kathleen and Frank</u> was written so that its author might
      examine the relationship between his art and his life....
      With humor and grace, Isherwood the rebel pays final homage
      to his mother and father, finding in their vigorous natures
      his own instinct for not only enduring life but...enjoying
      it."

16   CONSTABLE, ROSALIND. "Home Again." <u>Book World</u>, 6 (23 Janu-
      ary), 5.
      Review of <u>Kathleen and Frank</u>: "This often moving auto-
      biography of [Isherwood's] family in relation to himself is
      an act of piety and even of atonement."

17   COOK, BRUCE. "Isherwood: 'I Tried to See My Parents as Peo-
      ple in a Novel.'" <u>National Observer</u>, 11 (19 February), 29.
      Interview with Isherwood and review of <u>Kathleen and
      Frank</u>: "[B]ooks about parents are seldom satisfying. The
      worst are acts of filial devotion; the best are a kind of
      settling of accounts.... Although it is closer in spirit
      to the second sort, <u>Kathleen and Frank</u> is quite different
      in shape from both. It is very like a novel...; it is very
      much a Nineteenth Century novel."

18   COOPER, ARTHUR. "Bringing up a Camera." <u>Newsweek</u>, 79
      (17 January), 77-79.
      While the title characters of <u>Kathleen and Frank</u> "emerge
      as stuffy, very dull Victorians," the "central character of
      this literary psychodrama is novelist Isherwood," who "re-
      veals himself in a graceful narrative about the diaries and
      letters and in a penetrating, cathartic afterword."

19   CRAFT, ROBERT. <u>Stravinsky: Chronicle of a Friendship 1948-
      1971</u>. New York: Alfred A. Knopf, pp. 9, 11-13, 19, 48,
      93, 105, 298, 356, 369.
      Reprints diary entries from 1969.23; adds one or two
      mentions of Isherwood.

20   DELDERFIELD, R. F. "70 Years of English Foibles." <u>Life</u>, 72
      (28 January), 18.
      <u>Kathleen and Frank</u> is "an outstanding memorial to the
      day-to-day lives of [Isherwood's] mother and his war-hero

1972

father...." Isherwood saw the faults in his relatives "with a candor of a rebel revolting against the cult of the past and accepted these oddly fascinating people as considerable characters in their own right."

*21 DELFINO, RITA. "The Camera Speaks." New York Post (17 February), p. 45.
Interview. Cited: Orphanos, 1976.25.

22 DRAKE, SYLVIE. "'River' Billed at the Mark Taylor." Los Angeles Times (23 April), Sunday "Calendar" section, p. 38.
Report on the anticipated opening of the dramatic version of A Meeting by the River at the Mark Taper Forum in Los Angeles; includes comments by Isherwood, who describes the work as a "religious comedy."

23 DUCHENE, FRANÇOIS. The Case of the Helmeted Airman: A Study of W. H. Auden's Poetry. London: Chatto & Windus, pp. 48, 50, 64, 73-75, 85, 98-99, 104, 110, 115-116, 120.
The Dog Beneath the Skin is the "most interesting" of the Auden-Isherwood plays. But its "surrealist abruptness owes less to anarchic depths than to the fact that its looseness of structure and freedom from the unities make it an ideal vehicle for dramatising moral abstractions."

24 DZENITIS, SIGURDS. Die Rezeption deutscher Literatur in England durch Wystan Hugh Auden, Stephen Spender und Christopher Isherwood. Geistes- und Sozialwissenschaftliche Dissertationen 21. Hamburg: H. Lüdke, pp. 22-57.
Brecht was Auden and Isherwood's leader in the development of a new dramatic form, and he recognized their kinship with him. Isherwood's translations of Brecht's mottoes (in A Penny for the Poor) do not lack a certain verbal felicity, but they go beyond the literal meanings, making the verses more accessible but giving them a more general significance. [In German.]

25 EARLE, ANITA. "Writing for the Stage Is 'Like Painting with a Broom.'" San Francisco Sunday Examiner and Chronicle (21 May), "Date Book" section, pp. 7-8.
Isherwood discusses the play version of A Meeting by the River: "I think we've opened out the characters so that you hear from Patrick's victims, as you never do in the book. And I do like the idea at the end, both sides think they've won, and that's spelled out in the play."

26 EDWARDS, SYDNEY. "Sally: Still No. 1 with Isherwood." London Evening Standard (4 February), p. 18.
Interview: Isherwood comments on his creation of Sally Bowles and expresses his optimism about the film version of

<u>Cabaret</u>, especially about the choice of Michael York to play the "Isherwood" character.

*27 FLEMING, ANNE TAYLOR. "Christopher Isherwood, He Is a Camera." <u>LA: Womens' Liberation Newsletter</u>, 23 (9 December), 14-16.
Cited: Orphanos, 1976.25.

28 GEHERIN, DAVID J. "An Interview with Christopher Isherwood." <u>Journal of Narrative Technique</u>, 2 (September), 143-158.
Interview took place 17 March 1972 in Isherwood's home in Santa Monica. Discusses the use of narrators, point of view, autobiographical content, and other matters of technique.

29 GILL, RICHARD. <u>Happy Rural Seat</u>. New Haven: Yale University Press, pp. 135, 160-163.
In <u>The Memorial</u> Isherwood documented "the malaise which spread through England after the war.... For Isherwood, as for Huxley and Lawrence and Waugh, the demise of the country house dramatizes the material, social, and moral bankruptcy of the old order in a new era."

30 GRESH, BERNARD S. Review of <u>Kathleen and Frank</u>. <u>America</u>, 126 (19 February), 184.
"Although <u>Kathleen and Frank</u> is worth reading, one only wishes that Isherwood's commentary, not the diaries and letters, dominated the book."

31 KARL, FREDERICK R. <u>A Reader's Guide to the Contemporary English Novel.</u> Revised edition. New York: Farrar, Straus, Giroux, pp. 9, 274, 288-290.
Revision of 1962.53; no change in the text on Isherwood.

32 KAUFFMANN, STANLEY. "The Past in the Present." <u>New Republic</u>, 166 (15 January), 25-27.
Beyond the "obvious pleasure" of seeing change and advent as they happen, <u>Kathleen and Frank</u> offers "four other kinds of reward": "social insight"; "the way the diaries were written"; the comments of "Isherwood the observer"; and "the seen-unseen protagonist, Isherwood himself."

33 KIRSCH, ROBERT. "Writer Confronts His Past, Debunks Childhood Myths." <u>Los Angeles Times</u> (18 January), part IV, p. 3.
"Myths of childhood die hard. People use them defensively. To confront them is an act of courage and that is precisely what Christopher Isherwood does in <u>Kathleen and Frank</u>, part a memoir of his parents, part an essay in self-analysis."

1972

34 KURDYS, DOUGLAS B. Form in the Modern Verse Drama. Salzburg
    Studies in English Literature: Poetic Drama, No. 17.
    Salzburg: Institut für Englische Sprache und Literatur,
    pp. 168-192.
        Reprint, somewhat revised, of 1969.13.

35 LASK, THOMAS. "Isherwood Looks at an English Era." New York
    Times (15 February), p. 26.
        Isherwood discusses the writing of Kathleen and Frank
    and his present life in America; he also comments on his
    homosexuality and his teaching.

36 LASK, THOMAS. "Some Notes for the Record." New York Times
    (21 January), p. 43.
        In Kathleen and Frank, Isherwood is "able to perform an
    act of piety, make a gesture of reconciliation to his par-
    ents he would not have been able to make when they were
    alive and younger.... His own comments are puckish and far
    from reverential, but the book is a memoir that is also an
    apology."

37 [LOTTMAN, EILEEN]. Review of Kathleen and Frank. Publisher's
    Weekly, 202 (4 December), 63.
        The letters, diaries, and Isherwood's "interjected mem-
    ories" in Kathleen and Frank "form the living pattern of a
    true story of generations that combines mystery, biography,
    romance, tragedy--and all the other parts of well-lived
    lives."

38 LUMLEY, FREDERICK. New Trends in 20th Century Drama: A Survey
    Since Ibsen and Shaw. 4th revised edition. New York: Ox-
    ford University Press, p. 81.
        Revised version of 1956.3.

39 McLEOD, STUART R. Modern Verse Drama. Salzburg Studies in
    English Literature: Poetic Drama, No. 2. Salzburg: In-
    stitut für Englische Sprache und Literatur, pp. 85, 88,
    150-155, 281-283.
        Reprint, somewhat revised, of 1961.4.

40 MATLAW, MYRON. "Isherwood, Christopher," in his Modern World
    Drama: An Encyclopedia. New York: E. P. Dutton, p. 398.
        Biographical summary.

41 MAUGHAM, ROBIN. Escape from the Shadows: His Autobiography.
    London: Hodder and Stoughton, pp. 106, 203.
        Maugham records his first meeting with Isherwood, his
    associations with Auden, and his encounters with Gerald
    Hamilton.

42   MITCHELL, DONALD and HANS KELLER, eds. <u>Benjamin Britten: A</u>
      <u>Commentary on His Works from a Group of Specialists</u>. West-
      port: Greenwood Press, pp. 12, 289, 298, 299, 311.
          Reprint of 1952.5.

*43   MOAN, MARGARET A. "Auden and His Audience: A Stylistic Study
      of W. H. Auden's Poetry in the Nineteen Thirties." Ph.D.
      dissertation, Temple University.
          Chapter Three includes a discussion of <u>The Dog Beneath</u>
      <u>the Skin</u>; Chapter Four includes <u>Journey to a War</u>. [<u>Disser-</u>
      <u>tation Abstracts International</u>, 32 (June 1972), 6991A.]

44   NAGARAJAN, S. "Christopher Isherwood and the Vedantic Novel:
      A Study of <u>A Single Man</u>." <u>Ariel: A Review of International</u>
      <u>English Literature</u>, 3, no. 4, 63-71.
          "The Vedanta of Samkara cannot, by definition, be real-
      ized in a novel. Pure consciousness is beyond the <u>chitta-</u>
      <u>vrittis</u>--which are all that language can cope with--and <u>A</u>
      <u>Single Man</u> copes with them very successfully indeed....
      The <u>chitta-vrittis</u> are described as if they were objects of
      perception, leading to the inference that there is per-
      ceiver other than the <u>chitta</u>. This is the Vedantic core of
      Isherwood's novel."

45   OLSON, RICHARD D. Review of <u>Kathleen and Frank</u>, in <u>The Li-</u>
      <u>brary Journal Book Reviews 1971</u>. New York: R. R. Bowker,
      p. 114.
          Reprint of 1971.13.

46   PARKER, DOROTHY L. "Love in the Afternoon's Mail." <u>Christian</u>
      <u>Science Monitor</u> (17 February), p. 9.
          In <u>Kathleen and Frank</u>, Isherwood "takes an urbane,
      slightly roguish pleasure in his own youthful rebellion
      against the rigid caste system into which he was born; he
      is a model of temperate reasonableness about his decision
      to become expatriate and his early escapade with Marxism."

47   SCOBIE, W. I. "England in Los Angeles." <u>National Review</u>, 24
      (4 August), 859-860.
          The play version of <u>A Meeting by the River</u> is "bril-
      liant," "quizzical," and a "confrontation piece." In the
      end neither side wins, but the meeting has altered and en-
      hanced the participants.

48   SHEPARD, RICHARD F. "Stage: A Series Begins." <u>New York</u>
      <u>Times</u> (20 December), p. 54.
          Review of a New York performance of the play version of
      <u>A Meeting by the River</u>: "The authors are really interested
      in relationships among people, between two brothers, the
      wife, the mother, the boy, the swamis in the monastery. A
      layer of hypocrisy is peeled off to find a layer of honesty,

which turns out to be another layer of insincerity....
These constantly shifting triangles and relationships make
an over-all interesting but wordy evening, one that slumps
into troughs of tedium."

49 SIGGINS, CLARA M. Review of Kathleen and Frank. Best Sellers,
31 (15 February), 503.
"Christopher's comments show him to be subtle, refined,
accurate and penetrating."

50 SNOW, C. P. "'Kathleen and Frank': True-to-Life 'Forsythe
Saga.'" Washington Post (22 January), p. B6.
"All the emotional entanglements of this story...Isher-
wood affectionately scrutinizes, analyzes, comments on,
with delicacy but extreme shrewdness, the effect totally
free of insipidity...."

51 THOMAS, DAVID P. "Goodbye to Berlin: Refocusing Isherwood's
Camera." Contemporary Literature, 13 (Winter), 44-52.
The "I am a Camera" passage should not be equated with
the role that Isherwood plays as narrator of his novels.
The true theme of Isherwood's work is "a search for con-
tact, for participation in the lives of others."

52 WENNERSTEN, ROBERT. "Christopher Isherwood." Transatlantic
Review, nos. 42 & 43 (Spring-Summer), pp. 5-21.
Isherwood discusses many of his works--Kathleen and
Frank, Prater Violet, A Meeting by the River, and A Single
Man; also talks of homosexuality, Forster, the difference
between British and American writers, and his film writing.

53 WORTH, KATHARINE J. Revolution in Modern English Drama. London: G. Bell & Sons, pp. ix, 58, 105, 108-112, 117.
The Dog Beneath the Skin and The Ascent of F6 cannot be
properly appreciated without the music hall/revue treatment. They deserve more attention from the professional
theatre.

1973

1 ANON. "Isherwood, Christopher (William)," in Current Biogra-
phy Yearbook 1972. Edited by Charles Moritz. New York:
H. W. Wilson, pp. 235-238.
Reprint of 1972.2.

2 ANON. "Paperback Short List." The Sunday Times (1 July),
p. 39.
Publication notice of paperback edition of Journey to a
War: Auden and Isherwood "chose to report on the Sino-
Japanese War in a long, lucid travel diary, gentle among
the grimmest scenes."

3 ANON. Review of <u>Frankenstein: The True Story</u>. <u>Publisher's</u>
   <u>Weekly</u>, 204 (1 October), 84.
   "The story here is more complex and Freudian [than
   older versions]...."

4 BEDFORD, SYBILLE. <u>Aldous Huxley: A Biography, Volume One:</u>
   <u>1894-1939</u>. London: Chatto and Windus, pp. 361, 376-377,
   381.
   "Christopher Isherwood first came to Hollywood that
   summer [1939], under contract to a studio. As an old
   friend of Gerald [Heard]'s he soon met Aldous and Maria
   who quickly became very fond of him. They liked him, as
   the saying goes, for himself." [Reprinted as part of
   1974.3.]

5 BELL, ARTHUR. "Christopher Isherwood: No Parades." <u>New York</u>
   <u>Times Book Review</u> (25 March), pp. 10, 12, 14.
   Isherwood responds to questions about gay liberation,
   his revelation of his own homosexuality in <u>Kathleen and</u>
   <u>Frank</u>, and his 19-year relationship with his male lover.
   Comments on <u>A Single Man</u> and <u>Cabaret</u>.

6 BELL, ARTHUR. "An Interview with Christopher Isherwood."
   <u>Fag Rag</u> (Boston), no. 5 (Summer), pp. 4-5.
   Isherwood discusses his homosexuality, the autobiographical element of his work, political fiction, and the effect
   of "concealment" on creating literature. <u>The Berlin Stor-</u>
   <u>ies</u> is the only work discussed.

7 BLADES, JOE. "The Evolution of <u>Cabaret</u>." <u>Literature/Film</u>
   <u>Quarterly</u>, 1 (Spring), 226-238.
   "Sally Bowles and her compatriots have...had more incar-
   nations than almost any other figures of contemporary literature." The incisive character portraits and the strong
   evocation of period and mood have contributed to the successful translations of Isherwood's stories into other
   media.

8 BROCKETT, OSCAR G. and ROBERT R. FINDLAY. <u>Century of Innova-</u>
   <u>tion: A History of European and American Theatre and Drama</u>
   <u>Since 1870</u>. Englewood Cliffs, N.J.: Prentice-Hall,
   pp. 476-477.
   The major works of the Group Theatre were those of Auden
   and Isherwood, the most successful of which was <u>The Ascent</u>
   <u>of F6.</u>

9 BUELL, FREDERICK. <u>W. H. Auden as a Social Poet</u>. Ithaca, N.Y.:
   Cornell University Press, pp. 43-54, 131-135 and passim.
   Isherwood is frequently cited for interpretation of
   Auden's poetry, particularly the "gang myth" of the Mortmere

stories that <u>Lions and Shadows</u> explicates. The development in the political thought of the Auden/Isherwood plays is also discussed.

10 FUEGI, JOHN. [Critical essay on Auden's plays] in <u>Contemporary Dramatists</u>. Edited by James Vinson. New York: St. Martin's Press, pp. 54-56.

"The extreme and explicit social, indeed socialist commentary which totally permeates every line of <u>Dance of Death</u> and <u>The Dog Beneath the Skin</u> is somewhat modified in Auden and Isherwood's <u>The Ascent of F6</u>.... The drift towards religion and away from politics that is evident in <u>The Ascent of F6</u> is somewhat less apparent in...<u>On the Frontier</u>...."

11 GERSTENBERGER, DONNA. <u>The Complex Configuration: Modern Verse Drama</u>. Salzburg Studies in English Literature: Poetic Drama, No. 5. Salzburg: Institut für Englische Sprache und Literatur, pp. 78-90.

Reprint, somewhat revised, of 1958.3.

12 JURAK, MIRKO. "Dramatic Concepts of the English Group Theatre: The Totality of Artistic Involvement." <u>Modern Drama</u>, 16 (June), 81-86.

Auden and Isherwood closely followed the stated norms of the Group Theatre in <u>The Dog Beneath the Skin</u>, and to a lesser degree in their other two plays.

13 KRAMER, HILTON. <u>The Age of the Avant-Garde: An Art Chronicle of 1956-1972</u>. New York: Farrar, Straus, and Giroux, p. 468.

In the double portrait of Isherwood and Don Bachardy, David Hockney "offers us pictorial sociabilities of a high order, at once amused and disabused, very much a part of the milieu they depict and yet detached enough to be witty, precise, and...a little cruel."

14 LEYLAND, WINSTON. "Christopher Isherwood: An Interview." <u>Gay Sunshine: A Newspaper of Gay Liberation</u>, no. 19 (September-October), pp. 1-3.

Isherwood discusses his works, especially <u>The Berlin Stories</u> and <u>Kathleen and Frank</u>, and comments on his homosexuality and how he portrayed it in his early works.

15 RILEY, CAROLYN, ed. <u>Contemporary Literary Criticism</u>. Volume 1. Detroit: Gale Research Co., pp. 155-157.

Excerpts from seven critical books and articles on Isherwood: 1962.53; 1964.2; 1967.19; 1970.5; 1971.19; 1972.15; 1972.51.

16 SCOBIE, W. I. "Theatre: Fat Hollywood in Hungry Bengal."
London Magazine, NS 13 (April/May), 137-144.
Discusses Isherwood's early life in America, his involvement with Vedantic philosophy, and, primarily, his
dramatic adaptation of A Meeting by the River. The play is
summarized and commented upon, particularly its differences
from the novel.

17 SEYMOUR-SMITH, MARTIN. Funk & Wagnalls Guide to Modern World
Literature. New York: Funk & Wagnalls, pp. 263, 290, 293.
[British title: Guide to Modern World Literature.]
"Christopher Isherwood (1904), once a great hope of English fiction, petered out into a skilful and intelligent
entertainer--a novelist of high quality, but not of the
first or perhaps even the second rank. His genius all but
vanished, possibly under the pressure of personal problems,
in a cloud of mysticism...."

18 SMITH, CECIL. "He Walks While a Monster Stalks." Los Angeles
Times (23 May), part IV, p. 18.
Interview in which Isherwood discusses the TV production
of Frankenstein: The True Story and the Writers Guild
strike, for which he walked the picket line.

19 SMITH, S. M. "Isherwood, Christopher," in Webster's New World
Companion to English and American Literature. London:
International Press; New York: World Publishing, pp. 355-
356.
Survey of Isherwood's career with brief critical comments
on both the plays and novels: "When his writing is more
personal, it parades a bruised vulnerability which limits
its appeal...." [Reprinted: 1976.34.]

20 WATSON, ALAN HULL. "Mysterious East." Spectator, 231 (8
September), 316.
Review of Vedanta for Modern Man: "a rare garland of
priceless jewels, gathered together in exposition and interpretation of Vedanta." Comments on the study of Vedanta
as an aid in the interpretation of Christianity.

1974

1 ANON. "Isherwood, Christopher," in The Reader's Adviser: A
Layman's Guide to Literature. 12th edition. Edited by
Sarah L. Prakken. New York: R. R. Bowker, vol. 1, pp. 214,
462-463; vol. 2, p. 76; vol. 3, pp. 145, 147.
Brief biographical summary and bibliographical listings.

2 BECKHAM, NANCY H. "Kathleen and Frank," in Masterplots 1973
Annual. Edited by Frank N. Magill. Englewood Cliffs, N.J.:
Salem Press, pp. 210-215.

1974

"Although ostensibly nonfiction, <u>Kathleen and Frank</u> might be considered Proustian. It has more in common, however, with the New Journalism and other contemporary genres such as the nonfiction novel."

3 BEDFORD, SYBILLE. <u>Aldous Huxley: A Biography</u>. New York: Alfred Knopf/Harper & Row, pp. 361, 376-377, 381, 392, 394, 403, 404-405, 426-427, 432, 441, 491, 494-495, 588, 607, 618, 636, 638, 691, 734, 741.
    Brief references to Isherwood's association with the Huxleys and with Gerald Heard; includes some comments on movie-script collaboration between Huxley and Isherwood and some excerpts from the correspondence of both Aldous and Maria that mentions Isherwood. [Reprints material from 1973.4.]

4 BORETZ, MARIANNE STANLEY. "The Discreet and Conspiratorial Convention: The Autobiographical Writings of Christopher Isherwood." Ph.D. dissertation, University of Southern California, 261 pp.
    Treats Isherwood's two autobiographies and four novels that have narrators who bear his name. "<u>Lions and Shadows</u> ends with the young Isherwood in full flight from all the formative influences of his youth.... The autobiographical novels which follow trace the course of his flight. Throughout these works, Isherwood has maintained a certain duality, a division between younger self--seriously flawed and naive--and the older narrator who reports these adventures, with a self-concept that is most loathsome in <u>Lions and Shadows</u> and most tolerant in <u>Down There on a Visit</u>. The movement of the novels is toward a self-understanding and forgiveness which reaches its culmination in <u>Kathleen and Frank</u>...."

5 HALPERN, DANIEL. "A Conversation with Christopher Isherwood." <u>Antaeus</u>, 13/14 (Spring-Summer), 366-388.
    Discusses contemporary writing, his own reading, his life in Berlin, his trip with Auden to China, his interest in Eastern philosophy, his association with the Quakers, and his present life.

6 HEINEY, DONALD and LENTHIEL H. DOWNS. <u>Essentials of Contemporary Literature of the Western World</u>. Vol. 2. Woodbury, N.Y.: Barron's Educational Series, Inc., pp. 38, 51-52, 234-235, 239.
    Revision of 1954.24.

7 JOHNSTONE, IAIN and JENNY REES. "Bowles Players." <u>Radio Times</u> (18 April), pp. 54-55, 57, 59.
    Interviews with Isherwood and with four actresses who have played Sally Bowles: Liza Minnelli, Dorothy Tutin, Judi Dench, and Julie Harris.

156

8   JURAK, MIRKO. "Commitment and Character Portrayal in the
     British Politico-Poetic Drama of the 1930s." <u>Educational</u>
     <u>Theatre Journal</u>, 26 (October), 342-351.
          The social criticism of the plays of the Group Theatre
     is still relevant today. The decline of the governing
     class and its supporters is depicted in all the plays.
     The three Auden/Isherwood plays are discussed.

*9   KAPLAN, CAROLA M. "The Search for Belief in the Novels of
     Christopher Isherwood." Ph.D. dissertation, Cornell Uni-
     versity, 264 pp.
          "The nine novels of Christopher Isherwood center about
     the problems associated with defining and achieving authen-
     tic selfhood. What distinguishes the struggles of Isher-
     wood's characters is that they try to resolve their prob-
     lems of self-definition not through continuous introspection
     but by attempting to find outside of the individual a system
     of belief within which the problems of personality are
     transcended and resolved." [<u>Dissertation Abstracts Inter-</u>
     <u>national</u>, 35 (1975), 4527A.]

10   KENNEDY, ALAN. "Christopher Isherwood's Psychological Make-
     up," in his <u>The Protean Self: Dramatic Action in Contem-</u>
     <u>porary Fiction</u>. London: Macmillan Press, pp. 213-229.
          Undertakes "to study closely one of Isherwood's recent
     novels, <u>A Single Man</u>, with reference to the meaning in it
     of dramatic metaphors." This focus "is most useful in the
     investigation in fiction of the dualism of body and spirit
     (or mind)...."

11   MORSEBERGER, ROBERT and KATHERINE. "Everybody's Favorite
     Monster in Fact and Science Fiction." <u>Los Angeles Times:</u>
     <u>The Book Review</u> (22 September), p. 4.
          "The teleplay 'Frankenstein: The True Story' by Chris-
     topher Isherwood and Don Bachardy is not 'the true story'
     as Mary Shelley wrote it, though it comes closer in set-
     ting, characterization and scope than the [Boris] Karloff
     version.... Isherwood's is forceful drama, and the script
     is good reading...."

*12 PIAZZA, PAUL V. "Christopher Isherwood: Myth and Anti-Myth."
     Ph.D. dissertation, University of Maryland, 232 pp.
          "The novels of Christopher Isherwood are all part of an
     intensely personal world--a world given continuity and sub-
     stance by Isherwood's lifelong creating of his own myth,
     or anti-myth as he calls his vision in <u>Kathleen and Frank</u>.
     This anti-myth forms the foundation of Isherwood's fiction
     and instills pattern into his nine novels...." [<u>Disserta-</u>
     <u>tion Abstracts International</u>, 36 (1975), 908A.] Revised
     and expanded in 1978.1.

1974

13 SCOBIE, W. I. "Art of Fiction: Interview." Paris Review, 14
    (Spring), 138–182.
        Discussion centers on A Meeting by the River and Isher-
    wood's involvement with Vedanta; also touches on Isherwood's
    writing habits and his opinions about a variety of topics
    and people: Forster's Maurice, the gay liberation move-
    ment, Gerald Heard, Stravinsky, Virginia Woolf, the Auden
    collaboration, life in Southern California. Most of his
    other works are mentioned. [Reprinted: 1976.31.]

14 SPENDER, STEPHEN. "On Being a Ghost in Isherwood's Berlin."
    Mademoiselle, 79 (September), 138–139, 197.
        Personal recollection of an incident that diverges from
    the ending of the story "Sally Bowles," although Spender
    admits that he may have remembered it all wrong. Also dis-
    cusses some of the "transformations" of the Sally Bowles
    story (i.e., I Am a Camera, Cabaret).

15 WYNDHAM, FRANCIS. "Twenty-five Years of the Novel," in The
    Craft of Letters in England. Edited by John Lehmann.
    Westport, Conn.: Greenwood Press, pp. 44–59.
        Reprint of 1957.6.

                              1975

1 BARDEN, THOMAS EARL. "W. H. Auden: The Poet's Use of Drama."
   Ph.D. dissertation, University of Virginia, pp. 71–121.
       The Auden/Isherwood plays are important to the modern
   theatre because they strengthened "the link between drama
   and pre-war activism" and "helped to establish the limits
   of viability of modern poetic drama" by means of their
   "experimental verve."

2 CUNNINGHAM, VALENTINE. "Cabaret." New Statesman, 90 (22 August), 229–230.
       In The Berlin of Sally Bowles "the juxtaposing of ordi-
   nary lives or feckless careers against the mounting bru-
   talities of the Nazis makes a tellingly radical critique
   of the politically innocent, romantic, or careless."

3 DOUGLAS, DON. "Christopher Isherwood Speaks Out." Gay Scene,
   5 (February), 4–5.
       Report of an interview with Isherwood in which he talks
   about the book he is at work on (Christopher and His Kind),
   his life in pre-War Berlin, and his homosexuality. He also
   comments on Auden's attitude toward homosexuality.

4 FINNEY, BRIAN. "Christopher Isherwood--A Profile." The New
   Review, 2 (August), 17–24.
       A review of Isherwood's literary career with observa-
   tions and data on his recent life and work: "One can

choose to see all Isherwood's fiction as a search for self-knowledge, involving him in an increasingly ruthless immersion into the past of his friends, his parents and himself."

5   FUSSELL, PAUL. The Great War and Modern Memory. New York:
     Oxford University Press, pp. 23, 24, 109-112, 197, 271,
     283.
          Lions and Shadows illustrates the "subliminal persistence" of World War I in British fiction; it documents "the persistence of the binary sense and the prevalence of the conception of 'the enemy,' first at school and later at university just after the war." The Memorial registers Isherwood's feelings about the "persisting war" in a novel.

6   GUILES, FRED LAWRENCE. Hanging on in Paradise. New York:
     McGraw-Hill, pp. 16-17, 32, 159, 183-185, 196, 313-314.
          Gives information on Isherwood's life in Hollywood, especially his association with Berthold Viertel. Quotes Isherwood on writing for films. Lists thirteen films for which Isherwood wrote.

7   HOLLOWAY, JOHN. "Narrative Structure and Text Structure:
     Isherwood's A Meeting by the River and Muriel Spark's The
     Prime of Miss Jean Brodie." Critical Inquiry, 1 (March),
     581-604.
          Analyzes the structure of A Meeting by the River in linguistic terms; shows how individual "runs" (sequences of events) are combined into a unified narrative through transformations and de-transformations. Contrasts Isherwood's narrative with that of Spark.

8   KINSMAN, CLARE D., ed. Contemporary Authors: A Bio-Biblio-
     graphical Guide to Current Authors and Their Work. Vols.
     13-16. First revision. Detroit: Gale Research Co.,
     pp. 420-421.
          Updates 1965.16 and 1969.9.

9   KNODT, KENNETH. "Goodbye to Berlin: The Diaries as Struc-
     ture." Descant, 20 (Fall), 40-48.
          Problems of the diary structure are overcome by the use of image patterns: motifs developed in the first diary are repeated later in the internal chapters. For instance, the theme of the progressive dehumanization of Berlin is reflected in the animal imagery.

10 LODGE, DAVID. "Metaphor and Metonymy in Modern Fiction."
     Critical Quarterly, 17 (Spring), 75-93.
          Isherwood and other realistic writers of the 30s made a conscious revolt against the experimental, "aesthetic," modernist novel and used the metonymic mode, rather than

the metaphorical, expressing their analogies through simi-
les. [This discussion is incorporated into 1977.23.]

11 NIN, ANAIS. <u>The Diary of Anaïs Nin, 1947-1955</u>. Edited by
Gunther Stuhlmann. New York: Harcourt Brace Jovanovich,
p. 58.
One entry on Isherwood (Summer 1950); quotes from a
letter that Isherwood wrote to Nin, explaining why he felt
that her <u>Four-Chambered Heart</u> could not be dramatized.

12 PLOMER, WILLIAM. <u>The Autobiography of William Plomer</u>. London:
Jonathan Cape, pp. 273, 297-298, 302, 314.
Repeats comments made in 1958.5.

13 SCOBIE, W. I. "Christopher Isherwood: A Lively Exchange with
One of Our Greatest Living Writers." <u>The Advocate</u> (Los
Angeles), no. 179 (17 December), pp. 6-8.
Isherwood discusses his life and writing, especially the
relation of his homosexuality to his work: "Being gay has
given me an oblique angle of vision on the world. Without
it, I might never have been a writer."

14 SMITH, ELTON EDWARD. <u>The Angry Young Men of the Thirties</u>.
Carbondale, Ill.: Southen Illinois University Press,
pp. 17, 38, 44, 63-64, 84, 86, 93, 97, 98, 100, 102, 104,
106, 111, 114, 116-118, 119, 121, 122-126, 143-145, 153.
Discusses the themes and techniques of the Auden/Isher-
wood plays. Some mentions are also made of <u>Journey to a</u>
<u>War</u> and <u>Lions and Shadows</u>.

15 SMITH, SARAH and MARCUS. "To Help along the Line: An Interview with Christopher Isherwood." <u>New Orleans Review</u>, 4,
no. 4, 307-310.
Isherwood answers questions about his Vedantic studies
and beliefs, his opinion of <u>Cabaret</u>, his treatment of death
in <u>A Single Man</u>, and his work-in-progress.

16 SPENDER, STEPHEN, ed. <u>W. H. Auden: A Tribute</u>. New York:
Macmillan, pp. 9-11, 31-32, 36, 40, 46, 69-70, 72, 80, 93,
103, 155, 175, 250.
Various essays contain random comments on Isherwood's
association with Auden.

17 STOOP, NORMA McLAIN. "Christopher Isherwood: A Meeting by
Another River." <u>After Dark</u>, 7 (April), 60-65.
Isherwood discusses <u>Cabaret</u>, <u>A Single Man</u>, and the play
version of <u>A Meeting by the River</u>. Includes several photos
of Isherwood and scenes from theatrical versions of his
works.

18   WADE, ROSALIND. "Quarterly Fiction Review." <u>Contemporary Review</u>, 227 (October), 214-215.
Review of <u>The Berlin of Sally Bowles</u>; comments only on <u>Mr. Norris Changes Trains</u>: "If the reader is left pondering uneasily on the paucity of genuine characterization and narrative skill in the contemporary espionage novel, it is reassuring to turn back to one of the very first in the <u>genre</u>."

19   WILDE, ALAN. "Language and Surface: Isherwood and the Thirties." <u>Contemporary Literature</u>, 16 (Autumn), 478-491.
"[I]t is clear that the language of <u>Mr. Norris</u> and <u>Goodbye to Berlin</u> is meant to establish a norm against which the reader gradually comes to measure the linguistic (and, by extension, the social, political, and psychological) situation in prewar Berlin.... Style, then, does its judgmental work throughout <u>The Berlin Stories</u>...."

20   WILLIAMS, TENNESSEE. <u>Memoirs</u>. Garden City, N.Y.: Doubleday, pp. 77, 79.
Comment on Williams' relationship with Isherwood: "There was an almost sentimental attachment between us but it didn't come to romance: instead, it turned into a great friendship, one of the continuing friendships in my life, and one of the most important ones."

21   YOUNG, PERRY DEANE. "Some Things I've Wanted to Say." <u>MS</u> (March), pp. 115-116, 120.
Deane says Isherwood advised him to write openly about homosexuality and the gay life in Saigon: "[Isherwood] said it was the mistake he had made in the Berlin stories." Also quotes from Isherwood's encouraging comments on the manuscript of the book, <u>Two of the Missing</u>, which was published in 1975.

1976

1   ADAIR, GILBERT. "Isherwood in Hollywood." <u>Sight & Sound</u>, 46 (Winter), 25.
Interview which focuses on Isherwood's movie career, including comments about his work with Aldous Huxley and other film projects, including the television film of <u>Frankenstein</u>.

2   ANON. "Briefly Noted: Fiction." <u>New Yorker</u>, 52 (27 December), 68.
In <u>Christopher and His Kind</u> the "public events of the thirties--so important to the writings of Isherwood and Auden--rather recede into the background. The best moments are those in which the stream of facts suddenly slows and forms a deft sketch of a person or state of mind."

1976

3   ANON. "People." <u>Time</u>, 108 (13 December), 69.
    "Christopher Isherwood, setting the tone for his new
    book <u>Christopher and His Kind</u>.... Debunking impressions
    that his interest in politics drew him into pre—World War
    II Germany, Isherwood reveals that he was propelled by a
    tip from his sometime lover and collaborator W. H. Auden
    about the boy bars in Berlin."

4   ANON. Review of <u>Christopher and His Kind</u>. <u>Booklist</u>, 73
    (1 December), 515.
    "Frank, especially as he describes the expression of
    what was for him natural sexuality (but never does his
    homosexuality become a chip on his shoulder), Isherwood
    has re-created [in <u>Christopher and His Kind</u>] the flavorful
    experiences that engendered many of his works of fiction."

5   ANON. Review of <u>Christopher and His Kind</u>. <u>Kirkus Reviews</u>, 44
    (15 October), p. 1158.
    In <u>Christopher and His Kind</u>, "[p]assion does surface in
    Christopher's correspondence...and in Isherwood's present-
    day homosexual militance, but readers should not expect the
    emotional pull of <u>Goodbye to Berlin</u> or <u>Down There on a
    Visit</u>."

6   BORKLUND, ELMER. "Isherwood, Christopher," in <u>Contemporary
    Novelists</u>. Edited by James Vinson and D. L. Kirkpatrick.
    Second edition. New York: St. Martin's Press, pp. 703–
    707.
    Reprint of 1972.13.

7   BRESLIN, JOHN B. "A Season of Books: The Literary Editor
    Previews This Fall's Prospects in Publishing." <u>America</u>,
    135 (2 October), 195.
    "More literary lives are revealed by, among others,
    Christopher Isherwood in <u>Christopher and His Kind</u>..., use-
    ful background for fans of <u>Cabaret</u>."

8   BROGAN, HUGH. "Lions and Shadows." <u>Twentieth Century Litera-
    ture</u>, 22 (October), 303–311.
    A personal response to <u>Lions and Shadows</u>: "I was two
    years old when the book was published, yet, again and
    again, I find it throwing light on the specifics of my own
    experience. England changes, but very slowly; <u>Lions and
    Shadows</u> will long remain a valuable guide to her charac-
    ter...."

9   FINNEY, BRIAN. "Laily, Mortmere and All That." <u>Twentieth
    Century Literature</u>, 22 (October), 286–302.
    Description of unpublished "Mortmere" material: this
    fantasy "offered both writers [Isherwood and Upward] less
    an escape from reality than a means of exploring their own

values and their own modes of literary expression, magically
freed from the conventions which oppressed them as writers
and as individuals in search of their adult identities."

10 FOX, TIMOTHY X. "Auden Parted the Curtain." <u>Village Voice</u>,
    21 (6 December), 96.
        "Neither an apologia nor a flaunting, self-justifying
    confession, [Christopher and His Kind] is singularly cheer-
    ful, unhysterical, and free of...adolescent sexual boast-
    ing.... [It] is at its best--funny, enlightening, and
    disconcerting--when it offers us material that is new:
    portraits of the young Auden and Spender, above all the
    portrait of the young Isherwood himself, who turns out to
    have been a good deal more than a camera."

11 FRYER, JONATHAN H. "Sexuality in Isherwood." <u>Twentieth Cen-
    tury Literature</u>, 22 (October), 343-353.
        "There is...a traceable development in the approach of
    [Isherwood's] novels to sex, as if each time he has felt
    justified in going one little step further, swimming with
    the current of enlightened public opinion rather than lead-
    ing it.... [H]is significance in this field comes from
    the way he has helped to make respectable topics previously
    unmentionable in polite society."

12 GLICKSBERG, CHARLES I. <u>The Literature of Commitment</u>. Lewis-
    burg, Pa.: Bucknell University Press, pp. 261-263, 265-
    266.
        Comments on the political motives and purposes of the
    Auden/Isherwood plays and <u>Journey to a War</u>.

13 GREEN, MARTIN. <u>Children of the Sun: A Narrative of "Deca-
    dence" in England after 1918</u>. New York: Basic Books,
    pp. 4, 5, 9, 13, 44-45, 247, 252, 280, 285-288, 292, 396.
        "Isherwood's fascination with...mature and discreet
    cynicism complements his fascination with young flamboyant
    corruption, and together they alert the reader to the subtle
    and deceitful resonances ever present in Isherwood's naive-
    ly candid prose."

14 GRIFFIN, ERNEST. "Conversation with Edward Upward." <u>Modernist
    Studies: Literature & Culture 1920-1940</u>, 2, no. 2, 19-35.
        Upward discusses the "Mortmere" stories and his associa-
    tions with Isherwood at Cambridge: "Isherwood had a very
    keen sense of the concrete and of detail. That's what he
    gave to me, I think, and I gave to him, to some extent, an
    interest in abstract ideas, in what we used to call 'the
    externals.'"

1976

15   HEILBRUN, CAROLYN G.   "Christopher Isherwood: An Interview."
     Twentieth Century Literature, 22 (October), 253-263.
          Isherwood discusses Ramakrishna, homosexuality, atti-
     tudes toward Jews; his friendships with J. R. Ackerley,
     Dr. Evelyn Hooker, and Maria Huxley; and his plans for fu-
     ture writing.

16   HEILBRUN, CAROLYN G.   "An Interview with Gavin Lambert."
     Twentieth Century Literature, 22 (October), 332-342.
          Lambert comments on Isherwood's religion, his homosex-
     uality, his life and work in Hollywood, his relationship
     with Don Bachardy, and his attitude toward women.

17   JOHNSTON, ALBERT H.   Review of Christopher and His Kind. Pub-
     lisher's Weekly, 210 (1 November), 67.
          "This highly personal memoir offers a wealth of private
     and literary revelations along with an evocation of Europe
     on the verge of holocaust...." But the book will "dismay"
     some because of its "self-indulgent" tone and its "distor-
     tions"; Isherwood's "ultimate measure of the world seems
     to be sexual." [This review is quoted in 1977.7.]

18   KING, FRANCIS. Christopher Isherwood. Writers and Their
     Work, No. 240. Longman Group, 28 pp.
          "Possessed of an insight into character, an incisiveness
     of style and an architectural sense all far superior to his
     powers of invention, [Isherwood] belongs essentially to
     what might be called the 'suppose-if' category of novelists.
     For such novelists the process of creation begins with
     something that they have either experienced or observed at
     close quarters. Taking this foundation of reality, they
     then proceed to build on it imaginatively by a series of
     'suppose-ifs'--suppose if I had done that and not this,
     suppose if so-and-so had said this and not that.... There
     should be a word for writing of this kind, poised half way
     between fact and fiction. Perhaps 'faction' would do."

19   LEHMANN, JOHN. "Two of the Conspirators." Twentieth Century
     Literature, 22 (October), 264-275.
          Lehmann recalls his seven-year association with Isher-
     wood as his editor, publisher, and friend. Most of the
     early works, from The Memorial to Goodbye to Berlin, are
     touched on.

20   LEONARD, JOHN. "Isherwood Revises Record." New York Times
     (9 December), p. 45.
          Isherwood seems to be criticizing himself in Christopher
     and His Kind: "If he had been braver, the 'I' seems to be
     saying, the novels wouldn't have been so empty at their
     centers; their author would not seem so much a tourist in
     his own life."

21   MARVIN, JOHN R. Review of <u>Christopher and His Kind</u>. <u>Library</u>
      <u>Journal</u>, 101 (1 December), 2478.
            In <u>Christopher and His Kind</u>, Isherwood "impresses this
      reviewer as a sort of latter-day Oscar Wilde, but, unfor-
      tunately, with little of Wilde's talent and force." [Re-
      printed: 1977.26.]

22   MENDELSON, EDWARD. "The Auden-Isherwood Collaboration."
      <u>Twentieth Century Literature</u>, 22 (October), 276-285.
            Offers "a historical note on what happened in the [Auden-
      Isherwood] collaboration and when"; includes a "Biblio-
      graphical Note" about typescripts and variant versions of
      the plays.

23   MESIC, PENELOPE. "Young Christopher Isherwood and the Company
      He Kept." <u>Book World</u>, 10 (12 December), 1.
            "The result of Isherwood's frankness is satisfyingly un-
      tidy, almost embarrassingly intimate. Reading [<u>Christopher</u>
      <u>and His Kind</u>] is like being led into a room and made to
      feel the imprint of the author's body in a tumbled bed."

24   MULLIN, DONALD. "The 'Decline of the West' as Reflected in
      Three Modern Plays." <u>Educational Theatre Journal</u>, 28
      (October), 363-369.
            "One finds, in <u>The Dog Beneath the Skin</u>, a rejection of
      contemporary illusion and pretense.... The authors wish,
      however, to suggest a Higher Moral Purpose than satire or
      reportage. The protagonist not only rejects, he also re-
      jects utterly. It is not his wish to revise, correct, or
      improve, but to cut loose."

25   ORPHANOS, STATHIS. "Christopher Isherwood: A Checklist 1968-
      1975." <u>Twentieth Century Literature</u>, 22 (October), 354-361.
            Lists both primary works—books, articles, paperback
      editions, reissues, and foreign editions; and secondary
      sources—two books, nine articles, 21 interviews, and 43
      reviews.

26   PIAZZA, PAUL. "Isherwood: A Remembrance of Things Past."
      <u>Washington Post</u> (23 November), section C, p. 2.
            <u>Christopher and His Kind</u> "is far more than Isherwood's
      truth-game, a making public of private facts and faces.
      Though the impulse may be autobiographical, the product is,
      finally, artistic.... After a career of more than 50 years
      in which Isherwood has transformed life into art, art pre-
      vails: fiction merges into reality."

27   PIAZZA, PAUL. "So Many Isherwoods." <u>The Chronicle of Higher</u>
      <u>Education</u>, 13 (20 December), 9.
            In <u>Christopher and His Kind</u>, "Isherwood is systematical-
      ly trying to separate fact from fiction in the intricate

1976

puzzle he has pieced together over half a century.... But
now the puzzle won't come undone. There are so many cross-
overs between art and reality in Isherwood's books, and so
many ghost-like Isherwoods who refuse to vanish, that the
new autobiography has all the complexity and ironic dis-
sonance of his fiction."

28   REUVEN, BEN. "Christopher Isherwood: Reading the Sands of
      Time." Los Angeles Times: The Book Review (5 December),
      pp. 3, 16.
         Interview: Isherwood talks about Christopher and His
      Kind, his life in California, the film and play versions
      of The Berlin Stories, and his aims and goals as a writer.

29   ROVE, JOHN HOWARD. "The Berlin Stories, I Am a Camera, Caba-
      ret: An Analysis and Comparison." Master's thesis, Mem-
      phis State University, 143 pp.
         The four dramatic productions based on Goodbye to Berlin
      "altered the Isherwood images to suit the creative needs of
      the playwrights, producers, directors, performers and medi-
      ums involved. Yet, because the characters and situations
      of Goodbye to Berlin are so compelling, four distillations
      of the material carefully preserved its theme and charac-
      ters."

30   S., P. H. "The Times Diary: Cabaret." London Times
      (25 June), p. 16.
         Reports on Isherwood's visit to the National Portrait
      Gallery exhibit on the life and works of five authors of
      the 1930s. Includes comments by Isherwood about the let-
      ters and other materials on display.

31   SCOBIE, W. I. "Christopher Isherwood," in Writers at Work:
      The Paris Review Interviews. 4th series. Edited by George
      Plimpton. New York: The Viking Press, pp. 209-242.
         Reprint of 1974.13.

32   SCOBIE, W. I. "Christopher Talks about 'His Kind.'" The Ad-
      vocate (Los Angeles), no. 205 (15 December), pp. 20, 22-23.
         Isherwood discusses his friends of the 30s, explains why
      he came to America, and answers questions about the lit-
      erary and ethical aspects of his writings.

33   SCOBIE, W. I. "Isherwood's Power Is Undiminished." The Advo-
      cate (Los Angeles), no. 205 (15 December), pp. 21, 23-24,
      49.
         Isherwood's "power of dramatizing his predicament at any
      given moment" is undiminished in Christopher and His Kind:
      "Had one never heard the names of the author and other
      well-known people who inhabit these pages, the book might
      be read as a work of fiction. This is because its leading

character is such an eminently suitable hero for a comic
novel. 'Christopher' may infuriate, dismay, or embarrass
us, but he never bores."

34 SMITH, S. M. "Isherwood, Christopher," in Webster's New World
Companion to English and American Literature. Edited by
Arthur Pollard. New York: Popular Library, pp. 355-356.
Reprint of 1973.19.

35 STANSKY, PETER. "Christopher and His Kind." New York Times
Book Review (28 November), pp. 31-34.
Christopher and His Kind is, in some ways, "a revenge on
the 'camera' image, the author as no more than photographer,
so irrevocably identified with the earlier version.... But
in 'Christopher and His Kind' he is down front. The importance of the observer, and in particular his sexual tastes
and matings, so neutralized in the novels as to be invisible, have come increasingly into prominence."

36 THOMAS, PETER. "'Camp' and Politics in Isherwood's Berlin
Fiction." Journal of Modern Literature, 5 (February), 117-
130.
"If Mr. Norris Changes Trains and Goodbye to Berlin are
read from the starting-point of their literary allegiances
and not with a view of their political pedigree, they ac-
quire a richer metaphorical texture and, finally, a deeper
political meaning.... 'Camp' provided a mode of specific
political truth, and Isherwood was the brilliant chronicler
of Berlin in the early Thirties because of literary and not
strictly political loyalties."

37 TOLLEY, A. TREVOR. The Poetry of the Thirties. New York: St.
Martin's Press, pp. 30, 31, 33, 35, 44, 46-47, 52, 85-87,
89-90, 93, 99, 104-105, 108, 113, 122, 158, 161, 166-168,
296-298, 300, 304-305, 311, 320-321, 323, 348, 374.
The Mortmere fantasies and the "imaginative concerns"
which Isherwood developed while at Cambridge--particularly
the concepts of 'The Test' and 'The Truly Strong Man'--
figure prominently in the poetry and plays of "a not necessarily self-conscious group" of writers, including Auden,
Isherwood, Spender, Day Lewis, Rex Warner, and Edward Upward.

*38 TOYNBEE, PHILIP. "Five Young Writers Who Changed My World."
London Observer Magazine (20 June), 17-19.
Cited: British Humanities Index 1976, p. 260.

39 VIDAL, GORE. "Art, Sex, and Isherwood." New York Review of
Books, 23 (9 December), 10-18.
"Art and sex: the two themes intertwine in Isherwood's
memoirs but in [Lions and Shadows] we do not know what the

1976

> sex was all about: the reticences of the Thirties forbade candor. Now in Christopher and His Kind, Isherwood has filled in the blanks; he is explicit about both sex and love."

40 WILSON, COLIN. "An Integrity Born of Hope: Notes on Christopher Isherwood." Twentieth Century Literature, 22 (October), 312–331.

> Isherwood's "own peculiar virtue as a novelist" is that he is not an egoist: "on the basis of [his] refusal to be an 'ego,' he has slowly built up a 'true personality,' a 'real I.' The interesting result is that he is one of the very few modern novelists...who has escaped the slide into defeat or negation."

1977

1 ADAMS, PHOEBE-LOU. Review of Christopher and His Kind. Atlantic, 239 (January), 93.

> In Christopher and His Kind, Isherwood has "undertaken to tell what really happened, and what really happened, homosexual love affairs and all, proves dull going for the reader."

2 ANNAN, GABRIELE. "The Issyvoo Years." Times Literary Supplement (1 April), pp. 401–402.

> "When you look at Isherwood's work as a whole...you see that one way or another, first as an act of defiance and then as a fight for equal rights, it has always been a homosexual campaign. A guerilla campaign at first, with the Christopher figure...camouflaged as an implausible hetero. In Christopher and His Kind Isherwood explains that the reason for camouflage was not caution alone: there was an artistic reason as well. The narrator has to be 'as unobtrusive as possible' so that the reader can identify with him, or rather share his reactions to the weird goings-on around him."

3 ANON. "Goings On: Candid Camera." The Sunday Times (16 January), p. 35.

> Report on a 40-minute film "Over There on a Visit," featuring Isherwood and Don Bachardy, to be screened on February 5.

4 ANON. "Notes on Current Books." Virginia Quarterly Review, 53 (Spring), 54.

> In Christopher and His Kind, "some of the social comments and depictions of noted individuals offer a modicum of general interest [but] most of the book is merely a more complete accounting of who did what to whom and where."

5   ANON. "Paperbacks: New and Noteworthy." <u>New York Times Book Review</u> (6 November), p. 59.
     <u>Christopher and His Kind</u>: "This shrewd and candid memoir...throws new light on an ambiguous era."

6   ANON. Review of <u>Christopher and His Kind</u>. <u>Choice</u>, 14 (April), 200.
     In <u>Christopher and His Kind</u>, Isherwood analyzes "his own interior self, seeking to learn how he came to be what he is today. The results are fascinating, both as an interior picture and as a view of the literary world of the '30s."

7   ANON. Review of <u>Christopher and His Kind</u>. <u>Publisher's Weekly</u>, 212 (26 September), 136.
     Notice of the forthcoming paperback edition of <u>Christopher and His Kind</u>. Quotes 1976.17.

8   AUSTEN, ROGER. "The Lighter Touch of Christopher Isherwood," in his <u>Playing the Game: The Homosexual Novel in America</u>. Indianapolis, Ind: Bobbs-Merrill, pp. 207-209.
     "In some of his earlier works, [Isherwood] had so interwoven gayness as quietly supplemental to other themes that homophobes were left with very little to attack. Even in his bolder novels of the sixties, <u>Down There on a Visit</u> and <u>A Single Man</u>, his homosexuals were sketched with such happy nonchalance and intelligence that they provoked little alarm, inside or outside of the covers."

9   BAILEY, JEFFREY. "Interview: Christopher Isherwood." <u>California Quarterly</u>, 11-12 (Winter/Spring), 87-96.
     Excerpts from a conversation recorded at Isherwood's home shortly after his seventieth birthday: Isherwood comments on his association with Auden, Spender, and Upward; his life in Berlin; his conversion to Vedanta; why <u>A Single Man</u> is his favorite book; and his life in America.

10 BAYLEY, JOHN. "Thinking about Erich." <u>Manchester Guardian Weekly</u>, 116 (10 April), 22.
     In <u>Christopher and His Kind</u>, the "intensity of [Isherwood's] romance with Germany--as a place of pure otherness--comes across in every word.... But what makes everything [Isherwood] writes compulsively readable seems not connected with homosexuality as such but with states of mind and awareness common to all kinds of threshold excitement 'irradiated with sex.'"

11 BRONSKI, MICHAEL. "Surviving Fame." <u>Boston Gay Review</u>, no. 2 (Spring), pp. 4-5.
     What is "most reassuring and trustworthy" about <u>Christopher and His Kind</u> is the "sense of growth" that it demonstrates: "By the end of the book Isherwood has gone through

1977

several social and political metamorphoses and has blos-
somed into what might be called a homosexually-identified
pacifist."

12   CONRAD, PETER. "The Trouble with Christopher." Spectator,
      238 (2 April), 20-21.
          Review of Christopher and His Kind: Isherwood and Auden
      "adopted opposite but congruent strategems of self-revela-
      tion.... Isherwood's lacerating frankness about his sexual
      truancies is as evasive and oblique as Auden's reticence
      was a coy technique of self-dramatisation."

13   COOK, BRUCE. "What Happened in Berlin? Isherwood Tells All."
      National Observer, 16 (22 January), 23.
          Christopher and His Kind "proves to be, for the most
      part, a chronicle of the author's homosexual activities
      during the '30s.... [Isherwood] writes as a man let loose,
      allowed by our new frankness regarding sexual matters to
      tell the truth for the first time about what really hap-
      pened in Berlin...."

14   ELLMANN, MARY. "Five Lives." Yale Review, 67 (Autumn), 131-
      133.
          Christopher and His Kind "is confessional, and it lacks
      some of the elusive quality which unstatedness gives to
      [Lions and Shadows]. Insofar as it gives the situations in
      real life that underlie Isherwood's fictions, there is an
      impression of clothes being repeatedly taken off to dis-
      close something less interesting than the tailored crea-
      tures formerly visible."

14a   ELLMAN, RICHARD. "The Year's Books: Richard Ellmann on Bio-
      graphy." New Republic, 177 (26 November), 28.
          Christopher and His Kind is well written, "but rather
      off-putting however admirable its candor."

15   FIRCHOW, PETER E. "Private Faces in Public Places: Auden's
      The Orators." Publications of the Modern Language Associa-
      tion, 92 (March), 253-272.
          The primary audience of The Orators was the "Auden
      group" of the 30s. Isherwood is "one of the best guides
      through the strange topography" of this poem. Makes ex-
      tended use of and commentary on Lions and Shadows.

16   FORD, CHRISTOPHER. "Christopher's Jungle Book." Manchester
      Guardian Weekly, 116 (10 April), 22.
          Isherwood discusses Christopher and His Kind and com-
      ments, coincidentally, on the difference between memoirs
      and autobiography, his work habits, his writing for Holly-
      wood, and his present projects.

17 FRYER, JONATHAN. <u>Isherwood: A Biography of Christopher Ish-
    erwood</u>. London: New English Library, 300 pp.
        "Reading through files of old newspaper cuttings about
    Isherwood made me realise how little even a self-confessed
    admirer knew of the man, his work in the film world, his
    pacifist activities or his crusading for homosexual rights.
    For most people, indeed, he remains Herr Issyvoo of his
    classic Berlin stories, yet this is only one aspect of a
    many-faceted and extraordinary personality. So the idea
    for this book was born, the aim of it being to present a
    clear picture of a man who has quietly made a significant
    contribution to twentieth-century life...."

18 GINGERICH, MARTIN E. <u>W. H. Auden: A Reference Guide</u>. Ref-
    erence Guides in Literature, edited by Ronald Gottesman.
    Boston: G. K. Hall & Co., passim.
        Numerous entries deal with works on which Isherwood and
    Auden collaborated.

19 HEWISON, ROBERT. <u>Under Siege: Literary Life in London 1939-
    1945</u>. New York: Oxford University Press, pp. 7-8, 145,
    182.
        The departure of Auden and Isherwood for America in 1939
    was "the most important literary event since Spain" and re-
    sulted in the breakup of the "Popular Poets' Front." De-
    moralization resulted and "literature became non-combatant."

20 HYNES, SAMUEL L. <u>The Auden Generation: Literature and Poli-
    tics in England in the 1930s</u>, pp. 21, 28, 34-37, 50, 52,
    72, 85, 126-127, 177-186, 228, 236-241, 292, 307-310, 322-
    325, 341-349, 353-359.
        Discusses the social and political significance of Ish-
    erwood's works of the thirties: <u>The Memorial</u>, <u>Mr. Norris
    Changes Trains</u>, <u>Goodbye to Berlin</u>, and <u>Lions and Shadows</u>.
    Also analyzes the four works of the Auden/Isherwood col-
    laboration.

21 KERMODE, FRANK. "In the Best Sense, Silly." <u>Listener</u>, 97
    (31 March), 419-420.
        "Isherwood finds it impossible not to shape his narra-
    tion in familiar ways. But it could be said that the pur-
    suit of absolute fidelity to the facts has done some harm;
    for, interesting as it must be to everybody who knows the
    novels or remembers the Thirties, <u>Christopher and His Kind</u>
    strikes me as inferior to <u>The Memorial</u>, in which some of
    its facts were fictionalized."

22 LAMBERT, J. W. "Isherwood: The Candid Conspirator." <u>The
    Sunday Times</u> (3 April), p. 41.
        For all its candor, <u>Christopher and His Kind</u> does not
    tell the "whole truth" about Isherwood. "All the same, it

offers an hypnotic study of a human spirit, both tremulous
and diamond-hard, at odds with a crumbling world from 1929
to 1939."

23 LODGE, DAVID. The Modes of Modern Writing: Meton-
    ymy, and the Typology of Modern Literature. Ithaca, N.Y.:
    Cornell University Press, pp. ix, 46-48, 110, 191, 193-194,
    199-200, 201-204, 206-207, 211-212, 224, 258, 268-269.
        The fiction of Isherwood and other "realistic" writers
    of the 30s "is based on the assumption that there is a com-
    mon phenomenal world that may be reliably described by the
    methods of empirical history." Isherwood's use of selec-
    tive detail is "a staple device of realism" and his use of
    the simile illustrates how a synecdochic or metonymic re-
    lationship can be presented "as if it were metaphorical."
    [Incorporates the discussion in 1975.10.]

24 LONGFORD, FRANK. "Two Autobiographies." Contemporary Review,
    230 (June), 328-330.
        Although Christopher and His Kind is full of "delightful
    touches" and humorous portraits of famous persons, the
    story of Isherwood's life in Berlin "is a horrifying tale.
    To say that is not to denigrate homosexuals as such....
    But the general ethos was one of total promiscuity, sexual
    exploitation of young working-class men and callous disre-
    gard of their interests...."

25 McCABLE, BERNARD. "The Isherwood Generation." Commonweal,
    104 (28 October), 683-685.
        "Unfortunately what has happened in Christopher and His
    Kind is a shift from the exterior objects of Isherwood's
    attention to an absorbed interest in Isherwood.... Whereas
    Mr. Norris, for example, manipulates a fine balance between
    observer and observed, this book is only a re-telling...of
    Isherwood's personal life in the thirties."

26 MARVIN, JOHN R. Review of Christopher and His Kind. The
    Library Journal Book Review 1976. New York: R. R. Bowker,
    p. 109.
        Reprint of 1976.21.

27 MITCHISON, NAOMI. "The Not So Gay World." Books and Bookmen,
    22 (May), 34-35.
        "Christopher and His Kind is a balanced and fascinating
    experiment in the writing of an autobiography, or rather
    part of one. All the early Isherwood books were more or
    less autobiographical, but everything was fictionalised.
    In this one, nothing is; there is a very cool watching eye.
    The literary device by which 'I' is Isherwood today and
    Christopher is Isherwood then, is entirely successful."

28   PASCHALL, DOUGLAS. "Goose-Stepping on Thin Ice." Sewanee Re-
     view, 85 (Spring), 346-351.
          In Christopher and His Kind, Isherwood is "remarkably
     adept at turning to the immediate purpose of present truth-
     telling the 'angle of vision' that he had employed as a
     writer of fiction.... For here are the boasts and the
     tricks of modesty all at once, while the whole book remains
     a steady, crisp, and luminous album of self-exposure."

29   REUVEN, BEN. "The Beginnings of Isherwood." Los Angeles
     Times: The Book Review (12 June), p. 11.
          Lions and Shadows "was originally subtitled 'An Educa-
     tion in the Twenties'--an accurate description, but one
     that conceals the color, wit and vitality of Isherwood's
     writing." This early work "reveals a treasure trove of
     literary banknotes and historical jewels."

30   RUSSO, TONY. "Interview with Christopher Isherwood." Chris-
     topher Street, 1 (March), 6-10.
          Isherwood discusses the "gay sensibility" in his earlier
     works, the issue of gay writers' "coming out" in their
     works, and a recent play by Harold Pinter, No Man's Land,
     which may contain a dramatic portrait of Auden.

31   RYAN, STEPHEN P. Review of Christopher and His Kind. Best
     Sellers, 37 (April), 11-12.
          "It is difficult to approach a book like this. One
     simply must reject moral indignation, condescension, and
     any form of outright disapproval of Mr. Isherwood's sexual
     preferences; yet Christopher and His Kind strikes me as a
     dreary, unhappy revelation...."

32   S., P. H. "The Times Diary: Christopher and His Golden
     Goose." London Times (7 April), p. 16
          Report on a literary luncheon for Isherwood. Responds
     to the "moral" question of attending, posed by a columnist
     in the Sunday Express because of Isherwood's homosexuality.
     Isherwood is quoted briefly.

33   SCOBIE, W. I. "The Youth That Was 'I': A Conversation in
     Santa Monica with Christopher Isherwood." London Magazine,
     NS 17 (April/May), 23-32.
          The interview centers on Christopher and His Kind and
     the autobiographical material therein.

34   SNOW, C. P. Review of Christopher and His Kind. Financial
     Times (7 April), p. 14.
          Christopher and His Kind is a "distasteful" book. Pre-
     fers a recent biography of Noel Coward, because Coward and
     his circle, although sometimes tiresome, at least "took
     their taste for granted, neither feeling themselves perse-
     cuted nor wishing to persecute others."

1977

35   SPENDER, STEPHEN. "Notebook--XII." London Magazine, NS 17
     (April/May), 46-51.
         "Isherwood is a novelist whose best work is based on
     autobiography.... At the same time...they are not egotis-
     tic. Nor are they journalism. Something is always created
     which is fiction. The Isherwood character is not just a
     camera-eye observer. He is a living presence constantly
     transforming the material of observed life into art."

36   STANFORD, DEREK. Review of Christopher and His Kind. British
     Book News (June), p. 484.
         In Christopher and His Kind, Isherwood "sees the unlove-
     ly young man he was but preaches us no tiresome sermons.
     His value judgements are precise and to the point without
     being consciously sententious. Neither has his sharp eye
     nor his sly self-humour deserted him."

37   TOYNBEE, PHILIP. "Herr Issyvoo Comes Clean." London Observer
     (3 April), 26.
         Christopher and His Kind is "a lively, interesting and
     very amusing presentation of the raw material out of which
     [the Berlin] novels were hewn. There is much for hetero-
     sexuals to learn here about the curiosities of homosexual
     life, including some things--such as the charming ease of
     love-making between friends--which heterosexuals may well
     envy."

38   UPWARD, EDWARD. "The Resolute Anti-Hero." New Statesman, 93
     (1 April), 434.
         Christopher and His Kind "is something much more than a
     collection of wonderful chapters. It is a complete and
     subtly constructed work of art, building up to the climax
     of the arrest of Heinz, and it needs to be considered as an
     artistic whole if its stature is to be properly appreciated."

39   WAUGH, AUBERON. "Out in the Open." Books and Bookmen, 22
     (May), 6-7.
         "I must say that although I found [Christopher and His
     Kind] distasteful for a number of reasons..., it is also
     extraordinarily readable. More than that, it is fascinating
     for those like myself with a keen if not invariably friendly
     interest in the left wing homosexual literary cliques of
     the 1930s...."

40   WEST, REBECCA. Review of Christopher and His Kind. London
     Sunday Telegraph (3 April).
         "The unworthy Mr. Isherwood and his friends" are not
     typical homosexuals, but are "swinish" and "squalid" and
     can be divided into two groups: "The first consists of
     male prostitutes, children and adolescents who are dirty,
     drunken, often afflicted with unpleasant diseases, and

treacherous. The second group consists of their patrons,
grown men of all ages, possessing the same characteristics.
These two groups unite in [Christopher and His Kind] to
lead an existence which is one long symphony of squalor."

41 WINDHAM, DONALD, ed. Tennessee Williams' Letters to Donald
Windham, 1940-1965. New York: Holt, Rinehart and Winston,
pp. 63-64, 71-72, 77, 85n, 93-94, 102, 106, 117, 121, 185,
195, 199, 204, 221-222, 253.
Letter of 12 May 1943: "I met Christopher [Isherwood]
today.... I recognized him at once, just by instinct, and
he does look just the way I imagine myself to look--it was
funny. I like him awfully, and I think he must have thought
me rather school-girlish about his writing which I place
with Chekhov's."

42 Y., D. W. Review of Christopher and His Kind. West Coast Review, 3 (March), 32.
"[W]e're certain that [Isherwood's] other works will
outlast this effort to set the record straight. For most
of Isherwood's readers, we are sure, would rather believe
the fantasy than the fact."

1978

1 PIAZZA, PAUL. Christopher Isherwood: Myth and Anti-Myth.
New York: Columbia University Press, 245 pp.
"The anti-myth, begun as a revolt in the nursery, or
anti-nursery, materialized at Repton, and was expanded at
Cambridge with Upward and after Cambridge with Auden. It
forms the foundation of Isherwood's fictional output and
instills patterns into works which might otherwise appear
distinct and unconnected, a mere farrago. Isherwood's
anti-myth splits the world into two camps: the Enemy, or
the Others, and the conspiratorial clique of the writer and
his friends.... Isherwood's antagonism is translated into
the novels in terms of the alienated protagonist at odds
with society.... Not until Isherwood's conversion to
Vedanta is the Enemy seen not as other people but as one's
self, one's own lack of love." [Substantial revision of
1974.12.]

Index

W

W., B., 1967.65
W., D., 1937.40
W., H. A., 1964.67
W., L. G., 1967.66
Wade, Rosalind, 1975.18
Wain, Joseph, 1954.45
Walker, Peregine, 1954.46
Wall Street Journal, 1962.83
Walpole, Horace, 1933.1
Walton, Edith, 1939.91
Ward, A. C., 1970.18
Ware, James M., 1969.26
Warner, Rex, 1976.37
Washington Evening Star, 1946.29;
    1962.4; 1964.6; 1965.35
Washington Post, 1967.67;
    1972.50; 1976.26
Waterbury Republican [CT],
    1964.64
Watson, Alan Hull, 1973.20
Watts, Alan, 1965.36
Waugh, Auberon, 1966.26; 1977.39
Waugh, Evelyn, 1939.92; 1968.4
The Way of All Flesh, 1962.44;
    1970.8
Weatherby, W. J., 1960.13
Webb, W. L., 1971.18
Webster, Harvey Curtis, 1946.39
Weeks, Edward, 1946.40
Weintraub, Stanley, 1965.37
Weisgerber, Jean, 1958.6
Wennersten, Robert, 1972.52
West, Paul, 1963.9; 1965.38
West, Rebecca, 1977.40
Westby, Selmer, 1968.16
West Coast Review of Books,
    1977.42
Wheildon, L., 1962.98
Whistler, Laurence, 1937.41
White, E. W., 1937.42
White, Eric Walter, 1949.18;
    1970.19
Whitehead, John, 1965.39
Wickes, George, 1965.40
Wilde, Alan, 1970.20; 1971.19;
    1975.19
Wiley, Paul, 1963.10
Willett, John, 1970.21
Williams, Raymond, 1952.11;
    1968.17

Williams, Russell, 1964.69
Williams, Tennessee, 1975.20;
    1977.41
Williamson, Audrey, 1956.5
Wilmington News [DE], 1954.9;
    1966.29
Wilson, Angus, 1954.47; 1966.37-
    38; 1971.20
Wilson, Colin, 1971.21; 1976.40
Wilson, Edmund, 1937.43; 1939.93;
    1945.14; 1947.30; 1950.3-4;
    1952.12
Windham, Donald, 1977.41
Wingate, Gifford W., 1954.48
Winston-Salem Journal and Senti-
    nel [NC], 1962.61
Wisconsin Studies in Contemporary
    Literature, 1963.10; 1964.60;
    1965.25
Wolff, Geoffrey A., 1967.67
Wood, Frederick T., 1963.11
Woodburn, John, 1946.41
Woodcock, George, 1965.41;
    1967.68
Woolf, Leonard, 1953.4; 1967.69;
    1970.22
Woolf, Virginia, 1948.16;
    1953.4; 1967.70
Worcester Telegram [MA], 1954.35;
    1962.54; 1964.44; 1967.66
Wordsworth, Christopher, 1967.71
The World in Books: A Magazine
    of Life and Letters, 1947.6
The World in the Evening,
    1952.1, 3; 1953.3; 1954.1,
    3-12, 14-21, 23, 25-47, 50-
    51; 1955.4; 1957.6; 1958.6;
    1960.6, 8, 10; 1961.6;
    1962.53, 56; 1964.2, 29-30;
    1965.39; 1966.19, 27, 31;
    1967.19, 59; 1968.8; 1969.8,
    14; 1970.5, 7, 12, 14, 16-17;
    1971.1, 8, 11, 19; 1972.13,
    28, 31; 1973.19; 1974.9, 12,
    15; 1975.4; 1976.6, 11, 34,
    40; 1978.1
Worsley, T. C., 1954.49
Worth, Katharine J., 1972.53
Wright, George T., 1969.27
Wright, Ralph, 1938.22
Writers Guild of America, 1970.1;
    1973.18